The Mother Tongue
Adapted for Modern Students

George Lyman Kittredge
Sarah Louise Arnold

Adapted By
Amy M. Edwards and Christina J. Mugglin

BLUE SKY DAISIES

The Mother Tongue: Adapted for Modern Students
By Amy M. Edwards and Christina J. Mugglin © 2014
Second printing, 2015

The Mother Tongue: Book II, An Elementary English Grammar
By George Lyman Kittredge, Sarah Louise Arnold © 1901, 1908

Published by Blue Sky Daisies
blueskydaisies.net

Cover design: © Blue Sky Daises 2021

ISBN-13: 978-0-9905529-0-1
ISBN-10: 099055290X

Table of Contents

FOREWORD
2014

THE MOTHER TONGUE

The Mother Tongue, Book II, An Elementary English Grammar is over one hundred years old, yet it still has a loyal following. For some, it is a supplemental grammar reference; for others, it is a primary grammar text used for students in the middle grades, somewhere between fifth and tenth grades. This text, written by George Lyman Kittredge and Sarah Louise Arnold, was originally published in 1901, but was published in a revised edition in 1908. It is known as *Book II* because its companion book *The Mother Tongue Book I* was written for younger children. *Book I* is not a prerequisite to *The Mother Tongue Book II.* Any further reference to *The Mother Tongue* will refer to *Book II* by Kittredge and Arnold.

Why republish a century-old grammar book? We were drawn to *The Mother Tongue* following the recommendation of grammarians who knew better than we, but we found the vintage format difficult to utilize in our homeschools. We wanted the excellent content of *The Mother Tongue*, but in a more readable, modern font and layout.

The written exercises in *The Mother Tongue* are excellent and unlike those found in any recent grammar book. The sentences in these exercises, most of which are taken from literature, are an outstanding ingredient of *The Mother Tongue*. Students with a sharp eye will recognize lines from Shakespeare, Brontë, Dafoe, and many others. These sentences not only give students challenging

practice working with English grammar, they will expand their vocabulary and build writing skills.

We wanted our students to complete the excellent practice exercises, but found it particularly time-consuming for them to work the exercises from the old format. In republishing this classic, we wanted to bring these exercises to a new generation of students.

METHODOLOGY IN ADAPTING A CLASSIC

The reformatted and revised edition of *The Mother Tongue* that you hold in your hands, as well as the companion workbooks, is our answer. We preserved the original text of the first edition almost exactly, making only insignificant changes to make it more readable. We incorporated exercises and improvements from the 1908 revised edition. If you are a fan of the revised edition, you will notice that the structure of this book is patterned on the first edition, but the written exercises include improvements from the revised edition. We also have included the very useful appendices on capitalization, punctuation, and syntax that are found in the revised edition.

You will find all of the same outmoded (yet wonderful) terms and all of the same challenging exercises that were in the original *The Mother Tongue*.

Certain examples and student exercises will seem dated to today's students, but we have kept them intact. For instance, modern grammar books have dispensed entirely with teaching students the pronouns *thee* and *thou* or the verb forms *shalt* and *wert*. This could be distracting, but we find that it is very valuable for students to understand these old forms of English, enabling them to read old books without fear. Likewise, *The Mother Tongue* uses old-fashioned terms such as "genitive case" for possessive case and "preterite," for past tense. These terms remain in place, with footnotes, margin boxes, or parenthetical reminders of what that term means. There is value in knowing these old terms, particularly for those students who will study other languages.

New features. We have added some features that we think modern students will find particularly helpful. **Margin boxes** contain definitions or summary information from chapters to make it easier to study and to remember the key information from that chapter. **New footnotes** throughout the text assist the teacher with unfamiliar terms that have fallen out of use.

We have also added **punctuation and capitalization practice exercises** to the student workbooks. Appendices on capitalization and punctuation rules, which are from *The Mother Tongue Revised Edition,* are included in the textbook. For students who need practice in applying punctuation and capitalization rules, our student workbooks contain extra practice exercises. We created these exercises by removing all capitals and punctuation from sentences taken from *The Mother Tongue* and from literature. Students are asked to copy the sentences, correcting all punctuation and capitalization.

THE COMPANION BOOKS

The Mother Tongue Adapted for Modern Students is a textbook with over 350 pages of grammar instruction, reference, and practice exercises.

The Mother Tongue Student Workbook 1 and *The Mother Tongue Student Workbook 2* provide all of the written exercises in a consumable format. Students are given space to complete the work directly on the page.

The Mother Tongue Student Workbook Key 1 and *2* provide answers for the workbook exercises. Until now, no key has been available for *The Mother Tongue.*

FOR THE TEACHER

The Mother Tongue is organized by chapter. Main points in each chapter are divided into numbered sections and are often referenced by section number. The section numbering continues chronologically to the end of the book and are used as a handy reference. This section numbering comes directly from *The Mother Tongue* first edition.

Most chapters include written exercises so the student can put the concept into practice. Some chapters have more practice than others, and some chapters do not have written practice exercises.

Scope and Sequence. *The Mother Tongue* teaches students the fundamentals of English grammar, as well as advanced grammar concepts. Students learn parts of speech, sentence analysis, noun cases, verb tenses, inflection and syntax. The chapters are progressively more challenging.

The Mother Tongue is an ideal resource for your student after he has completed an elementary grammar program.

How to Use *The Mother Tongue*. Some homeschooling families prefer to use *The Mother Tongue* as an oral grammar resource, reading aloud the sections and working the exercises together, a little bit each day.

Others like to use *The Mother Tongue* as a primary grammar text. The text can be used for three to four years in the middle grades, beginning as early as 5th grade and taking a slow pace, or beginning in high school taking an accelerated pace.

We have taught our multiple-age kids *The Mother Tongue* together by reading the chapter aloud in a group after which students work the written exercises independently. Occasionally we work the exercises together orally only.

The Mother Tongue is also an excellent grammar reference book to keep on your shelf.

Managing the Workload

The exercises provide students with plenty of opportunity to sharpen their grammar skills. Some students will not require all of the exercises to master the skill or concept. As the teacher, you must feel free to assign the appropriate amount to your students.

In the following pages, we offer three paces: a three-year plan, a two-year plan, and an accelerated one-year plan. These paces are only a guideline to help get you started.

Amy M. Edwards
Christina J. Mugglin
Editors

TEACHING SCHEDULES

Three Year Plan

The three year plan covers the first half of *The Mother Tongue* in one year and the last half in two years. In this plan, the early lessons are assumed to be review and the pace slows down considerably as the more challenging concepts are introduced. Additional capitalization and punctuation practice exercises can be done at the teacher's discretion.

Year One: Complete *The Mother Tongue Student Workbook 1,* which covers the first 75 chapters of *The Mother Tongue.*

Year Two: Complete chapters 76-110 of *The Mother Tongue Student Workbook 2.*

Year Three: Complete chapters 111-143 of *The Mother Tongue Student Workbook 2.*

Year 1: First Semester		Year 1: Second Semester		Year 2: First Semester		Year 2: Second Semester		Year 3: First Semester		Year 3: Second Semester	
Wks	Chap	Wks	Chap	Wks	Chap	Wks	Chap	Wks	Chap	Wks	Chap
1	1-2	19	37-38	1	76	19	93	1	111	19	128
2	3-4	20	39-40	2	77	20	94	2	112	20	129
3	5-6	21	41-42	3	78	21	95	3	113	21	130
4	7-8	22	43-44	4	79	22	96	4	114	22	131
5	9-10	23	45-46	5	80	23	97	5	115	23	132
6	11-12	24	47-48, Review	6	81	24	98	6	Review	24	133
7	13-14	25	49-50	7	82	25	99	7	116	25	134
8	15-16	26	51-52	8	83	26	100	8	117	26	135
9	17-18	27	53-54	9	84	27	101	9	118	27	136
10	19-20	28	55-56	10	85	28	102	10	119	28	137
11	21-22	29	57-60	11	86	29	103	11	120	29	138
12	23-24	30	61-62	12	87	30	104	12	121	30	139
13	25-26	31	63-64	13	88	31	105	13	122	31	140
14	27-28	32	65-67	14	89	32	106	14	123	32	141
15	29-30	33	68-70	15	Review	33	107	15	124	33	142
16	31-32	34	71-72	16	90	34	108	16	125	34	143
17	33-34	35	Review, 73	17	91	35	109	17	126	35	
18	35-36	36	74-75	18	92	36	110	18	127	36	

Two Year Plan

The two year plan covers *The Mother Tongue Student Workbook 1* in one year, and *The Mother Tongue Student Workbook 2* in one year. Students cover about two chapters a week. Additional capitalization and punctuation practice exercises can be done at the teacher's discretion.

Year 1: First Semester		Year 1: Second Semester		Year 2: First Semester		Year 2: Second Semester	
Weeks	Chapters	Weeks	Chapters	Weeks	Chapters	Weeks	Chapters
1	1-2	19	37-38	1	76-77	19	109-110
2	3-4	20	39-40	2	78-79	20	111-112
3	5-6	21	41-42	3	80-81	21	113-114
4	7-8	22	43-44	4	82-83	22	115-116
5	9-10	23	45-46	5	84-85	23	117-118
6	11-12	24	47-48, Review	6	86-87	24	119-120
7	13-14	25	49-50	7	88-89	25	121-122
8	15-16	26	51-52	8	Review, 90-91	26	123-124
9	17-18	27	53-54	9	92-93	27	125-126
10	19-20	28	55-56	10	94-95	28	127-128
11	21-22	29	57-60	11	96-97	29	129-130
12	23-24	30	61-62	12	98-99	30	131-132
13	25-26	31	63-64	13	100-101	31	133-134
14	27-28	32	65-67	14	102-103	32	135-136
15	29-30	33	68-70	15	104	33	137-138
16	31-32	34	71-72	16	105	34	139-140
17	33-34	35	Review, 73	17	106	35	141-142
18	35-36	36	74-75	18	107-108	36	143

One Year Accelerated Plan

This plan will help advanced grammar students quickly get through *The Mother Tongue* in one year. *The Mother Tongue Student Workbook 1* is covered in 12 weeks and *Student Workbook 2* is covered in the remaining 24 weeks. This plan assumes that chapters 1-75 will be review for the student. Additional capitalization and punctuation practice exercises can be done at the teacher's discretion. Students work about five days a week.

Week Q1	Chapters	Week Q2	Chapters	Week Q3	Chapters	Week Q4	Chapters
1	1-10	10	61-67	19	97-98	28	116-117
2	11-15	11	68-71	20	99	29	118-119
3	16-23	12	72-75	21	100-101	30	120-122
4	24-31	13	76-80	22	102-104	31	123-124
5	32-39	14	81-84	23	105-106	32	125-126
6	40-46	15	85-88	24	107-109	33	127-128
7	47-50	16	89-90	25	110-111	34	128-136
8	51-53	17	91-94	26	112-114	35	137-140
9	54-60	18	95-96	27	115	36	141-143

PREFACE TO THE ORIGINAL *MOTHER TONGUE BOOK II*
1901

The purpose of this book is to set forth the elements of English grammar in their relation to thought and the expression of thought. This object has been the guiding principle in the selection and arrangement of material, in the treatment of forms and constructions, and in the fashioning of the very numerous illustrative exercises.

The Introduction explains in simple language certain general conceptions too often ignored in the study of grammar: the nature of language, its relation to thought and to style, the processes which affect its growth and decay, the province of grammar, and the relation of grammar to usage. These chapters are intended to be read aloud by the pupils or by the teacher and to serve as the basis for informal discussion in the classroom. The pupil should not be allowed to study them mechanically. Above all things, he should not try to learn them by heart. The main principles which they embody are summed up in chapter 1, page 1, with which the definite study of grammar begins.

Chapters 2-58 deal primarily with the parts of speech and with their combination into sentences in the expression of thought. In this part of the book only so much inflection is included as is necessary for an understanding of the structure of sentences. As soon as the pupil has learned something of the nature of substantives and verbs, he is introduced to simple sentences, and from this point to the end of chapter 56, the study of analysis and synthesis is carried on in connection with the treatment of the parts of speech until all the main elements of sentence-structure have been exemplified. Chapter 57 sums up, by way of review, the analytical processes with which the pupil has become familiar in the chapters which precede.

With chapter 59 a more detailed study of inflection begins. This continues through chapter 115, and includes all the important phenomena of English inflection, which are explained, not as isolated facts, but as means of expressing varieties of human thought. The explanations are made as simple as possible, and this very simplicity necessitates a somewhat fuller treatment than is usual in school grammars. The paradigm of the verb has been much simplified by a careful discussion of verb phrases. A number of notes in fine type deal with some of the more striking facts of historical grammar, and may be used by the teacher at his discretion to illustrate the true nature of the forms and constructions of which they treat. The study of this part of the book implies constant reviews of the earlier chapters. For convenience, the point at which such reviews may be advantageously made is indicated in footnotes, but the teacher will of course use his own judgment. In particular, it will be found desirable to continue practice in analysis, and for this purpose abundant material is contained in the exercises appended to the several chapters.

A number of the more difficult syntactical questions are deferred until inflection has been mastered (see chapters 116-142). Their treatment at this point affords an opportunity for a thorough and systematic review of the structure of complex sentences.

The appendix contains a list of irregular verbs and other material intended for reference. The lists of irregular verbs may be used in connection with the lessons on the preterite and the participles (chapter 91-95). These lists differ from those furnished by most grammars in one important particular: they contain only such forms as are unquestionably correct in accordance with the best modern prose usage. Experience has shown that the attempt to include in a single list rare, archaic, and poetical verb- forms along with those habitually employed by the best prose writers of the present day is confusing and even misleading to the beginner.[1] Accordingly, such archaic and poetical forms as have to be mentioned are carefully separated from the forms regularly used in modern prose.

Exercises for practice are furnished in liberal measure. It is not intended that every pupil should necessarily work through all these exercises. Each teacher is the best judge of precisely how much practice his pupils require. The aim of the authors has been to provide such material in abundance and with due regard to variety.

In the choice of technical terms, the authors have preferred those names which are universally intelligible and have the

authority of long-continued usage in all languages, to other terms which are scarcely seen outside of the covers of elementary English grammars. Thus, for example, the term genitive has been preferred to possessive. One advantage of this plan is that it does not isolate the study of our own language from the study of foreign languages. Here again, however, the individual teacher can best judge of the needs of his pupils. Hence the alternative terms are regularly mentioned, and they may be substituted without inconvenience.

The authors make no apology for employing certain shorthand grammatical terms which cause no difficulty to the youngest pupils. A studious effort to separate the name from the thing named, for example, may be important for the philosopher, but it is only baffling to the beginner. No real confusion of thought can ever arise from speaking of an adjective, for example, as "modifying, or describing, a noun," instead of always taking pains to represent it as "modifying the meaning of the noun" or "describing the person or thing for which the noun stands." Scientific grammarians the world over have given their sanction to such shorthand expressions, and they have been unhesitatingly used in this book whenever directness could be gained thereby. Surely there is no danger that the youngest child will ever mistake the word *apple* for the object which bears that name!

[1] See Appendix B.

INTRODUCTION

LANGUAGE AND GRAMMAR

> Language is the **expression of thought** by means of spoken or written **words**.

The English word *language* comes from the Latin word *lingua*, "the tongue," and was originally applied to oral speech. But the art of writing is now so common that it is quite as natural for us to speak of the **language** in which a book is written as of the language in which an address is delivered or a conversation carried on.

Many savage tribes (for example, the North American Indians) have a method of conversing in gestures without speaking at all. This is called the **sign-language**. All language, however, is really **the expression of thought by means of signs**; for spoken words are signs made with the voice, and written words are signs made with the pen.

Thus when we speak or write the English word *dog*, we are just as truly making a sign as an Indian is when he expresses the idea *dog* by his fingers. Our spoken or written sign for *dog* cannot be understood by anybody who does not know the English language; for different languages have different words, that is, different signs, for the same thing or idea. Thus the German word for *dog* is *Hund*; the Latin word for dog is *canis*, and so on.

> Most **words** are the **signs** of definite **ideas**.

For example, *soldier, sailor, dog, cat, horse, tree, river, house, shop*, call up in our minds images of persons or things; *run, jump, write, travel*, suggest kinds of action; *red, black, tall, studious, careful*, suggest qualities belonging to persons or things.

By the aid of such distinct and picturesque words as these, we can express many thoughts and ideas; that is, we can talk or write after a fashion. But we cannot talk in a connected manner. If, for example, we wish to say that the house is on fire, we can express our thought imperfectly by saying simply, "House burn!" or "House! fire!" as a young child, or a foreigner who knew very little English, might do. But if we wish to express our thought fully, it would be natural to say, "The house is on fire." That is, besides the words that express distinct ideas, we should use little words, *the, is, on*, which do not call up any clear picture in the mind.

To express thought, then, language needs not merely words that are the signs of distinct ideas, but also a number of words like *is, was, in, to, but, if*, which serve merely to **join words together** and to **show their relations** to each other in connected speech.

> The **relations of words to each other in connected speech** are shown in three ways:
>
>   (1) by their **form**;
>   (2) by their **order** or **arrangement**;
>   (3) by **the use of words** like *and, if, to, from, by*, etc.

I. In the phrase "John's hat," the **form** of the word *John's* shows the **relation** of *John* to the *hat*; that is, it shows that John is the **owner** or **possessor** of the hat.

II. Compare the two sentences:

> John struck Charles.
> Charles struck John.

The meaning is entirely different. In the first sentence, *John* gives the blow and *Charles* receives it; in the second, *Charles* does the striking and *John* gets hit. Yet the forms of the three words *John, Charles,* and *struck* are the same in both sentences. In each case the relation of the three words to each other is shown by the **order in which they stand**; the word which comes first is the name of the striker, and the word which follows *struck* is the name of the person who receives the blow.

III. Let us examine the use of such words as *of, by, to, from,* and the like. In the following phrase,

> The honor of a gentleman,

the relation of *honor* to *gentleman* is shown by the word *of*. The *honor*, we see, **belongs to** the *gentleman*.

The relation in which a word stands to other words in connected speech is called its **construction.**
Grammar is the science which treats of the **forms** and the **constructions** of words.

The study of grammar, then, divides itself into two parts:

(1) the study of the different **forms** which a word may take (as *John* or *John's*; *walk* or *walks* or *walked*; *he* or *him*);

(2) the study of the different **constructions** which a word may have in connected speech.

(3) The first of these parts is called the study of **inflection**, the second the study of **syntax**.

The **inflection** of a word is a **change in its form** to indicate its construction.
Syntax is that department of grammar which treat of the **constructions of words.**

In some languages, the constructions of words are shown to a great extent by means of **inflection**. Thus, in Latin, *lapis* means "a stone"; *lapidis,* "of a stone"; *lapide,* "with a stone"; *lapidum* "of stones," and so on. The word *lapis,* it will be seen, **changes its form** by inflection as its **construction changes**. English was formerly rich in such inflections, but most of these have been lost, so that in modern English the constructions of many words have to be shown either by their order or by the use of various little words such as *of, with.*

The **rules** of grammar get their authority from **usage**.

By **usage** is meant the practice of the best writers or speakers, not merely the habits of the community in which a person happens to live. There are, of course, varieties in usage, so that it is not always possible to pronounce one of two expressions grammatical and the other ungrammatical. In some cases, too, there is room for difference of opinion as to the correctness of a particular form or construction. But in a language like English, which has been written and studied for centuries, all the main facts are well settled. Usage, then, is practically uniform throughout the English-speaking world. Pronunciation differs somewhat in different places, but educated Englishmen, Americans, and Australians all speak and write in accordance with the same grammatical principles.

> Since language is the expression of thought, the **rules of grammar agree**, in the main, with **the laws of thought.**

In other words, **grammar** accords, in the main, with **logic**, which is the science that deals with the processes of reasonable thinking.

There are, however, some exceptions. Every language has its peculiar phrases or constructions which appear to be irregular or even illogical, but which, because they have become established by **usage**, are not ungrammatical. These are called **idioms** (from a Greek word meaning "peculiarities").

For example, if we say "When *are you going* to study your lesson?" we use the word *going* in a peculiar way without any reference to actual motion or *going*. We mean simply "When *shall you* study?" This use of "are you going" for "shall you" is, then, an **English idiom**.

One may speak or write **grammatically** and still not speak or write in what is called a **good style**. In other words, language may be grammatical without being clear, forcible, and in good taste.

Thus in the sentence "Brutus assassinated Caesar because he wished to become king," no rule of grammar is broken. Yet the style of the sentence is bad because the meaning is not clear; we cannot tell who it was that desired the kingship — Caesar or Brutus. Again, "He talks as fast as a horse can trot" is perfectly grammatical, but it would not be an elegant expression to use of a great orator.

Good style, then, is impossible without grammatical correctness, but grammatical correctness does not necessarily carry with it good style.

The ability to speak and write correctly does not depend on a knowledge of grammatical rules. It is usually acquired by unconscious imitation, as children learn to talk. Yet an acquaintance with grammar is of great help in acquiring correctness of speech. In particular, it enables one to criticize one's self and to decide between what is right and what is wrong in many doubtful cases. *Grammar, then, is useful as a tool*.

But the study of grammar is also valuable as training in observation and thought. Language is one of the most delicate and complicated instruments which men use, and a study of its laws and their application is a worthy occupation for the mind.

DEVELOPMENT OF LANGUAGE

Language never stands still. Every language, until it *dies* (that is, until it ceases to be spoken at all), is in a state of continual change. The English which we speak and write is not the same English that was spoken and written by our grandfathers, nor was their English precisely like that of Queen Elizabeth's time. The farther back we go, the less familiar we find ourselves with the speech of our ancestors, until finally we reach a kind of English which is quite as strange to us as if it were a foreign tongue.

Such changes take place gradually—so slowly indeed, that we are hardly aware that they are going on at all—but in the long run they may transform a language so completely that only scholars can recognize the old words and forms as identical, at bottom, with the new. Indeed, the changes may go so far that entirely new languages are formed.

Thus from Latin, the language of the ancient Romans (which is now dead) have come, by these gradual processes, a whole group of living modern languages, including French, Italian, and Spanish, differing from each other so much that a Frenchman cannot understand an Italian or a Spaniard any better than he can an Englishman or a German.

The changes which a language undergoes are of many different kinds. Most of them, however, we can observe in our own experience if we stop to think of what takes place about us. They affect

> (1) **vocabulary**, that is, the stock of words which a language possesses,
> (2) the **meanings of words**,
> (3) their **pronunciation** and **spelling**,
> (4) their forms of **inflection**,
> (5) their **construction**, that is, the manner in which they are put together in expressing thought.

I. Many words and phrases which once belonged to the English language have gone out of use entirely. Such words are said to be obsolete (from a Latin word which means simply "out of use").

Thus *holt* ("wood"), *couth* ("known"), *thilk* ("that same"), *achatour* ("buyer"), *warray* ("to wage war"), are obsolete English words.

Many words and phrases, though obsolete in spoken English and in prose writing, are still used in poetry. Such words are called **archaic** (that is, *ancient*).

Examples are *ruth* ("pity"), *sooth* ("truth"), *wot* ("know"), *ween* ("think"), *eke* ("also").

But changes in **vocabulary** are not all in the way of **loss**. New words and phrases are always springing up, whether to name new things and ideas or merely for the sake of variety in expression. Thus within the memory of persons now living the words *telegraph telegram, telephone, dynamo*, and the like, have come into existence and made good their place in the English language.

Both of these processes—the **rise** and the **disappearance** of words—may be observed by every one in the case of what we call **slang**. Slang words spring up almost daily, are heard for a time from the lips of old and young, and then vanish (become *obsolete*), only to be replaced by newcomers. Now and then, however, a slang word gets a footing in good use and so keeps its place in the language. Thus, *mob, snob, boss, chum*, were originally slang, but are now recognized members of the English vocabulary.

II. Changes in meaning. The words of a living language are constantly **changing in sense**. Old meanings disappear and new meanings arise. Thus, in the following passages from Shakespeare, the italicized words all bear meanings which, though common three hundred years ago, are now out of use {*obsolete*):

She is of so sweet, so gentle, so blessed a *condition*. [*Condition* here means "character" or "nature."]

Advance your standards. [*Advance* means "lift up."]

Make all the money thou canst. [*Make* here means "collect," "get together," not, as in modern English, "earn" or "gain."][2]

III. Changes in pronunciation and spelling. The business of spelling is to indicate pronunciation. In a perfect system, words would be spelled as they are pronounced. Such a system, however, has never been in use in any language, and, indeed, is impracticable, for no two persons pronounce exactly alike. Even if a perfect system could be devised, it would not remain perfect forever, since the pronunciation of every language is constantly changing so long as the language is alive at all. In the last five hundred years the pronunciation of English has undergone a complete transformation. Our spelling, also, has been much altered, but, as everybody knows, it is far from doing its duty as an indicator of the sounds of words.

IV. Inflection, as we have learned, is a change in the form of a word indicating its construction (or relation to other words in the sentence). Thus, are all inflectional forms of the same verb.

In the time of Alfred the Great, in the ninth century, our language had many **inflectional forms** which it has since lost. Its history, indeed, is in great part the history of these losses in inflection. English of the present day has very few inflectional forms, replacing them by the use of various phrases (see preface, p. ii). The study of such changes does not come within the scope of this book; but a few of them must be mentioned, from time to time, to illustrate modern forms and constructions.

V. The changes to which our language has been subjected in the matter of grammatical **construction** are numerous and complicated. The general tendency, however, especially for the past two hundred years, has been in the direction of law and order. Hence very many constructions which are now regarded as errors were in former times perfectly acceptable. In reading Shakespeare, for instance, we are continually meeting with forms and expressions which would be ungrammatical in a modern English writer. Two practical cautions are necessary:

(1) A construction which is ungrammatical in modern English cannot be defended by quoting Shakespeare.

(2) Shakespeare must not be accused of "bad grammar" because he does not observe all the rules of modern English syntax.

The language which one uses should always fit the occasion.

Colloquial English (that is, the language of ordinary conversation) admits many words, phrases, forms, and constructions which would be out of place in a dignified oration or a serious poem.

---

[2] Any large dictionary will afford abundant illustration of obsolete words and senses of words. See, for example, such a dictionary under *bower, cheer, favor, secure, convince, instance, insist, condescend, wizard, comply, soon, wot, mote, whilom, trow, hight.*

On the other hand, it is absurd always to "talk like a book," that is, to maintain, in ordinary conversation, the language appropriate to a speech or an elaborate essay. We should not "make little fishes talk like whales."

In general, written language is expected to be more careful and exact than spoken language. A familiar letter, however, may properly be written as one would talk.

The **poetical style** admits many **archaic** (that is, *old*) words, forms, and constructions that would be out of place in prose. It is also freer than prose with respect to the order or arrangement of words.

The **solemn style** resembles in many ways the style of poetry. In particular it preserves such words as *thou* and *ye*, and such forms as *hath, doth, saith findest, findeth,* and the like, which have long been obsolete in everyday language.

English Grammar

CHAPTER 1
General Principles [3]

Language expresses thought by using words.

❧

Construction refers to the way words are put together in connected speech.

❧

Inflection is a change in a word's form to change the word's meaning.

❧

Grammar is the science of the forms and construction of words.

❧

Rules of grammar take their authority from usage.

1. **Language is the expression of thought by means of spoken or written words.**

    Words are signs made to indicate thought.

2. Some words express **definite ideas**: as, *horse, sunset, run, headlong.*

    Other words (like *to, from, at, is, was, though*) express thought vaguely or in a very general way. Their use in language is to **connect** the more definite words, and to show their **relations** to each other.

3. **The relation in which a word stands to other words in connected speech is called its construction.**

    The **construction** of English words is shown in three ways:
    1. by their form;
    2. by their order;
    3. by the use of little words like *to, from, is,* etc.

4. **Inflection is a change in the form of a word which indicates a change in its meaning:**

    George, George's
    man, men
    kills, killed

5. **Grammar is the science which treats of the forms and the constructions of words.**

6. The **rules of grammar** derive their authority from custom or **usage**. They agree in general with the processes of thought.

---

[3] This chapter summarizes some of the general principles explained in the introductory chapters.

CHAPTER 2
The Parts of Speech

8 Parts of Speech
1. Noun
2. Pronoun
3. Adjective
4. Verb
5. Adverb
6. Preposition
7. Conjunction
8. Interjection

7. The curfew tolls the knell of parting day;
The lowing herd wind slowly o'er the lea;
The plowman homeward plods his weary way,
And leaves the world to darkness and to me.

A study of this stanza of poetry shows that different words in it have different tasks to perform in expressing the poet's thought.

Thus, *tolls, wind, leaves* **assert** or **declare** that somebody or something is **acting** in some manner. *Herd, plowman, world* are the **names** of persons or things. *Weary* is not the name of anything, but it **describes** the *way. And* calls up no picture in our minds, as *plowman*, or *herd*, or *darkness* does; it merely **connects** the fourth line of the stanza with the third. *Of* in the first line **shows the relation** between *knell* and *day. Me* is not the name of anybody, but it nevertheless **stands for** a person, — the speaker or writer of the poem.

Every **word** has **its own work** to do in the **expression of thought**. To understand the different tasks performed by different kinds of words is the first business of all students of language.

8. **In accordance with their various uses, words are divided into classes called parts of speech.**

9. **There are eight parts of speech: nouns, pronouns, adjectives, verbs, adverbs, prepositions, conjunctions, and interjections.**[4]

---

[4] The definitions that follow should not be committed to memory at this point. They are for reference, and for use as a review lesson after chapter 26.

THE PARTS OF SPEECH

A NOUN **is the name of a person, place, or thing.**
EXAMPLES: Charles, John, Mary, man, woman, boy, girl, London, Paris, city, town, street, horse, cat, dog, wood, iron, hammer, shovel, goodness, truth.

A PRONOUN **is a word used instead of a noun. It designates a person, place, or thing, without naming it.**
EXAMPLES: I, you, he, she, it, this, that, who, which, whoever.

Nouns and pronouns are called **substantives**.

An ADJECTIVE **is a word which limits or defines a substantive, usually by attributing some quality.**
EXAMPLES: good, bad, red, green, blue, heavy, large, pleasant, disagreeable, mysterious, idle.

A VERB **is a word which can assert something (usually an act) concerning a person, place, or thing.**
EXAMPLES: runs, jumps, travels, study, dig, fly, swim, try.

An ADVERB **modifies the meaning of a verb, an adjective, or another adverb.**
EXAMPLES: quickly, slowly, angrily, carefully, here, up, down.

A PREPOSITION **shows the relation of the substantive which follows it to some other word or words in the sentence.**
EXAMPLES: of, in, by, from, with, during, over, under.

A CONJUNCTION **connects words or groups of words.**
EXAMPLES: and, or, but, for, because, however, if.

An INTERJECTION **is a cry or exclamatory sound expressing surprise, anger, pleasure, or some other emotion or feeling.**
EXAMPLES: oh! ah! pshaw! fie! ha! alas! bravo!

CHAPTER 3
Nouns

10. One of the first duties of language is that of **naming** persons and things. It is impossible to express our thoughts unless we can, as the saying is, "call things by their right names."

In the following passage the italicized words are the **names** of various objects. Such words are called **nouns**.

> There was a most ingenious *architect*, who had contrived a new method for building *houses*, by beginning at the *roof* and working downward to the *foundation*; which he justified to me by the like practice of those two prudent *insects*, the *bee* and the *spider*. — SWIFT.

The word *noun* is derived from the French word for "name."

11. **A noun is the name of a person, place, or thing.**

> EXAMPLES: Charles, Mary, man, woman, boy, girl, horse, cow, cat, camel, city, town, village, kitchen, shop, Chicago, Texas, California, house, box, stable, car, boat, curtain, hatchet.

12. **Nouns are divided into two classes:**

> 1. **Proper nouns**
> 2. **Common nouns**

The difference may be seen in the following examples:

> *Charles* rode the horse to water.
> The *boy* rode the horse to water.

Charles is a person's own name, — the name which belongs to him and by which he is distinguished from other persons. It is therefore called a **proper name** or **proper noun**, "proper" in this use meaning "one's own."

Boy, on the other hand, is not the name of a particular person. It is a **general term** for any one of a large **class** of persons, — male human beings below the age of manhood. Hence it is called a **common noun**, that is, a name common to a whole class of objects.

The same distinction is found in the names of places and things. *Boston, Cincinnati, London, Paris, Germany, France, Mt. Washington, and Sahara* are proper nouns. *City, country, mountain, and desert* are common nouns.

A **noun** is a person, place, or thing.

There are two classes of nouns: **common** and **proper**.

<table>
<tr><td>

Two Noun Classes

ક

Proper: special name for a particular person, place or thing.

Common: a name for a whole class of similar persons, places or things.

</td></tr>
</table>

13. **A proper noun is the special name by which a particular person, place, or thing is distinguished from others of the same kind or class.**

> EXAMPLES: John, James, Mary, Elizabeth, Washington, Grant, Shakespeare, Milton, Rome, London, Cuba, Rocky Mountains, Cape Hatteras, Klondike.

14. **A common noun is a name which may be applied to any one of a whole class of similar persons, places, or things.**

> EXAMPLES: man, woman, child, dog, cow, fairy, street, house, monument, knife, bookcase.

In writing, proper nouns begin with a capital letter and common nouns usually begin with a small letter.

15. The English word "thing" is not confined in its use to objects that we can see, hear, taste, or touch. We may say, for example:

> *Patriotism* is a good thing.
> *Cowardice* is a contemptible thing.
> I wish there were no such thing as *sorrow*.

Such words as *patriotism* and *cowardice*, then, come under the general heading of names of things, and are therefore nouns.

16. When the name of a person, place, or thing consists of a number of words, the whole group may be regarded as a single noun. Thus,

> *Charles Allen* is my brother.
> *William Shakespeare* is the author of "Hamlet."
> *"The Rime of the Ancient Mariner"* was written by *Samuel Taylor Coleridge.*
> *North America* is connected with *South America* by the *Isthmus of Panama.*

Chapter 3 Exercise

In the following passages pick out as many nouns as you can find, and tell whether each is a common or a proper noun.

1. Drake with his one ship and eighty men held boldly on; and, passing the Straits of Magellan, untraversed as yet by any Englishman, swept the unguarded coast of Chili and Peru, and loaded his bark with gold-dust and silver-ingots of Potosi, and with the pearls, emeralds, and diamonds which formed the cargo of the great galleon that sailed once a year from Lima to Cadiz.

2. In that same village, and in one of these very houses (which, to tell the precise truth, was sadly time-worn and weather-beaten), there lived many years since, while the country was yet a province of Great Britain, a simple, good-natured fellow, of the name of Rip Van Winkle. He was a descendant of the Van Winkles who figured so gallantly in the chivalrous days of Peter Stuyvesant and accompanied him to the siege of Fort Christina.

3. An inhabitant of Truro told me that about a fortnight after the St. John was wrecked at Cohasset, he found two bodies on the shore at the Clay Pounds.

4. Oliver Goldsmith was born on the tenth of November, 1728, at the hamlet of Pallas, or Pallasmore, county of Longford, in Ireland.

CHAPTER 4
Special Classes of Nouns[5]

Abstract noun: name of a quality or idea.

Collective noun: name of a group, class, multitude, but not a single person, place or thing.

17. Certain classes of common nouns receive special names. Particularly important classes are **abstract nouns** and **collective nouns**.

18. In Section 15 we learned that words like *patriotism*, *cowardice*, and *sorrow*, which are the **names** of **ideas** or **qualities**, are nouns. Further examples follow:

> *Pity* is akin to *love*.
> *Order* is heaven's first law.
> A soft answer turneth away *wrath*.
> *Virtue* is bold, and *goodness* never fearful.

Such names as *pity*, *wrath*, etc., are called **abstract nouns**.

19. **An abstract noun is the name of a quality or general idea.**

> EXAMPLES: goodness, sweetness, wisdom, ignorance, truth, amiability, sauciness, folly, virtue, wickedness, liberty.

Many abstract nouns end in *-ness* and *-ty*.

20. In the following sentences the italicized nouns are the **names** of **groups** or **collections** of persons:

> A *crowd* gathered almost in an instant.
> The whole *class* studied the wrong lesson.
> The *crew* of the wrecked steamer were all saved.
> These boys formed a *club* to practice rowing.
> Captain Smith is an officer in the *navy*.

Such names are called **collective nouns**.

21. **A collective noun is the name of a group, class, or multitude, and not of a single person, place, or thing.**

> EXAMPLES: class, fleet, army, host, gang, company, regiment, party, people, nation, multitude, flock, herd, set, lot.

---

[5] This chapter should not be studied until the pupil is thoroughly familiar with the two main classes of nouns, proper and common. The teacher may prefer to postpone it until after chapter 16 or after.

22. Collective nouns are usually common nouns, but they become proper nouns when they are used as the special name of a particular group, class, or company. Thus,

> The *Congress* of the United States meets in Washington.
> The *Philadelphia Base Ball Club* will play at New York tomorrow.
> The *First Class* will recite at ten o'clock.

23. Any word, when mentioned merely **as a word**, is a noun. Thus,

> *Is* is one of the shortest words in our language.
> *Was* is a verb.
> *And* is a conjunction.

Chapter 4 Exercises

I.

In the following passages pick out all the abstract and all the collective nouns that you can find.

1. A number of young people were assembled in the music room.
2. He leads towards Rome a band of warlike Goths.
3. By ten o'clock the whole party were assembled at the Park.
4. Have I not reason to look pale and dead?
5. People were terrified by the force of their own imagination.
6. The Senate has letters from the general.
7. You misuse the reverence of your place.
8. There is hardly any place, or any company, where you may not gain knowledge if you please.
9. Here comes another troop to seek for you.
10. Their mastiffs are of unmatchable courage.
11. Our family dined in the field, and we sat, or rather reclined, round a temperate repast.
12. Our society will not break up, but we shall settle in some other place.
13. Let nobody blame him; his scorn I approve.
14. The Senate have concluded
    To give this day a crown to mighty Caesar.
15. He is banished, as enemy to the people and his country.
16. Society has been called the happiness of life.
17. His army is a ragged multitude
    Of hinds and peasants, rude and merciless.
18. There is a great difference between knowledge and wisdom.

19. All the country in a general voice cried hate upon him.
20. The king hath called his Parliament.
21. Let all the number of the stars give light to thy fair way!

II.

Give some collective noun which stands for a number or group of something. Thus,

Men — A company of men

Men, birds, cows, thieves, marbles, school children, sailors, soldiers, football players, musicians, robbers, pirates, books, postage stamps, senators, Members of Congress, partners in business.

III.

Give an abstract noun which names the idea or quality suggested by each of the words in the following list. Thus,

True — The noun is *truth*.

True, false, good, bad, lazy, careless, free, brave, sinful, cautious, just, beautiful, amiable, insane, passionate, natural, hasty, valiant, angry, grieving, sorry, holy, evil, unjust, accurate, simple.

CHAPTER 5
Pronouns

24. In expressing our thoughts we often have occasion to **mention** a person, place, or thing without **naming** it. Thus,

> The boy found a ball on the ground. *He* picked *it* up and put *it* into *his* pocket.

Here the boy and the ball are mentioned at the outset, but we do not wish to keep repeating the nouns *boy* and *ball.* Hence we use *he* and *his* to designate the boy, and *it* to designate the ball. These words are not nouns, for they do not **name** anything. They are called **pronouns**, because they stand **in the place of nouns** (*pro* being a Latin word for "instead of").

25. **A pronoun is a word used instead of a noun. It designates a person, place, or thing without naming it.**

26. Pronouns are not absolutely necessary to the expression of thought; but they make it possible to avoid awkward and confusing repetition. Compare the passages in the parallel columns below.

THOUGHT EXPRESSED WITH PRONOUNS	THOUGHT EXPRESSED WITHOUT PRONOUNS
The savages had two canoes with *them. They* had hauled *them* up on the shore.	The savages had two canoes with the savages. The savages had hauled the canoes up on the shore.

If you try to talk without using *I, you, he, she,* or *it,* you will soon discover what pronouns are good for.

27. The main classes of pronouns are:

> Personal,
> Relative,
> Interrogative,
> Demonstrative.

Their distinction and uses will be studied in later chapters.

For the present, we may content ourselves with recognizing some of the most important pronouns when we see them. Such are: *I, me, you, we, he, his, him, she, her, they, their, them.*

A **pronoun** is a word used in place of a noun. It designates a person, place or thing without naming it.

≈

Main classes of pronouns:
Personal
Relative
Interrogative
Demonstrative

Nouns and pronouns are called **substantives**.	28. Since the chief use of pronouns is to replace nouns, the constructions of these two parts of speech are almost always the same. It is therefore convenient to have a term which means "noun or pronoun," and the term used for this purpose is **substantive**.

29. Nouns and pronouns are called substantives.

Chapter 5 Exercises

I.

In the following passages pick out what nouns and pronouns you can find.

If you can, tell what noun is replaced by each pronoun.

1. Goneril, the elder, declared that she loved her father more than words could give out, that he was dearer to her than the light of her own eyes.
2. Bassanio took the ring and vowed never to part with it.
3. The floor of the cave was dry and level, and had a sort of small loose gravel upon it.
4. Having now brought all my things on shore, and secured them, I went back to my boat, and rowed, or paddled her along the shore, to her old harbor, where I laid her up. — *Robinson Crusoe.*
5. Heaven lies about us in our infancy.
6. Blessed is he who has found his work.
7. In fact, Tom declared it was of no use to work on his farm; it was the most pestilent little piece of ground in the whole country; everything about it went wrong, and would go wrong, in spite of him.
8. When Portia parted with her husband, she spoke cheeringly to him, and bade him bring his dear friend along with him when he returned.

II.

Fill the blanks with pronouns.

1. A thought struck _____, and _____ wrote a letter to one of _____ friends.
2. The flowers were bending _____ heads, as if _____were dreaming of the rainbow and dew.
3. We make way for the man who boldly pushes past _____.
4. "That's a brave man," said Wellington, when _____ saw a soldier turn pale as _____ marched against a battery: " _____ knows _____ danger, and faces _____ ."
5. I know not what course others may take; but, as for _____, give _____ liberty, or give _____ death.

6. There, in _____ noisy mansion, skilled to rule,
   The village master taught _____ little school.
7. Wordsworth helps us to live _____ best and highest life; _____ is a strengthening and purifying influence like _____ own mountains.
8. As the queen hesitated to pass on, young Raleigh, throwing _____ cloak from his shoulder, laid _____ on the miry spot, so as to ensure _____ stepping over _____ dryshod.
9. Tender-handed stroke a nettle,
   And _____ stings you for _____ pains;
   Grasp _____ like a man of mettle,
   And _____ soft as silk remains.
10. Whatever people may think of _____, do that which _____ believe to be right.
11. No man is so foolish but _____ may give another good counsel sometimes, and no man so wise but _____ may easily err.

CHAPTER 6
Verbs and Verb Phrases

Verbs:
Express or
assert action,
state, or
condition.

30. In order to express our thoughts we must be able not only to "call things by their right names," but to make statements, — that is, to **assert**.

31. Let us examine the following groups of words:

> Birds *fly*.
> Fishes *swim*.
> The boy *played* ball well.

Each of these expressions contains a word (*fly, swim, played*) which expresses **action**. Thus, *fly* expresses the action of the birds; *swim*, that of the fishes; *played*, that of the boy.

But these three words, *fly, swim,* and *played*, not only **express** action, they **state** or **assert** the action. Thus, in "Birds fly," it is the word *fly* which makes the assertion that the birds act in a certain way.

Such words are called **verbs**.

Language, then, must furnish us not only with **nouns**, by means of which we can **name** persons, places, or things, but with words of another kind, by means of which we can **state** or **assert** something about persons, places, and things.

32. **A verb is a word which can assert something (usually an act) concerning a person, place, or thing.**

In each of the following examples pick out the word which states or asserts some act:

> The travelers climbed the mountain.
> Wellington defeated Napoleon at Waterloo.
> The snow fell in great flakes all day long.

33. Most verbs express **action**. Some, however, merely express **state** or **condition**. Thus,

> You *lack* energy.
> This lake *abounds* in fish.
> The soldier *lay* dead on the battlefield.

Verb Phrases:
When an **auxiliary verb** is combined with a verb, a **verb phrase** is formed.

❧

Auxiliary verbs are also known as **helping verbs.**

❧

Auxiliary verbs:
forms of *to be*, *may, can, must, might, shall, will, could, would, should, have, has, had, do, did*

34. *Is (are, was, were,* etc.*), may, can, must, might, shall, will, could, would, should, have, had, do, did,* have a peculiar use in what are called **verb phrases**: as,

> The company *is charging* up the hill.
> The house *may fall* at any moment.
> We *can swim* to the boat.
> Our friends *will search* the woods in vain.

In the first of these sentences the assertion is made by means of the phrase *is charging*; in the second it is the phrase *may fall* that asserts the action, and so on.

Each of these phrases is formed by combining *is, may, can,* etc., with some word that expresses action, *charging, fall, swim, search.*

English has many verb phrases, by means of which it is able to express action in various ways. They will be studied in later chapters.

35. *Is (are, was, were,* etc.*), may, can, must, might, shall, will, could, would should, have, had, do, did,* when used in **verb phrases**, are called **auxiliary** (that is, "aiding") **verbs**, because they help other words to express action or state of some particular kind.[6]

36. The auxiliary verb may be separated from the rest of the verb phrase by other words. Thus,

> Tom *may* perhaps *find* his purse.
> We *were* rapidly *drifting* down the river.
> Washington *has* never *lost* the affection of his
>   countrymen.

Chapter 6 Exercises

I.
In each of the following passages pick out all the verbs and verb phrases that you can find.

1. Count Otto stares till his eyelids ache.
2. But so slowly did I creep along, that I heard a clock in a cottage strike four before I turned down the lane from Slough to Eton.
3. Like as the waves make towards the pebbled shore,
   So do our minutes hasten to their end.

---

[6] Editor's note: Auxiliary verbs are often called "helping verbs."

4. If it rains, we converse within doors.
5. The book you mention lies now upon my table.
6. The fleet in the Downs sent their captains on shore, hoisted the King's pennon, and blockaded the Thames.
7. The little company of the "Pilgrim Fathers," as after-times loved to call them, landed on the barren coast of Massachusetts, at a spot to which they gave the name of Plymouth, in memory of the last English port at which they touched.

II.
Pick out all the verbs and verb phrases that you can find in chapter 5, Exercise II.

III.
Fill each blank with a verb or verb phrase.

A young friend of mine _____ a clever little dog, whose name _____ Jack. He _____ his master whenever he _____ to school, and always _____ for him until the children _____. Then the dog _____ along at the boy's heels until home _____ in sight. Once some rascal _____ Jack and _____ him up in a cellar a long way from home. But Jack _____ and _____ his master again. I never _____ a dog that _____ on his hind legs so gracefully as my friend's Jack.

CHAPTER 7
Sentences

> A **sentence** is a group of words that expresses a single thought in a complete way.

37. Language, as we have already learned, is **thought expressed in words.**

In speaking or writing, however, we do not utter our thoughts in single words, but in **groups of words** which are so put together as to express **connected ideas**. Thus,

Birds fly.	Iron sinks.
Wood floats.	Lions roar.

These are very simple groups, but each expresses some thought and is, in a manner, complete in itself.

38. If we study a longer passage, we see at once that it may be broken up into a number of groups, some larger and some smaller, each of which is a kind of unit. Thus,

> The soldier awoke at break of day. | He sprang up from his hard couch on the ground. | The drums were beating. | It was time to fall in for the day's march.

The passage falls into four of these groups, each standing by itself and expressing a single thought.

Such groups of words are **sentences** of a very simple kind.

39. In the next chapter we shall study the **structure of sentences**, — that is, the parts out of which they are composed and the way in which those parts are put together.

For the present, we may content ourselves with framing a few sentences for practice. This we can easily do, for we have spoken in sentences ever since we learned to talk.

40. Make a short statement about each of the persons and things mentioned in the list below. Thus,

Lions	Lions are found in Africa.
Tree	A large tree grew in the square.

Ball, kite, top, doll, carriage, dogs, cats, schoolhouse, John, Mary, tigers, fisherman, carpenters, book, history, sugar, leather, vinegar, apples, plums, melon, salt.

In each of the statements you have **expressed a thought in language**. This you have done by means of putting together (**combining**) **words** into **sentences**.

Chapter 7 Exercises

Chapter 7 written work is included in Section 40, above, and may be done orally in the lesson time if desired.

CHAPTER 8
Sentences: Subject and Predicate

41. In the expression of ideas words are combined into sentences.

42. In its simplest form a sentence is the statement of a single fact. Thus,

Fire burns.	The king reigns.
Water freezes.	Victoria is queen.

Each of these sentences consists, it will be observed, of two parts:

> (1) a word or words designating the person or thing that is **spoken of** (*fire, water, the king, Victoria*);
> (2) a word or words **telling something about** that person or thing (*burns, freezes, reigns, is queen*).

The first of these parts is called the **subject** of the sentence, and the second is called the **predicate**.

43. Accordingly we have the following rules:

> **(1) Every sentence consists of a subject and a predicate.**
> **(2) The subject of a sentence is that person, place, or thing which is spoken of;**
> **(3) the predicate is that which is said of the subject.**

44. A declarative sentence is a sentence which declares or asserts something as a fact.

There are several forms of the sentence besides the declarative sentence. These will be studied later.

45. In such a sentence as

> Victoria reigns,

we have a very simple form of both subject and predicate. *Victoria*, the subject, is a single noun; and *reigns*, the predicate, is a single verb. So in

Fire burns.	Ships sail.
Horses gallop.	Truth prevails.

The subject may, however, be not a noun but a pronoun; for the office of pronouns is to stand in the place of nouns. Thus, in the sentence

---

A **sentence** contains a **subject** and a **predicate**.

❧

The **subject** is a person, place, or thing which is spoken of.

❧

The **predicate** is that which is said of the subject.

❧

A **declarative sentence** declares or asserts something as fact.

He laughs,

he is the subject, and *laughs* is the predicate.

If we examine a somewhat longer sentence, we shall see that it is still made up of the same two parts, — **subject** and **predicate**. Thus, in

The old chief of the Mohawks | fought desperately,

the whole subject is *The old chief of the Mohawks*, and the whole predicate is *fought desperately*.

46. The subject usually precedes the predicate; but not always. Thus,

Down came the rain.   Up flew the window.
Ran Coll, our dog.   Sad was the day.

Chapter 8 Exercises

I.

Fill the blanks with verbs, verb phrases, nouns, or pronouns, so as to make each example a complete sentence. Tell what it is that you have inserted in each case.

1. The teacher _____ at her desk writing.
2. The captain _____ his company in the suburbs of the town.
3. The strife _____ with unremitting fury for three mortal hours.
4. The first permanent settlement on the Chesapeake _____ in the beginning of the reign of James the First.
5. I _____ an aged beggar in my walk.
6. The English army _____ too exhausted for pursuit.
7. The owls _____ all night long.
8. A crow _____ a nest in one of the young elm trees.
9. A famous man _____ Robin Hood.
10. In the confusion, five or six of the enemy _____.
11. The eyes of the savage _____ with fury.
12. A little leak _____ a great ship.
13. The blacksmith _____ the red-hot iron.
14. A sudden _____ clouded the sky.
15. My _____ was then in London.
16. The _____ followed us over the moor.
17. _____ commanded the American army.
18. The _____ have wandered about nearly all day.
19. A high _____ blew hats and bonnets about.

20. The _____ fired a broadside at the enemy.
21. Many _____ were swimming in the pool.
22. Down _____ the timber with a crash.
23. Higher and higher _____ the sun.

II.

By means of a vertical line divide each of your completed sentences in **I,** above, into subject and predicate.

For example: The teacher │_____ at her desk writing.

CHAPTER 9
Complete and Simple Subject and Predicate

47.   Examine once more the sentence studied in Section 45:

The old chief of the Mohawks | fought desperately.

The **whole subject** is *the old chief of the Mohawks*, and the **whole predicate** is *fought desperately*.

The most important word in the subject is the **noun** *chief*; the most important word in the predicate is the **verb** *fought*. If we omit *old*, the sentence still makes sense. So we may omit *of the Mohawks*, or *desperately*, without destroying the sentence. But if we omit either *chief* or *fought*, the remaining words no longer make any statement.

> The old _____ of the Mohawks | fought desperately; or
> The old chief of the Mohawks | _____ desperately,

would be nonsense, for it would not express a thought.

In this sentence, then, a single noun, *chief*, names the person concerning whom the assertion is made, and a single verb, *fought* declares or asserts the action.

The noun *chief* is therefore called the **simple subject**, and the verb *fought* the **simple predicate** of the sentence.

The other words or phrases which go to make up the whole subject, — *the*, *old*, and *of the Mohawks*, — define more exactly the meaning of the simple subject *chief*.

The noun *chief* by itself may refer to any chief; but *the old chief of the Mohawks* is a well-defined person.

Similarly, the meaning of the simple predicate, the verb *fought* is defined or limited by the word *desperately* (telling *how* he fought).

48.   **The simple subject of a sentence is a noun or pronoun.**

The simple predicate of a sentence is a verb or verb phrase.

The simple subject, with such words as limit or define its meaning, forms the complete subject.

The simple predicate, with such words as limit or define its meaning, forms the complete predicate.

The **simple subject** is a noun or pronoun.

&

The **simple predicate** is a verb or verb phrase.

&

The **complete subject** is a simple subject and all the words that modify it (such as adjectives, appositives, etc.).

&

The **complete predicate** is a simple predicate and all the words that modify it (such as adverbs, objects, etc.).

A **sentence** expresses a **complete thought** and contains a **subject** and a **predicate.**

≈

A **noun** or **pronoun** which is the subject of a sentences is said to be in the **nominative case.** (More on this in chapter 70.)

≈

Analysis is a Greek word which means "the act of breaking up."

≈

In grammar, **analyzing a sentence** means to break it into its parts- **subject, predicate, and modifiers**.

In this book the **simple subject** and the **simple predicate** will generally be called the **subject** and the **predicate.** When the whole or complete subject or predicate is referred to, the terms **complete subject** and **complete predicate** will be used.

49.   The simple predicate may be a **verb phrase**. Thus,

Fire will burn.   John is running.

50.   In each of the following sentences the complete subject and the complete predicate are separated by a vertical line, and the simple subject and the simple predicate are printed in small capitals:

> Vast MEADOWS |STRETCHED to the eastward.
> The FARMER of Grand Pré | LIVED on his sunny farm.
> The rude FOREFATHERS of the hamlet | SLEEP.
> Each HORSEMAN | DREW his battle blade.
> The old DOCTOR | WAS SITTING in his armchair.
> The CLOCK | HAS STRUCK the hour of midnight.

51.   We are now able to define a sentence in a more accurate way than was possible before we knew the meaning of subject and predicate.

> **A sentence is a combination of words which expresses a thought and which contains a subject and a predicate.**

> **A noun or pronoun which is the subject of a sentence is said to be in the nominative case.**

52.   The exercises which follow are exercises in **analysis**.

Analysis is a Greek word which means "the act of breaking up." In grammar the term is applied to the "breaking up" or separation of a sentence into its parts, — **subject, predicate**, and **limiting words**. To dissect a sentence in this way is to **analyze** it.

In later chapters we shall learn more about the details of grammatical analysis.

53.   Analysis is useful not only because it helps us to get at the meaning of a thought, but because it sharpens our wits and tests our understanding of what we read. Practice in analysis ought also to assist us in expressing ourselves clearly and correctly.

Chapter 9 Exercise

By means of a vertical line divide the following sentences into their complete subjects and complete predicates.

In each sentence point out the substantive that is the simple subject and the verb or verb phrase that is the simple predicate.

1. She roams the dreary waste.
2. Ten thousand warblers cheer the day.
3. Thou climbest the mountain-top.
4. The river glideth at his own sweet will.
5. The rings of iron sent out a jarring sound.
6. The bolted gates flew open at the blast.
7. The streets ring with clamors.
8. The courser pawed the ground with restless feet.
9. Envy can never dwell in noble hearts.
10. His whole frame was trembling.
11. The wondering stranger round him gazed.

CHAPTER 10
The Copula (Linking Verb) "Is" [7]

54. One peculiar verb which is very important in the making of sentences, has so little meaning in itself that we might easily fail to recognize it as a verb at all.

This is the verb *is* (in its different forms), as seen in the following sentences:

I *am* your friend.   Tom *was* tired.
The road *is* rough.   You *were* merry.
These apples *are* mellow.   The soldiers *were* brave.

The verb *is* (in its various forms) is called the **copula.**

ેક

The term **copula** has been replaced with **linking** verb.

ેક

Am, is, are, was, were, are forms of the verb *to be.*

In all these examples the verb forms *am, is, are, was, were* do not in themselves tell us anything about the subject. The meaning of the predicate is really contained in the words that follow the verb (*your friend, rough, mellow,* etc.).

Yet if we omit the verb we no longer have sentences:

I _____ your friend.   Tom _____ tired.
The road _____ rough.   You _____ merry.
These apples _____ mellow.   The soldiers _____ brave.

55. The verb *is,* then, does two things:

> (1) It **asserts,** or **makes the statement** (for, omitting it, we have no statement);
> (2) It **connects** the **subject** with the word or words in the complete **predicate** that possess a distinct meaning.

Hence the verb *is* (in its various forms) is called the **copula,** that is, the "joiner" or "link."

56. The forms of the verb *is* are very irregular. They will be more fully studied in later chapters.

Meantime we should recognize *am, is, are, was, were,* as forms of this verb, and *has been, have been, had been, shall be,* and *will be,* as **verb phrases** belonging to it.

---

[7] Editor's Note: The term "copula" has fallen out of use, but it simply means, "a connecting word, in particular a form of the verb *be* connecting a subject and complement." Modern grammar texts generally speak of the linking verb "is."

57. In sentences like those in Section 54, the simple predicates are the verbs *am, is, are,* etc.[8]

58. The verb *is* (in its various forms) is not always a mere copula. It is sometimes emphatic and has the sense of *exist*. Thus,

I think. Therefore I *am*. [That is, I *exist*.]
Whatever *is*, is right. [That is, Whatever *exists*.]

Chapter 10 Exercises

I.

Make the following groups of words into sentences by inserting some form of the copula (*is, are,* etc.).

1. Fishes cold-blooded animals.
2. Milton a great poet.
3. Washington the Father of his Country.
4. You studious children.
5. Thou the man.
6. You a studious child.
7. He a colonel.

II.

Find the copula. Tell what it connects.

1. The stranger is an Austrian.
2. Your friends will be glad to see you.
3. We shall be too tired to walk home.
4. Seals are amphibious animals.
5. I am an American citizen.
6. The streets were wet and muddy.
7. Platinum is a very heavy metal.
8. Washington had been an officer under Braddock.
9. The Indians on Cape Cod were friendly.
10. We have been careless.
11. Sidney Lanier was a native of Georgia.

---

[8] Many grammarians regard *is* and the noun or adjective that follows it (*is rough, are mellow,* etc.) as the simple predicate; but the nomenclature here adopted is equally scientific and more convenient.

CHAPTER 11
Interrogative Sentences, Part 1

Interrogative sentences ask questions.

59. All the sentences which we have so far studied are **declarative sentences**; that is, they **declare** or **assert** something (see Section 44).

But we do not use language for the sole purpose of telling things. Whether we talk or write, we are continually **asking questions, giving orders**, and **making requests,** and we often give vent to our emotions by **exclaiming.**

There should, then, be special forms of the sentence to express some or all of these modes of thought. These special forms we shall now study under their several heads:

> (1) **interrogative** sentences;
> (2) **imperative** sentences;
> (3) **exclamatory** sentences.

60. If we examine the following sentences,

> Is John at home?
> Have these men a conscience?
> Who leads in the race?

we observe that they do not assert anything. On the contrary, they make inquiries; they are **questions**. Yet without doubt each of these examples is a sentence; for each expresses a thought and contains a subject and a predicate. Thus, in the first example *John* is the subject and *is at home* the complete predicate as truly as in the declarative sentence "John is at home." Such sentences are called **interrogative sentences.**

The word *interrogative* means merely "questioning." A *question* is often called an *interrogation.*

61. A sentence that asks a question is called an interrogative sentence.

Chapter 11 Exercises

I.
1. Ask questions about ten objects in the schoolroom.
2. Ask ten questions about some person or event famous in American history.
3. You have just made a number of **interrogative sentences**. Write an answer to each. These answers will be **declarative sentences.**

II.

Turn the following declarative sentences into interrogative sentences.

1. Our society meets once a fortnight.
2. Wellington defeated Napoleon at Waterloo.
3. They heard the din of the battle.
4. Swift wrote "Gulliver's Travels."
5. Shakespeare lived in the sixteenth and seventeenth centuries.
6. Our voyage was very prosperous.
7. Nothing dries more quickly than a tear.
8. Sir John Franklin perished in the Arctic regions.
9. The Hudson's Bay Company deals in furs.
10. John Adams was the second President of the United States.
11. Victoria is Empress of India.
12. William II is the German Emperor.
13. Siberia is a part of the Russian Empire.

III.

Compare the declarative and the interrogative sentences that you have made in I and II.
1.   Do you observe any difference in the order of words?
2.   With what words do many questions begin?
3.   See if you can frame a rough-and-ready rule for interrogative sentences.

CHAPTER 12
Interrogative Sentences, Part 2

In a question, the **simple subject** often follows the **simple predicate.**

Questions often use a verb phrase with the helping verb *do, does,* or *did.*

Questions often begin with the **interrogative pronouns** *who, whose, whom, which, what.*

62. The preceding exercise illustrates some of the peculiarities of **interrogative sentences**.

63. The simple subject of an interrogative sentence often follows the simple predicate. Thus,

> *Goes Caesar* to the capital tomorrow?
> *Know you* this man?
> *Is Thomas* your brother?

Change each of these sentences to the **declarative** form, and the difference in order is plain.

64. The predicate of an interrogative sentence is often a verb phrase with *do, does,* or *did.* Thus,

> *Do* I *blame* the man?
> *Do* you *feel* better?
> *Does* Charles *go* to school?
> *Did* they *find* your knife?

Here the predicates are the verb phrases *do blame, do feel, does go, did find.* The subjects (*I, you Charles, they*) come between the two parts of the verb phrases.

65. Interrogative sentences often begin with *who, whose, whom, which, what.* Thus,

> *Who* is on guard?   *Which* of you is ready?
> *Whom* did you see?   *What* troubles you?

These words are **pronouns**, for they point out or designate a person or thing (by asking a question about it).

When thus used to introduce a question, *who, whose, whom, which,* and *what* are called **interrogative pronouns.**

Chapter 12 Exercises

I.

Write ten interrogative sentences beginning with *do, does,* or *did.* Use as subjects some of the nouns in the lists below.

EXAMPLES: Does Henry skate well?
Do bananas grow in Africa?

Henry, Washington, Julia, river, lake, mountain, ship, England, Mr. Jackson, Lowell, bananas, coconuts, children, whales, lion, cotton, breadfruit, Kansas, Henry Clay

Write an answer to each of your questions.

II.

Write ten interrogative sentences beginning with *who, whose, whom, which,* or *what.* Write answers to your questions.

III.

Analyze the following sentences by designating:
- (1) the complete subject,
- (2) the complete predicate,
- (3) the simple subject,
- (4) the simple predicate.

1. Is wealth thy passion?
2. What shall I say in excuse for this long letter?
3. Is he not able to pay the money?
4. Urge you your petitions in the street?
5. Why was James driven from the throne?
6. Is this the welcome of my worthy deeds?
7. Why dost thou bend thine eyes upon the earth?
8. Why do you treat Alfred Burnham so defiantly?
9. Did you ever read anything so delightful?
10. Why would not you speak sooner?
11. Does this garden belong to the governor?

CHAPTER 13
Imperative Sentences

66. Each of the groups of words that follow expresses a **command** or a **request**:

> March forward!
> Drive the dog out.
> Sharpen my pencil for me, please.

Examining the form of these expressions, we observe certain peculiarities:

(1) There is a verb in each: *march, drive, sharpen.*
(2) No subject is expressed.
(3) A subject, however, is certainly in the speaker's mind, — namely, the person to whom he is speaking; and this subject may be expressed at will by prefixing to the verb the pronoun *you.* Thus,

> [You] march forward!
> [You] drive the dog out!
> [You] sharpen my pencil for me, please.

All these groups of words, then, are **sentences** of a peculiar kind, having a predicate expressed and a subject, *you,* understood.

(1) They are **directly addressed** to somebody.
(2) They express either a **command** or a **request**, the sole difference between the two consisting in the tone of voice in which the sentence is uttered.

Such sentences are called **imperative sentences**.

67. **An imperative sentence expresses a command or a request. The subject of an imperative sentence is usually omitted; when expressed, it is either *thou* or *you* (*ye*).**

> **Imperative sentences** make commands.
>
> ❧
>
> Commands or requests often have the implied subject *you* which is understood but not expressed.

Chapter 13 Exercises

I.

Make ten sentences expressing command or entreaty. How do the imperative sentences which you have made differ in form from declarative sentences?

II.

Make ten imperative sentences beginning with *do not*.
Observe that this is the common form of a **prohibition** (or negative command).

III.

Analyze the following imperative sentences thus:
    (1) mention the subject;
    (2) mention the complete predicate;
    (3) mention the simple predicate.

1. Go you before to Gloucester with these letters.
2. Follow thou the flowing river.
3. Go you into the other street.
4. Tomorrow in the battle think on me.
5. Do not lay your hand on your sword.
6. Bring forth the prisoners instantly.
7. Lend favorable ears to our request.
8. Call thou my brother hither.
9. Do not seek for trouble.
10. Spare my guiltless wife and my poor children.
11. See the wild waste of all-devouring years.
12. Don't measure other people's corn by your own bushel.
13. Teach not thy lips such scorn.
14. Give my regards to your brother.
15. Don't forget my message.
16. Remember never to be ashamed of doing right.
17. Do not saw the air too much with your hand.
18. Keep a firm rein upon these bursts of passion.
19. Do not spur a free horse.
20. Do not stand in your own light.

CHAPTER 14
Exclamatory Sentences

68. Any sentence, whatever its form, may be spoken as an **exclamation**; that is, may be uttered as a kind of cry expressing surprise or some other emotion. Such sentences are called **exclamatory sentences.**

An **exclamatory sentence** expresses surprise or strong emotion.

Thus, the sentences

> He comes!
> What do you mean?
> Go home!

are all exclamatory.

Declarative, interrogative, and **imperative** sentences can all be **exclamatory** sentences.

Yet these three examples are sentences of different kinds:

> the first is **declarative;**
> the second, **interrogative;**
> the third, **imperative.**

In the following sentences, however, we have exclamations expressed in a peculiar form:

> What a noise the boy makes!
> What beautiful flowers these are!
> How fast the horse runs!

Exclamatory sentences are followed by an **exclamation mark.**

These sentences are, it will be seen, essentially declarative, but they do not merely state a fact; they state a fact in the form of an exclamation. In other words, they are **exclamatory sentences.**

69. **Any sentence which expresses surprise, grief, appeal, or any strong emotion in the form of an exclamation or cry may be called an exclamatory sentence.**

An exclamatory sentence is followed by an **exclamation point (!)** if it is declarative or imperative.

Chapter 14 Exercise

Tell whether each of the following sentences is declarative, interrogative, or imperative, and give your reasons. If any of the sentences are also exclamatory, mention that fact.

1. Did you ever hear the streams talk to you in May, when you went a-fishing?
2. The white pavilions made a show,
    Like remnants of the winter snow.
3. But hark! what means yon faint halloo?
4. Things are stagnant enough in town.
5. But what's the use of delaying?
6. The Moors from forth the greenwood came riding one by one.
7. I was just planning a whole week's adventure for you.
8. At the Peckham end there were a dozen handsome trees, and under them a piece of artificial water where boys were sailing toy boats, and a poodle was swimming.
9. Look at the splendid prize that was to recompense our labor.
10. Don't think that my temper is hot.
11. The natives came by degrees to be less apprehensive of any danger from me.
12. Soldier, rest! thy warfare o'er,
    Sleep the sleep that knows not breaking.
13. How easily you seem to get interested in new people!
14. How little I thought what the quarrel would lead to!
15. How have you been employing your time?
16. "O, cease your sports," Earl Percy said,
    "And take your bows with speed."
17. He had been in business in the West End.
18. Abandon this mad enterprise.
19. Forgive my hasty words.
20. What black despair, what horror, fills his heart!

CHAPTER 15
Vocative ⁹

70. Examine the following sentence:

Thomas, you are a troublesome fellow.

Nouns used in **direct address** are called **vocatives.**

Vocatives are used in all kinds of sentences.

The vocative can be omitted without changing the meaning of the sentence.

A vocative is *not* part of the complete subject or the complete predicate.

In this sentence the noun *Thomas* is used as a **call** to attract the attention of the person addressed. It is not the subject of the sentence. Indeed, it has no connection of any kind with the verb.

Similarly, in each of the sentences in Section 72, the noun printed in italics is used merely to designate the person to whom we are speaking. It is quite independent of any verb.

Nouns thus used in **direct address** are said to be in the vocative (that is, the "calling") construction.

71. **A noun used for the purpose of addressing a person directly, and not connected with any verb, is called a vocative.**

A vocative is also called a *vocative nominative* or a *nominative of direct address.*

72. The vocative is common in sentences of all kinds, — declarative, interrogative, imperative, and exclamatory. Thus,

John, your father is calling.   [Declarative]
John, do you own a horse?   [Interrogative]
John, open the door.   [Imperative]
What a fellow you are, *John!*   [Exclamatory]

Omit the vocative *John,* and the meaning of these sentences is not changed. The vocative, then, stands by itself: that is, it is **independent** of the rest of the sentence.

73. Since imperative sentences are always directly addressed to some one, vocatives are very common in such sentences. Thus,

Look aloft, *Tom.*
Answer me, *Mary,* immediately.
John, lend me your rifle.

---

⁹ The vocative is treated at this point because it is common in imperative sentences and is often mistaken by beginners for the subject of an imperative.

Note that the **subject** of each of these sentences is the unexpressed pronoun *you* (Section 66), and *not* the **vocative** (*Tom, Mary, John*).

74. In **analyzing** a sentence containing a **vocative**, the vocative is mentioned by itself and is not regarded as a part of either the complete subject or the complete predicate.

Chapter 15 Exercises

I.

Fill the blanks with vocatives.

Observe that each sentence is complete already, and that therefore the vocatives are not necessary to the thought.

1. We shall miss you very much,_____.
2. Come hither,_____, and sit upon my knee.
3. What is your name,_____?
4. _____, can you tell me the road to Denver?
5. _____, spare that tree.
6. Don't disappoint me,_____. I trust you absolutely.
7. Jog on,_____, and we shall soon reach the stable.
8. Run,_____! The savages are after us!
9. Swim,_____, for your life. There's a shark chasing you!
10. Jump, _____! It's our last chance!

II.

In each of the following sentences mention the subject and the predicate.
Mention also any vocative nouns which the sentences contain.

1. O learned sir,
   You and your learning I revere.
2. The good old man
   Means no offense, sweet lady!
3. Goodbye! Drive on, coachman.
4. Why, Sir John, my face does you no harm.
5. Good cousin, give me audience for a while.
6. Yours is the prize, victorious prince.
7. "Wake, Allan-bane," aloud she cried
   To the old minstrel by her side.
8. Bid adieu, my sad heart, bid adieu to thy peace.
9. My dear little cousin, what can be the matter?
10. Come, Evening, once again, season of peace!
11. Plain truth, dear Murray, needs no flowers of speech.

12. Permit me now, Sir William, to address myself personally to you.

13. Go, my dread lord, to your great-grandsire's tomb.

14. Why do you stay so long, my lords of France?

15. My pretty cousins, you mistake me much.

16. Come on, Lord Hastings. Will you go with me?

17. O Romeo, Romeo, brave Mercutio's dead.

18. I will avenge this insult, noble queen.

19. O friend, I seek a harborage for the night.

20. My lord, I saw three bandits by the rock.

21. Father! thy days have passed in peace.

III.

Tell whether each of the following sentences is declarative, interrogative, or imperative. Divide each into the complete subject and the complete predicate. Mention the simple subject and the simple predicate. Mention any vocatives that you find.

1. I had a violent fit of the nightmare.
2. It was at the time of the annual fair.
3. My uncle was an old traveler.
4. The young lady closed the casement with a sigh.
5. The supper table was at length laid.
6. Hoist out the boat.
7. Are you from the farm?
8. She broke into a little scornful laugh.
9. Bring forth the horse.
10. When can their glory fade?
11. Shut, shut the door, good John!
12. Do you mark that, my lord?
13. Why sigh you so profoundly?
14. Within the mind strong fancies work.
15. The sun peeps gay at dawn of day.
16. The noble stag was pausing now
    Upon the mountain's southern brow.
17. Then through the dell his horn resounds.
18. Lightly and brightly breaks away
    The Morning from her mantle gray.
19. Fire flashed from out the old Moor's eyes.
20. The garlands wither on their brow.

IV.

Change the declarative sentences in III, above, into interrogative sentences. What changes do you make in the **form** of each sentence?

CHAPTER 16
Adjectives

> **Adjectives** describe nouns or pronouns.
>
> ❧
>
> Adjectives are said to **limit** or **modify** substantives.

75.   Examine the sentence that follows:

> The *golden* butterfly | glistened through the *shadowy* apartment.

In this sentence neither of the two nouns, *butterfly* and *apartment*, stands by itself. To the noun *butterfly* is attached the word *golden*, **describing** the butterfly; to the noun *apartment* is attached the word *shadowy*, **describing** the apartment.

Neither *golden* nor *shadowy*, it will be observed, is a noun. On the contrary, their task in the sentence is to **describe** or **define** the nouns *butterfly* and *apartment*; and this they do by **attributing** some **quality** to them. Such words are called **adjectives.**

76.   **An adjective is a word which limits or describes a substantive [noun or pronoun],[10] usually by attributing some quality.**

77.   **An adjective is said to belong to the substantive which it limits or describes.**

Thus, in the sentence at the head of the chapter, the adjective *golden* belongs to the noun *butterfly,* and the adjective *shadowy* belongs to the noun *apartment.*

78.   **How adjectives limit nouns** may be seen by writing down (1) a noun by itself, (2) a noun with one adjective, (3) a noun with two adjectives, (4) a noun with three adjectives. Thus,

> (1) apple;
> (2) red apple;
> (3) large, red apple;
> (4) large, red, mellow apple.

The noun *apple* in (1) may refer to any apple in the world, red or green or yellow, large or small, mellow or hard.

In (2) the adjective *red* limits the noun to apples of that particular color.

In (3) small apples are ruled out by the adjective *large.*

---

[10] Editor's note: This term was first introduced in Section 28. For now the student should remember that nouns and pronouns are substantives.

In (4) the adjective *mellow* makes still more limited the kinds of apples to which the noun can apply. Every additional adjective, then, narrows or **limits** the meaning of the noun.

Chapter 16 Exercises

I.
In the following sentences, point out all the adjectives and mention the noun or pronoun to which each belongs.

1. The sun is warm, the sky is clear.
2. Hope must have green bowers and blue skies.
3. His axe is keen, his arm is strong.
4. La Fleur instantly pulled out a little dirty pocket-book, crammed full of small letters.
5. His white hair floats like a snowdrift around his face.
6. A sorrowful multitude followed them to the shore.
7. My fugitive years are all hasting away.
8. The sails of this vessel are black.
9. The old officer was reading a small pamphlet.
10. He was almost frantic with grief.
11. We are weak and miserable.
12. A more striking picture there could not be imagined than the beautiful English face of the girl, and its exquisite bloom, together with her erect and independent attitude, contrasted with the sallow and bilious skin of the Malay, veneered with mahogany tints by climate and marine air, his small, fierce, restless eyes, thin lips, slavish gestures and adorations.[11]

II.
Fill each blank with an adjective limiting the simple subject of the sentence.
1. A _____ palace rose before us.
2. A _____ path led down to the brook.
3. _____ Indians attacked the village.
4. The _____ soldier was severely wounded.
5. _____ boys threw stones at the train.
6. A _____ lamp was burning in the room.
7. A _____ tower stood on the cliff.
8. Two _____ dogs guarded the house.
9. The _____ pupil has forgotten his book.
10. _____ walls surrounded the garden.

---

[11] Editor's note: This passage is taken from Thomas De Quincey's *Confessions of an English Opium-Eater* (1821).

11. The _____ elephant seized his tormentor.
12. This _____ merchant lived in Chicago.

III.

Complete each sentence by filling the blank with a noun as simple subject. Note that the noun must be such as the adjective preceding the blank may properly limit.

1. A fierce _____ sprang at the beggar.
2. Envious _____ are never happy.
3. The cowardly _____ deserted his companion.
4. A heavy _____ fell from the staging.
5. A bright _____ blazed on the hearth.
6. Smooth _____ covered the sidewalk.
7. A golden _____ was on his head.
8. Many _____ make light work.
9. My faithful _____ never left me.
10. Dark _____ shut out the sun.
11. A cold _____ is blowing.
12. The tall _____ was covered with snow.
13. A soft _____ turneth away wrath.
14. Angry _____ seldom give good advice.
15. Four black _____ drew the coach.

CHAPTER 17
Classes of Adjectives

Descriptive adjectives describe substantives.

꙾

Some adjectives **point out** or **designate** objects without describing them, indicating **place** or **number**.

꙾

Numeral adjectives indicate exact numbers.

꙾

Proper adjectives are formed from a proper noun.

79. Most adjectives are, like those which we have so far studied, **descriptive** words.

Others, however, serve merely to **point out** or **designate** objects in some way without actually describing them.

> You cannot swim to *yonder* rock.
> Mr. Ashe lives in the *next* house.
> The *right-hand* road leads to London.
> The *under* side of the cake is burned.
> *That* ice is dangerous.
> *These* grapes are very sour.
> *This* person was named Jeremy.
> *Some* dreams are like reality.
> *Each* man took a pear.
> *Every* rat abandoned the sinking ship.
> *Many* hands make light work.
> *Few* wars are really unavoidable.
> *All* men shrink from suffering.
> *No* camels were visible.
> *Innumerable* mosquitoes buzzed about us.

These adjectives, as the examples show us, usually indicate either **place** or **number**.

Adjectives that indicate number exactly (as, *one, two, twenty-five, forty-six*) are called **numeral adjectives**. (See chapter 89.)

80. An adjective formed from a proper noun is called a **proper adjective** and begins with a capital letter: as, *Roman, American, English.*

81. Tell which of the adjectives in Section 79 are descriptive, which indicate place, and which indicate number.

Chapter 17 Exercises

I.

Fill the blanks with appropriate adjectives.

1. Spring is cheery, but winter is _____.
2. A _____ fairy comes at night. Her eyes are _____, her hair is _____.
3. The _____ castle had never held half so many _____ knights beneath its roof.
4. Holly is _____ in the winter.
5. No _____ fire blazed on the hearth.
6. Wellington was an _____ general.
7. I wish you a _____ New Year.
8. Down he sank in the _____ waves.
9. The clothes and food of the children are _____ and _____.
10. His eyes are _____ with weeping.
11. "'Twas a _____ victory," said the _____ man.
12. _____ snow lay on the ground.
13. No footstep marked the _____ gravel.
14. Miss Bell seemed very _____.
15. John looks as _____ as a judge.

II.

Make twenty sentences, each containing one of these adjectives followed by a noun.

> Proud, tall, rusty, ruinous, anxious, careless, faithful, angry, blue-eyed, plentiful, purple, flowery, outrageous, accurate, fault-finding, swift, patriotic, athletic, torrid, American

III.

Mention a number of adjectives that might be used in describing each of the following objects.

> Iron, lead, robin, parrot, eagle, sparrow, bicycle, horse, oxen, cornfield, spring, summer, autumn, winter, butterfly, spider, carpenter, physician, sugar, marble

IV.

Use in a sentence each of the nouns in the list below. With each noun use an adjective. Thus,

> Noun: *dog*   Adjective: *shaggy*
> Sentence: That *shaggy dog* of John's needs clipping.

> Cat, engineer, game, hall, orange, lemon, sailor, architect, president, Washington, scholar, mechanic, board, saw, book, merchant, battle, charge, artillery, grove, prairie, mountain, lake

CHAPTER 18
The Two Articles

The two articles *a* and *an* are **indefinite articles.**

❧

The is a **definite article.**

82. **Two peculiar adjectives, *a* (or *an*) and *the* are called articles.**[12]

83. The general difference between the two **articles** *a* and *the* appears in the following sentences:

> *The* horseman galloped up.   *A* horseman galloped up.

In the first sentence the **article** *the*, belonging to *horseman*, shows that some particular horseman is meant. In other words, it **definitely** points out an individual person as distinguished from a whole class of persons. Hence *the* is called the **definite article.**

In the second sentence the **article** *a*, belonging to horseman, does not definitely point out the horseman as an individual; it simply designates him, **indefinitely**, as belonging to a class of persons, — horsemen. Hence *a* (or *an*) is called the **indefinite article.**

84. **The definite article *the* points out one or more individual persons or things as in some way distinct from others of the same general class or kind.**

Find the **definite articles** in the following passages, and observe that they each designate a particular object:

(1) You should have seen the wedding.
(2) The day of our vengeance was come.
(3) In the year fifty-nine came the Britons.
(4) As they entered the yard the flames were rushing out of the chimney.
(5) The old man looked wistfully across the table, the muscles about his mouth quivering as he ended.
(6) Harry shaded his eyes with his hand for a minute, as he stood outside the cottage drinking in the fresh, pure air, laden with the scent of the honeysuckle which he had trained over the porch, and listening to the chorus of linnets and finches from the copse at the back of the house.

---

[12] The articles are sometimes rated as a distinct class among the parts of speech; but it is better to include them among adjectives, in accordance with their origin, nature, and use.

An is used before words beginning with a vowel.

❧

A is used before words beginning with a consonant.

85. The indefinite article *a* (or *an*) designates a person or thing as merely one of a general class or kind, making no distinction between individuals.

The article *a* is simply a fragment of *ān* (pronounced *ahn*), the old form of the modern English numeral *one*. *An* preserves the old *-n*, which is lost in *a*.

In its meaning the indefinite article may still be recognized as a very weak "one." Compare the indefinite use of *one* in such phrases as "One John Smith is suspected of this robbery," that is, "*somebody, nobody knows who*, called John Smith," "*a* John Smith," "*a certain* John Smith."

86. *An* is used before words beginning with a vowel or silent *h*; *a* before other words. Thus,

an inkstand;	a box;
an elephant;	a cataract;
an hour;	a zebra.

87. Special Rules for *a* or *an*.

(1) Before words beginning with the sound of *y* or *w*, *a*, not *an*, is used. Thus,

a unison;	a European;
a unicorn;	a eucalyptus tree;
a universal genius;	such a one.

Under this head are included all words beginning with *eu* and many beginning with *u*. These form no exception to the general rule in Section 86, for *u* and *eu*, when pronounced like the pronoun *you*, do not express a vowel sound.

(2) Before words beginning with *h* and not accented on the first syllable, *an* is often used. Thus, we say,

a history;   BUT, *an historical* novel.

Here again we have no real exception to the rule in Section 86; for in the words in question, when the accent is not on the first syllable, the *h* is very weak in pronunciation and sometimes entirely disappears, so that the word practically begins with a vowel.

Chapter 18 Exercises

I.
Find the indefinite articles in the following passages, and observe whether the form is *a* or *an*.

1. Whenever there was sickness in the place, she was an untiring nurse.
2. We are going to have a great archery party next month, and you shall have an invitation.
3. But man of all ages is a selfish animal, and unreasonable in his selfishness.
4. There is a pleasure in the pathless woods.
5. At length I met a reverend good old man.
6. He was lying on a crimson velvet sofa, reading a French novel. It was a very little book. He is a very little man. In that enormous hall he looked like a mere speck.

II.
In the following sentences supply an article, either definite or indefinite. In case it is possible to supply either the definite or the indefinite article, tell what difference of meaning comes from using one rather than the other.

1. The schoolhouse was _____ low building rudely constructed of logs; _____ windows were partly glazed, and partly patched with leaves of old copybooks.
2. He was always ready for either _____ fight or _____ frolic.
3. It was, as I have said, _____ fine autumnal day. _____ sky was clear and serene.
4. _____ sloop was loitering in _____ distance, dropping slowly down with _____ tide, her sail hanging uselessly against _____ mast.
5. _____ musician was _____ old gray-headed negro.
6. On one side of _____ church extends a wide woody dell, along which raves _____ large brook.

III.
In the following passage, point out all the definite and all the indefinite articles and tell to what noun each belongs.

1. An acquaintance, a friend as he called himself, entered.
2. The town was in a hubbub.
3. The men were quiet and sober.
4. You see this man about whom so great an uproar hath been made in this town.
5. I disliked carrying a musket.
6. I sat down on one of the benches, at the other end of which was seated a man in very shabby clothes.
7. The ploughman whistles.
8. The mower whets his scythe.
9. Young and old come forth to play
    On a sunshine holiday.

CHAPTER 19
Adverbs

Adverbs
modify
verbs.

&.

Adverbs
change the
meaning of
verbs and
often end in
-*ly*.

88.   Examine the following sentence:

The statesman advised the king *wisely*.

In this sentence the word *wisely* is different, both in its form and its use, from any part of speech which we have so far studied.

It bears some resemblance to an adjective. It is not an adjective, however, for it does not **describe** or **limit** either of the two **nouns** in the sentence, *statesman* or *king*.

Indeed, its very form (*wise**ly***) shows that it is not an adjective. "The *wisely* statesman" is an impossible form of speech. *Wise* is the adjective form, not *wisely*.

Wisely, then, has no relations with the **nouns** in the sentence. On the other hand, it clearly *is* connected with the **verb**, — *advised;* for it tells **how** or **in what manner** the statesman advised the king.

Wisely, then, **modifies** (that is, affects the meaning of) the **verb** *advised*.

For *wisely* we may substitute *foolishly, rashly, treacherously, quickly,* or *respectfully,* and each of these words would change the meaning of *advised*.

The statesman advised the king
{
wisely.
foolishly.
rashly.
treacherously.

Such words are called **adverbs**, because of their frequent association with **verbs.**

The Mother Tongue

Chapter 19 Exercise

I.

Pick out the adverbs and tell what verb or verb phrase each modifies.

1. Carroll waved his whip triumphantly in the air.
2. This contemptuous speech cruelly shocked Cecilia.
3. Spring came upon us suddenly.
4. The king gained ground everywhere.
5. Every night in dreams they groaned aloud.
6. Northward he turneth through a little door.
7. I dimly discerned a wall before me.
8. Miss Sharp had demurely entered the carriage some minutes before.
9. Punctuality at meals was rigidly enforced at Gateshead Hall.
10. But here the doctors eagerly dispute.
11. The guardsman defended himself bravely.
12. Swiftly, swiftly flew the ship,
    Yet she sailed softly too:
    Sweetly, sweetly blew the breeze —
    On me alone it blew.
13. Kent had been looking at me steadily for some time.
14. By this storm our ship was greatly damaged.

II.

Change the meaning of each of the following sentences by substituting a different adverb.

1. Stevens laughed boisterously.
2. Merrily sang the birds in the wood.
3. You have acted unjustly toward your brother.
4. The ship settled in the water gradually.
5. Fiercely the chieftain made reply.
6. We rowed slowly up the stream.
7. Mr. Fleetwood entered the room noisily.
8. They waited patiently for better times.

III.

Fill each blank with an adverb and tell what it modifies.

1. This poor fellow has been _____ hurt.
2. All the pupils were _____ delighted with the entertainment.
3. The explosion did _____ great damage.
4. Joe passed his hand _____ over his aching forehead.
5. The prisoner struggled _____.

6. _____ many objections were heard.
7. I am not _____ unhappy, but still I am _____ uncomfortable.
8. Helen speaks _____ rapidly; John does not speak rapidly _____.
9. The wind howled _____ down the wide chimney.
10. My boat will hold six persons _____.
11. The room is not large _____ for the class.
12. The scout crept _____ through the thicket.
13. Jackson's salary is _____ small for his needs.
14. The river is rising _____ rapidly.
15. Such conduct will be _____ punished.

CHAPTER 20
Adverbs Modifying Adjectives

Adverbs may modify **adjectives.**

&

Adverbs change the meaning of adjectives and often end in *-ly*.

89. An adverb may modify the meaning of an adjective.

Thus, in the sentence

The man was *foolishly* confident,

the adverb *foolishly* modifies the adjective *confident* by indicating that the man was confident in a foolish way.

As before, we could substitute for *foolishly* other adverbs, such as *rashly, bravely, wisely, moderately,* and every such substitution would affect or modify the meaning of *confident* (see chapter 19).

The man was { *foolishly* *rashly* *bravely* *wisely* } confident.

Chapter 20 Exercise

Pick out the adverbs that modify adjectives.

1. Her language is singularly agreeable to me.
2. Mr. Sedley's eyes twinkled in a manner indescribably roguish.
3. The river walk is uncommonly pretty.
4. She had been going on a bitterly cold winter night to visit some one at Stamford Hill.
5. Mrs. Harrel was extremely uneasy.
6. The meeting was very painful to them both.
7. Kate had been unreasonably angry with Heatherleigh.
8. Be particularly careful not to stumble.
9. The poor fellow was pitifully weak.

CHAPTER 21
Adverbs Modifying Adverbs

Adverbs may modify another adverb.

❧

An **adverb** is a word that modifies the meaning of a **verb**, an **adjective**, or another **adverb**.

90. An adverb may modify the meaning of another adverb.

Thus, in

The governor predicted his own election *very* confidently,

(1) *confidently* is an adverb modifying the verb *predicted*, and (2) *very* is an adverb modifying *confidently*.

The pupil recited *very* badly.
The governor spoke *rather* rapidly.
Charles cannot dance *so* gracefully as John.

91. In accordance with what we have learned from chapters 19-20, we may now define the adverb:

An adverb is a word that modifies the meaning of a verb, an adjective, or another adverb.

Chapter 21 Exercise

Pick out the adverbs that modify other adverbs.

1. She told her distress quite frankly.
2. Cecilia then very gravely began an attempt to undeceive her.
3. This service she somewhat reluctantly accepted.
4. He fixed his eyes on me very steadily.
5. We strolled along rather carelessly towards Hampstead.
6. Do not speak so indistinctly.
7. The red horse trots uncommonly fast.
8. The commander rebuked his boldness half seriously, half jestingly.
9. The cotton must be picked pretty soon.
10. Why did King Lear's daughters treat him so unkindly?

CHAPTER 22
Classification of Adverbs

92. Adverbs may be divided according to their sense into four classes:

   (1) adverbs of **manner;**
   (2) adverbs of **time;**
   (3) adverbs of **place;**
   (4) adverbs of **degree.**

93. Adverbs of manner answer the question "How?" "In what way?"

They are very numerous, and most of them end in -*ly.*

> The starving man ate *greedily.*
> The wayfarer plodded *wearily* along.
> *Merrily* sang the boatmen.
> The queen was *foolishly* suspicious.
> The gift was *splendidly* generous.
> The nine plays *unexpectedly* well.

Several adverbs of manner have no ending -*ly* and are identical in form with adjectives of like meaning.

> The farmer always works *hard.*
> How *fast* the time flies!

Adverbs of manner usually modify either verbs or adjectives; they rarely modify adverbs.

See how many of the adverbs in chapter 19, Exercise I and II are adverbs of manner, and tell what they modify.

94. Adverbs of time answer the question "When?"

EXAMPLES: now, then, soon, formerly, today, tomorrow, by-and-by.

Adverbs of time usually modify verbs. Thus,

> James lives in San Francisco *now.*
> *Then* the sailor leaped into the sea.
> I shall return *tomorrow.*

95. Adverbs of place answer the question "Where?"

EXAMPLES: here, there, yonder, far, near, aloft, astern, forward, backward.

Adverbs of place usually modify verbs. Thus,

> *There* stands the Capitol.
> I shall wait for him *here.*
> The tired swimmer fell far *astern.*

Adverbs of Manner:
How?

Adverbs of Time:
When?

Adverbs of Place:
Where?

Adverbs of Degree:
To What Extent?

96. Adverbs of degree answer the question "To what degree or extent?"

EXAMPLES: so, very, much, little, exceedingly, hardly, barely, not (the negative adverb).

Adverbs of degree modify verbs, adjectives, and adverbs. They are the only class of adverbs that are much used to modify other adverbs.

> The reply pleased the king very *much.*

Here *much* modifies the verb *pleased,* indicating the degree or extent to which the king was pleased.

> The workman was *little* content with his lot.

Here *little* modifies the adjective *content.*

> I never saw him run *so* rapidly.

Here *so* modifies the adverb *rapidly.*

97. The four classes of adverbs are not separated by hard and fast lines. The same adverb may be used in different senses and thus belong to different classes. Sometimes, too, there is room for difference of opinion as to the classification of an adverb in a given sentence. The whole matter is simply a question of the thought expressed.

Chapter 22 Exercises

I.
Fill each blank with an adverb of degree and tell how it modifies the adjective or the adverb that follows.

1. The wind blew _____ hard.
2. The air bites shrewdly; it is _____ cold.
3. I was in the utmost astonishment, and roared _____ loud that they all ran back in fright.
4. I bowed _____ respectfully to the governor.
5. The peacock's voice is not _____ beautiful as his plumage.
6. We jogged homeward merrily _____.
7. Tom was _____ angry to measure his words.
8. The load was _____ too heavy for the horse to draw.
9. "My lesson is _____ hard. Is yours?" "No, not very; but still it is _____ difficult."
10. The physician was rather surprised to find his patient _____ lively.
11. This has been an _____ dry season.

II.

Very many adverbs end in -*ly*. These are usually derived from adjectives. Thus,

ADJECTIVES	ADVERBS
fair	fairly
bold	boldly
cordial	cordially
outrageous	outrageously

Form such adverbs from the adjectives in the following list. Use each adverb in a sentence.

> Fine, courageous, brave, splendid, eager, plain, doubtful, confusing, remarkable, heedless, careful, polite, rude, civil, violent, mild, meek, gentle, smooth, soft, boisterous.

III.

In the sentences which you have made in II, tell whether the adverb modifies a verb, an adjective, or another adverb.

IV.

Use each of the following verbs and verb phrases with several different adverbs, and see how the meaning varies. Let each of your examples be a sentence.

> Sings, runs, flies, talks, walks, works, acted, spent, played, rushes, has confessed, were marching, are writing, gazed, have examined, will study, devoured, shall watch, may hurt, can ride, has injured, will attack.

V.

Read the sentences which you have made in IV, omitting all the adverbs. Observe how this changes the meaning.

VI.

Pick out all the adverbs in chapter 19, Exercises I and II. Tell whether they are adverbs of time, place, manner, or degree, and indicate what verb, adjective, or adverb each modifies.

NOTE: In determining whether an adverb indicates **manner**, **time**, **place**, or **degree**, the student will do well to test the matter by asking himself whether the word answers the question *"how?" "when?" "where?"* or *"to what extent?"*

VII.

For each adverb in the sentences in chapter 19, Exercises I and II substitute some other adverb.

Observe what effect this change has on the meaning of each sentence.

CHAPTER 23
Analysis: Modifiers

> **To modify** is to change the meaning.
>
> ❧
>
> An **adjective** is often used as a modifier of the **subject.**
>
> ❧
>
> An **adverb** is often used as a modifier of the **predicate.**

98. You have already learned to take the first steps in the **analysis of a sentence.** You know how to divide it into the **complete subject** and the **complete predicate,** and to designate the **simple subject** (noun or pronoun) and the **simple predicate** (verb or verb phrase). Thus,

The honest farmer | worked diligently.

Here the complete subject is *the honest farmer;* the complete predicate is *worked diligently.* The simple subject is the noun *farmer;* the simple predicate is the verb *worked.*

99. We may now take another step in analysis and study some words which **change** or **modify** the meaning of the simple **subject** and the simple **predicate.**

100. In the sentence before us the subject *farmer* has attached to it the adjective *honest,* and the predicate *worked* has attached to it the adverb *diligently.*

Honest **changes** or **modifies** the meaning of *farmer* by describing the farmer's character. *Diligently* **modifies** *worked* by telling how or in what manner the farmer worked.

Hence *honest* is called a **modifier of the subject,** and *diligently* is called a **modifier of the predicate.**

101. **A word or group of words attached to the subject or the predicate of a sentence to modify its meaning is called a modifier of the subject or the predicate.**

An adjective is often used as a modifier of the subject.

An adverb is often used as a modifier of the predicate.

Chapter 23 Exercises

I.

Analyze the sentences below, as follows:

    (1) Divide each sentence into the complete subject and the complete predicate.

    (2) Point out the simple subject and the simple predicate.

    (3) Mention any adjectives that modify the subject.

    (4) Mention any adverbs that modify the predicate.

1. The large room was quickly filled.
2. A great wood fire blazed cheerfully.
3. Our dusty battalions marched onward.
4. The heavy gates were shut instantly.
5. A magnificent snow-fed river poured ceaselessly through the glen.
6. Back darted Spurius Lartius.
7. A meager little man was standing near.
8. This terrible winter dragged slowly along.
9. The cattle were feeding quietly.
10. Instantly a dire hubbub arose.
11. The red sun sank slowly behind the hills.
12. Many strange stories were told of this adventure.

II.

Expand the following short sentences by inserting modifiers of the subject and of the predicate.

1. Men work.
2. Pupils studied.
3. The wind howls.
4. Women were weeping.
5. Grapes hung.
6. Enemy resisted.
7. Crows were cawing.
8. Corn grew.
9. Fire spread.
10. Messenger rode.
11. Building fell.
12. Child cried.
13. Dog swam.
14. Tiger sprang.

CHAPTER 24
Prepositions

Propositions show the relation of the noun or pronoun to some other word in the sentence.

❧

The object of the preposition is a noun or pronoun following the preposition.

❧

The **substantive** that is an **object of the preposition** is in the **objective case.**

❧

Appendix H contains a list of common prepositions.

102. Among the words which do not themselves call up a distinct picture to the mind, but which serve to bind other words together and to show their relations to each other in connected speech,[13] the **prepositions** form a very important class. Their use is illustrated in the following sentences:

> The walls *of* the factory fell *with* a crash.
> The dog lay *by* the fire.
> The hat *on* the table is mine.
> This train goes *to* Chicago.
> He wrapped his cloak *about* me.

In the first sentence, for example, the word *of* not merely **connects** the two nouns *walls* and *factory*, but it shows the **relation** between them; the walls *belong to* the factory. Omit *of*, and we no longer know what the factory and the walls have to do with each other.

Again, in the same sentence, *with* shows the relation of the noun *crash* to the verb *fell*; the act of falling was accompanied by a loud noise. Omit *with*, and the sense of the passage vanishes.

So in each of the other sentences the italicized word (a **preposition**) shows the relation between the noun that follows it and some other word in the sentence.

Accordingly, we have the following definition:

103. **A preposition shows the relation of the substantive which follows it to some other word or words in the sentence.**

104. **The substantive which follows a preposition is called its object, and is said to be in the objective case.**

Thus, in the first example in Section 102, the noun *factory* is the object of the preposition *of,* and the noun *crash* is the object of the preposition *with.* In the last example the pronoun *me* is the object of the preposition *about.*

Other examples may be seen in the following sentences:

> The savages fought with fury.
> The anchor was made of iron.
> The train runs from Boston to New York.

---

[13] See Introduction

> Prepositions may have **two or more objects.**
>
> ❧
>
> **Be careful!** Sometimes words that are usually prepositions are used as **adverbial suffixes.**

The banner floated over the castle.

We shall arrive at Denver before morning.

105. A preposition may have two or more objects. Thus,

The fireman dashed *through* smoke and flame.

Here the two nouns *smoke* and *flame* are the objects of the preposition *through.*

He feathers his oars with skill and dexterity.

The father sought his lost boy in highways and byways.

The hunters galloped through field and forest.

The road runs over hill and plain.

106. Some words that are usually prepositions may be attached to certain verbs as **adverbial suffixes.** Thus,

The ship *lay to.*

A fierce storm *set in.*

The fainting man *came to.*

The darkness *came on.*

A friend of mine *came in.*

He *passed by* on the other side.

In this use the adverb is practically a part of the verb.

Chapter 24 Exercises

I.

Fill the blanks with prepositions showing the relation of the italicized words to each other.

1. John's hat *hung* _____ the *peg.*
2. The river *rises* _____the *mountains* and *flows* _____ a great *plain*_____ the *sea.*
3. The miseries of numbed hands and shivering skins no longer accompany every *pull* _____the *river.*
4. He *was* _____ a particularly *good-humor* with himself.
5. His conscience pricked him for *intruding* _____ *Hardy* during his hours of work.
6. Tom came to understand the *differences* _____ his two *heroes.*
7. Such cruelty *fills* us _____ *indignation.*
8. He was *haunted* _____ a hundred *fears.*
9. _____ a score of *minutes* Garbetts *came* back_____ an anxious and crestfallen *countenance.*

10. To *drive* the deer _____*hound* and *horn*
    Earl Percy took his way.
11. Cooks, butlers, and their assistants were *bestirring* themselves _____the *kitchen*.
12. The weary traveler *was sleeping*_____ a *tree*.
13. Jack *hid* _____ the *door*.
14. I will *call* _____ *dinner*.

II.

Use the following prepositions, with objects, in sentences:

> Of, in, upon, from, by, to, into, during, along, behind, within, without, till, up, down, round, at, beside, before, against, about, concerning, except, but (= except), beyond, through, throughout, after, above, beneath, over, under.

III.

In the following sentences:
  (1) find the prepositions;
  (2) mention their objects;
  (3) point out the word with which each preposition connects its object;
  (4) tell what part of speech that word is if you can.

1. The village maid steals through the shade.
2. His eyes burnt like coals under his deep brows.
3. Their vessels were moored in our bay.
4. The hounds ran swiftly through the woods.
5. They knocked at our gates for admittance.
6. I grew weary of the sea and intended to stay at home with my wife and family.
7. Several officers of the army went to the door of the great council chamber.
8. This seems to me but melancholy work.
9. The bowmen mustered on the hills.
10. Death lays his icy hand on kings.
11. Untie these bands from off my hands.
12. Down the wide stairs a darkling way they found.
13. He halts, and searches with his eyes
    Among the scattered rocks.
14. The cottage windows through the twilight blazed.
15. All shod with steel,
    We hissed along the polished ice.
16. He was full of joke and jest.
17. Lady Waldegrave swept her fingers over a harp which stood near.

IV.

Find fifteen prepositions in some poem in your reading book. Sir Walter Scott's "Lochinvar" is included in the student workbook. Mention the object of each preposition.

Between what other word and its object does each preposition show the relation?

CHAPTER 25
Conjunctions

107. **Conjunction** means "connective." Certain words which do not themselves express any distinct ideas, but which serve to make clearer the **connection** between ideas expressed by other words, are grouped together as **conjunctions.**

Their use is illustrated in the following sentences:

> Have you seen Jack *and* Tom this morning?
> The boy *and* his dog went up the road.
> Is New York *or* Philadelphia the larger city?
> The wildcat scratched *and* bit fiercely.
> The teacher struck a bell *and* the pupils all rose.
> You are strong, *but* I am weak.
> I will help him *if* he is poor.
> The people rebelled *because* they were abused.

A **conjunction** is a word that **connects** words or groups of words, sometimes even whole sentences.

❧

A sentence combined with another sentence by means of a conjunction is called a **clause.**

The italicized words in these sentences are conjunctions. Though they differ much in the amount and kind of meaning which they express, they are all alike in one respect — they are **connectives.**

Thus, in the first sentence, the two nouns *Jack* and *Tom* are connected by *and*; in the second, *and* connects *the boy* and *his dog*; in the fourth, two verbs are joined by means of *and*; in the sixth, *but* binds together two statements, "You are strong" and "I am weak."

Hence we have the following definition:

108. **Conjunctions connect words or groups of words.**

109. **The groups of words connected by conjunctions may be whole sentences.**

Thus, in the last example above, the conjunction *because* connects "The people rebelled" and "They were abused," each of which could stand by itself as a complete sentence.

When two or more sentences are thus combined to make one longer sentence, they are called **clauses.**

The study of clauses and the classification of conjunctions must be reserved for later chapters.[14]

---

[14] More in chapter 49.

110. The most important English conjunctions are:

> And (both . . . and), or (either . . . or), nor (neither . . . nor), but, for, however, nevertheless, therefore, wherefore, still, yet, because, since (= because), though, although, if, unless, that, whether, as (= because), than, lest.

111. **Prepositions,** as well as **conjunctions**, may be regarded as connectives; but there is a marked difference between the two parts of speech.

A **preposition** (as we have already seen in Chapter 24) not only connects its object with some other word in the sentence but indicates a close and definite grammatical relation between the two. A **conjunction**, on the other hand, has no object, and simply makes clear some connection of thought between two words or groups of words. Thus,

> Snow *and* ice are both cold.

[Here *and* simply connects the two nouns *snow* and *ice* without affecting the sense of either. It is therefore a *conjunction*.]

> Snow *on* ice makes poor skating.

[Here *on* shows some relation between the noun *ice*, its object, and the noun *snow*. It indicates the position of the ice with respect to the snow; the snow is above and the ice beneath. Hence *on* is a *preposition*.]

Chapter 25 Exercises

I.

Pick out the conjunctions, and tell what words, or groups of words, they connect.

1. The wind was high and the clouds were dark,
    And the boat returned no more.
2. It was the time when lilies blow
    And clouds are highest up in air.
3. Beating heart and burning brow, ye are very patient now.
4. The uncouth person in the tattered garments dropped on both knees on the pavement, and took her hand in his, and kissed it in passionate gratitude.
5. He rose, and stood with his cap in his hand.
6. She bowed to him, and passed on, grave and stately.
7. She was an amiable but strictly matter-of-fact person.

8. Brand became more and more convinced that this family was the most delightful family in England.
9. If there were any stranger here at all, we should not dream of asking you to sing.
10. Helen was on the lookout for this expected guest, and saw him from her window. But she did not come forward.
11. I am busy and content.
12. Carrying this fateful letter in his hand, he went downstairs and out into the cool night air.
13. For Romans in Rome's quarrel
    Spared neither land nor gold,
    Nor son nor wife, nor limb nor life,
    In the brave days of old.
14. He was neither angry nor impatient.
15. There were forty craft in Avès that were both swift and stout.
16. We knew you must come by sooner or later.
17. He continued his story, though his listener seemed singularly preoccupied and thoughtful.

II.

Make sentences containing:

1. Two nouns connected by *and*; by *or*.
2. A noun and a pronoun connected by *and*; by *or*.
3. Two adjectives connected by *and*; by *or*.
4. Two adverbs connected by *and*; by *or*.
5. Two verbs connected by *and*; by *or*.
6. Two adverbs connected by *and*; by *or*.
7. *Neither—nor* connecting nouns.
8. *Neither—nor* connecting pronouns.
9. *Neither—nor* connecting adjectives.
10. *Neither—nor* connecting adverbs.
11. *Neither—nor* connecting verbs.
12- 16. *Either—or*, used like *neither—nor* in 7-11.
17. Three nouns in a series, with two conjunctions; with one.
18. Three verbs in a series, with two conjunctions; with one.

III.

Make sentences, each containing one of the following conjunctions:

And, but, or, nor, neither, if, however, although, since, for, because, whether, than.

IV.

Find ten conjunctions in chapter 5, Exercise I, and tell what each conjunction connects.

V.

Fill each blank with a conjunction.

1. Iron, lead, _____ gold are metals.
2. _____ Jack nor Joe is at school.
3. _____ you do not hurry, you will miss the train.
4. Either Mary _____ Francis is to blame.
5. There are _____ lions _____ tigers in the jungle.
6. _____ one or the other of us must give way.

CHAPTER 26
Interjections

112. Examine the following sentences:[15]

> *Oh!* how sorry I am!
> *Ah!* my friend, here you are!
> *Hullo!* there are the dancing bears!
> *Bah!* this is disgusting.

In these sentences the italicized words are mere **cries** or **exclamatory sounds**. Indeed, they are hardly words at all, and may be compared with the bark of a dog or the mewing of a cat. They express **emotion** or **feeling** but have no distinct sense.

Thus, the single word *oh!* uttered in various tones of the voice, may suggest almost any kind of feeling, — anger, distress, surprise, delight, scorn, pity, and so on.

Such words are called **interjections** (that is, words interjected or "thrown in"), because they usually have no grammatical connection with the structure of the sentences in which they stand.

113. **An interjection is a cry or other exclamatory sound expressing surprise, anger, pleasure, or some other emotion or feeling.**

An interjection is often followed by an **exclamation point** (!).

114. **Interjections usually have no grammatical connection with the phrases or sentences in which they stand.**

115. In analyzing a sentence, any **interjections** that it contains are mentioned separately, since they have no genuine grammatical relation with the rest of the sentence.

116. The number of possible interjections is almost limitless. The following are among the commonest:

Oh (*or* O), ah, hullo (holloa, halloo), bah, pshaw, fie, whew, tut-tut, st (*often spelled* hist), ha, aha, ha-ha, ho, hey, hum, hem, heigh-ho, (heigh-o), alas, bravo.

An **interjection** is a cry or other exclamatory sound expressing emotion or feeling.

❧

Interjections have no grammatical connection with phrases or sentences.

---

[15] Editor's note: Modern capitalization rules require the sentences following an exclamatory interjection to be capitalized. For example: *Oh! How sorry I am!* Mild interjections are followed by a comma and a lower case word, such as *O, let us yet be merciful.* The editors have not changed the text to reflect modern rules, but teachers may wish to have students complete the exercises following modern convention.

Calls to animals (like *whoa, haw, gee*) and imitations of the voices of animals (like *mew, bow-wow*, etc.) are also interjections.

The spelling of an interjection is often a very imperfect representation of its sound.

Chapter 26 Exercises

I.

In the following sentences pick out the interjections and tell what emotion you think each expresses.

1. Fie, fie! they are not to be named, my lord.
2. Pish for thee, Iceland dog!
3. Lo! where the giant on the mountain stands.
4. "Ah me!" she cries, "was ever moonlight seen so clear?"
5. Pshaw! this neglect is accident, and the effect of hurry.
6. O, let us yet be merciful.
7. That I did love thee, Caesar, O, 't is true.
8. The Wildgrave winds his bugle-horn.
   To horse, to horse! halloo! halloo!
9. But psha! I've the heart of a soldier,
   All gentleness, mercy, and pity.
10. Louder rang the Wildgrave's horn,
    "Hark forward, forward! holla, ho!"
11. Huzza for the Arethusa! She is a frigate tight and brave.

II.

Try to think of some interjections that you are in the habit of using, and frame sentences containing them.
What emotion does each express?

CHAPTER 27
Phrases

117. To express thought we use, as you have already learned, words combined into sentences.

Sentences, however, are not the only groups of connected words which language employs in the expression of thought.

118. Examine the following sentences, noting the italicized words:

> The *President of the United States* | lives *in the White House.*
> The *Duke of Marlborough* | was victorious *at Blenheim.*
> A *girdle of gold* | encircled the sultan's waist.

In the first and second sentences, *President of the United States* and *Duke of Marlborough* are groups of words which serve as the names of persons; *in the White House* and *at Blenheim* are groups of words answering the question "Where?" In the third, *of gold* is a group describing the *girdle*; *girdle of gold* and *golden girdle* mean the same thing.

Each of these groups may be said to be used as a single **part of speech**.

Thus, *President of the United States* and *Duke of Marlborough* may be called **nouns**, for they are the names of persons; *of gold* is like an **adjective**, for it describes the noun *girdle*, as the adjective *golden* would do; *in the White House* and *at Blenheim* are like **adverbs of place**, for they modify verbs and answer the question "Where?"

The groups that we are studying are not **sentences**, for they do not contain a subject and a predicate.

Such groups are known as **phrases.**

119. A group of connected words, not containing a subject and a predicate, is called a phrase.

A phrase is often equivalent to a part of speech.

120. In the following sentences each group of italicized words is a phrase. See if you can tell why.

> That fireman *will be killed.*
> Jack hit the ball *with all his might.*
> The messenger was running up the road *at full speed.*
> The knight's armor was *of burnished steel.*

> A **phrase**
> is a group of
> connected
> words
> without a
> subject and
> predicate.
>
> ❧
>
> **Phrases** are
> used as a
> single part of
> speech, such
> as an
> adjective or
> adverb.
>
> ❧
>
> A **preposition
> and its
> object** form a
> phrase.

A man *of courage* surely *would have made* the attempt.
The *master of the school* was named Lawson.
The *mayor of San Francisco* has an office *in the City Hall*.

Tell, if you can, what part of speech each of these phrases stands for or resembles.

Chapter 27 Exercises

I.

Make sentences of your own containing the following phrases:

> Baseball club, Queen of England, will come, has traveled, North American Continent, Isthmus of Suez, in the street, on the playground, with an effort, of fur, of silver, had tried, at sea, at home, in school, of iron, of stone, with the exception of, out of, in front of, against my will.

II.

Tell, if you can, what part of speech each of the phrases in I, above, resembles in its use in your sentence.

III.

Take each of the phrases to pieces and name the parts of speech of which it consists.

IV.

Find one phrase in each of the following sentences. Tell, if you can, for what part of speech it stands.

1. The Declaration of Independence was signed in 1776.
2. The House of Representatives has adjourned.
3. Professor Edward Johnston is now in Sioux City.
4. The great Desert of Sahara is in the Continent of Africa.
5. All were on their feet in a moment.
6. The preparations for disembarking had begun.
7. The Pacific Mail Steamship Company has an office at this port.
8. Isabel shuddered with horror.
9. I am a man of peace, though my abode now rings with arms.
10. They were all running at full speed.
11. They had fixed the wedding day.
12. There are many thousand Cinderellas in London, and elsewhere in England.
13. The maddened, terrified horse went like the wind.
14. The Prince of Wales is heir to the crown of England.
15. "In two days," Cromwell said coolly, "the city will be in our hands."

16. The scene had now become in the utmost degree animated and horrible.
17. There were upwards of three hundred strangers in the house.
18. The dog is not of mountain breed.
19. The boys were coming out of the grammar school in shoals, laughing, running, whooping, as the manner of boys is.
20. My father walked up and down the room with impatience.
21. Mr. Thomas Inkle of London, aged twenty years, embarked in the Downs on the good ship called the Achilles, bound for the West Indies, on the 16th of June, 1647, in order to improve his fortune by trade and merchandise.

CHAPTER 28
Adjective Phrases

121. Instead of using an **adjective** to describe or limit a noun or pronoun, we may often use a **prepositional phrase**, — that is, a **phrase** consisting of a **preposition** and its **object**.

Thus, instead of "an *honorable* man," we may say "a man *of honor*"; instead of "a *bad-tempered* fellow," "a fellow *with a bad temper*"; instead of "a *Brazilian* Indian," "an Indian *from Brazil*."

Phrases thus used are called **adjective phrases**.

122. **A substantive[16] may be modified by a prepositional phrase which describes or limits it as an adjective would do and which is therefore called an adjective phrase.**

> A person *of experience* is usually a safe guide.
> The bale of cotton was held together by bands *of iron*.
> He received the freedom of the city in a box *of polished silver*.
> He rang the bell and a man *in black* came to the door.
> He received a book *with pictures* as a present.
> The judge was a man *without mercy*.
> Spices *from the East* were used to flavor the dish.
> The ring was made of gold *from Australia*.

123. An adjective phrase is, as we have seen, often a mere substitute for a single adjective. Thus, "a man *without mercy*" is "a *merciless* man"; "gold *from Australia* " is the same thing as "*Australian* gold"; "spices *from the East*" are "*Oriental* spices."

It is, however, not always possible to substitute an adjective for an adjective phrase. The descriptive ideas which have to be expressed in speech and writing are countless, and our stock of adjectives is limited. Hence the power to form adjective phrases freely adds enormously to the richness and variety of the English language.

> **Prepositional phrases** may be used to modify a noun or pronoun. They are then **adjective phrases.**

[16] Editor's Note: Recall that nouns and pronouns are *substantives*. See Section 29.

Chapter 28 Exercises

I.

Find the adjective phrases and tell what substantive each describes or limits.

1. A man of strong understanding is generally a man of strong character.
2. His flaxen hair, of sunny hue,
   Curled closely round his bonnet blue.
3. Eastward was built a gate of marble white.
4. He found a strong, fierce-looking Highlander, with an axe on his shoulder, standing sentinel at the door.
5. Hard by a poplar shook alway,
   All silver-green, with gnarled bark.
6. The gentleness of heaven is on the sea.
7. The balustrade of the staircase was also of carved wood.
8. Of stature fair, and slender frame,
   But firmly knit, was Malcolm Graeme.
9. It was a lodge of ample size.
10. This gentleman was a man of unquestioned courage.
11. An emperor in his nightcap would not meet with half the respect of an emperor with a glittering crown.
12. Our affairs are in a bad condition.
13. Vathek arose in the morning with a mind more at ease.
14. Her own mind was now in a state of the utmost confusion.
15. Griffiths was a hard business man, of shrewd, worldly good sense, but of little refinement or cultivation.

II.

Substitute for each italicized adjective an adjective phrase without changing the general meaning of the sentence. Thus,

> The cashier was a *strictly honest* man.
> The cashier was a man *of strict honesty.*

1. The cashier was a strictly *honest* man.
2. A very *deep* ravine checked our advance.
3. Brutus is an *honorable* man.
4. *Wooden* pillars supported the roof.
5. The wanderer's clothing was *ragged.*
6. The sailor carried an *ivory-handled* knife.
7. The runner was quite *breathless.*

8. The baron lived in his *ancestral* castle.
9. *Light-hearted* he rose in the morning.
10. Dr. Rush was a *skillful* and *experienced* physician.

III.

Replace the adjective phrases by adjectives without materially changing the sense.

1. Warrington was of a quick and impetuous temper.
2. The road was not of the most picturesque description.
3. Fanny left the room with a sorrowful heart.
4. You are a man of sense.
5. Upon the hero's head was a helmet of brass.
6. Bring forth the goblets of gold!
7. To scale the wall was a task of great difficulty.
8. The old soldier was in poverty.
9. We were all in high spirits.
10. A river of great width had to be crossed.
11. He told his fellow-prisoners, in this darkest time, to be of courage.
12. This is a matter of importance.
13. The beast glared at me with eyes of fire.

Additional Exercises

I.

Analyze the following sentences by identifying:
    (a) the complete subject,
    (b) the complete predicate,
    (c) the simple subject,
    (d) the simple predicate,
    (e) modifiers of the subject (adjectives and adjective phrases).

1. The men of Rome hated kings.
2. A thing of beauty is a joy forever.
3. Steps of marble led up to the palace door.
4. A ladder of ropes hung from the balcony.
5. A huge nugget of gold rewarded my search.
6. A book with heavy clasps was found in the chest.
7. The sword in his hand trembled violently.
8. A figure with three angles is a triangle.
9. The heights above us were shrouded in mist.
10. An animal with four legs is called a quadruped.

11. Diamonds from Africa lay in the casket.
12. The subject under discussion was fiercely argued.
13. Rough herdsmen from the mountains filled the square.
14. My friends at home write to me seldom.
15. My uncle in London sent me an urgent message.
16. Books by the best authors were his delight.
17. The silence of the prairie was well-nigh terrible.
18. The horse chestnuts in the sheltered square broke into blossom.
19. A group of strange children ran at his heels.
20. The light on the mantel piece had burnt low.
21. The customs of mankind are influenced by climate.
22. The tree before his window was a shabby sycamore.
23. Before him rose a gate of marble white.

II.

Analyze the following sentences as in Exercise I.

1. A giant with three heads lived in the cave.
2. A man with a scythe stood in the path.
3. A poodle with shaggy hair barked on the doorstep.
4. That castle on the cliff looks very ancient.
5. His money in the bank is his dearest possession.
6. The comrade by his side fell in the first attack.
7. The portraits on the wall frowned at him.
8. The bucket in the well was old and water-soaked.
9. A big dog under the table growled and showed his teeth.
10. The path by the brook wound pleasantly along.
11. The pain in his arm grew unendurable.
12. The road to ruin is all downhill.
13. My voyage among the islands lasted three days.
14. The smile on her lips faded.
15. The road through the forest is dangerous.
16. The man at the wheel was washed overboard.
17. The workmen in the factory struck for higher wages.

CHAPTER 29
Adverbial Phrases

124. In the preceding chapter we learned that a **phrase** may often be used instead of an **adjective**.

Similarly, a great variety of phrases may be used instead of **adverbs**, and such phrases are called **adverbial phrases**.

125. In the sentence,

> The lady received her visitor *graciously*,

graciously is an **adverb of manner** modifying the verb *received*.

Without changing the meaning of the sentence, we may substitute for the adverb *graciously* any one of several phrases. Thus,

> The lady received her visitor *in a gracious way*.
> The lady received her visitor *in a gracious manner*.
> The lady received her visitor *with graciousness*.
> The lady received her visitor *in a gracious fashion*.

In each of these sentences a prepositional phrase has been substituted for the adverb *graciously*, but the meaning has not been changed at all. In other words, the adverbial phrases *in a gracious manner*, *in a gracious way*, etc., **modify** the verb *received* just as the adverb *graciously* modifies it.

Substitute **adverbs of manner** for the italicized **phrases**:

> The hunter crept along *with caution*.
> I was received *in silence*.
> *Against my will* I obey you.
> Do you say this *in jest*?
> He struggled hard, but *without success*.

126. The number of **adverbs of time** or **place** in the English language is comparatively limited. Hence it is often necessary to express time or place by means of a phrase. Thus,

I. Adverbial phrases of time:

> He lived there *many years ago*.
> The letter will probably arrive *in a few days*.
> *At this instant* a large ship was sighted.
> King Alfred ruled England *in days of old*.
> We expect to settle this claim *in the future*.

<aside>
Phrases used instead of an adverb are called **adverbial phrases.**

❧

Adverbial phrases may serve as **adverbs of manner** or **adverbs of time** or **adverbs of place** or **adverbs of degree.**
</aside>

II. Adverbial phrases of place:

> The carpenter lives *in this neighborhood.*
> The governor of Massachusetts resides *in Boston.*
> Caesar conquered Pompey's sons *at Munda in Spain.*
> My mother is not *at home.*
> The building stands *in the square.*

All such phrases are, of course, adverbial phrases modifying the verb in the same way in which a single adverb of time or place would have modified it.

Adverbial phrases may modify **verbs, adjectives,** or **another adverb.**

❧

Adverbial phrases are often **prepositional phrases,** but may also be a **noun and its modifiers.**

127. Other examples of adverbial phrases of time or place are the following:

    I.   TIME: before long, in olden times, in youth, in age, in middle life, without delay, on the spot, of yore, of old.

    II. PLACE: in town, away from home, at a distance, in this vicinity, in front, at one side, to windward, to the eastward.

128. **Degree**, like manner, time, or place, may be expressed by means of an adverbial phrase. Thus,

> The strength of one's memory depends *to a great extent* on one's habits of thought.
> His report was *by no means* accurate.
> My friend always enjoys himself *in the extreme.*

129. In accordance with the examples in the preceding sections we have the following rule:

A verb, an adjective, or an adverb may be modified by a phrase used as an adverb.

Such phrases are called adverbial phrases.

130. Most adverbial phrases consist of a preposition and its object or objects, with or without modifiers; but many idiomatic phrases of other kinds are used adverbially. Thus,

> To and fro, now and then, up and down, again and again, first and last, full speed, full tilt, hit or miss, more or less, head first, upside down, inside out, sink or swim, cash down.

Many of these phrases may be regarded as compound adverbs.

131. A phrase consisting of a **noun** and its **modifiers** may be used adverbially. Thus,

> I have been waiting a *long time*.
> Jackson was *forty-three years* old.
> The river is almost *two miles* wide.
> The gun carries *five miles*.
> Move the table *this way*.
> This rope is *several fathoms* too short.
> They rode silently *the whole way*.
> You can do nothing *that way*.
> They marched *Indian file*.

In the first sentence, the phrase *a long time* modifies the verb phrase *have been waiting* as an adverb of time would do. The phrase consists of the noun *time* with its adjective modifiers the article *a* and the adjective *long*. In the second sentence, the phrase *forty-three years* modifies the adjective *old* as an adverb of degree would do.

Study the other phrases in the same way.

Chapter 29 Exercises

I.

Use each of the adverbial phrases in Section 127, I and II, in a sentence.
Do the same with those in Section 130.

II.

Here is a short list of adverbs with adverbial phrases which have the same meaning:

courageously: with courage	furiously: with fury
eloquently: with eloquence	easily: with ease, without effort
purposely: on purpose	fearlessly: without fear
unwillingly: against his will	vainly: in vain

Try to continue the list.
Make a sentence including each of these adverbs.
Substitute for the adverb the corresponding phrase.

III.

Pick out the adverbial phrases and tell what each modifies.

1. Early in the morning a sudden storm drove us within two or three leagues of Ireland.
2. These things terrified the people to the last degree.
3. At the first glimpse of dawn he hastened to the prison.
4. The wall fell with a crash.
5. By daybreak we had sailed out of sight of land.
6. The full light of day had now risen upon the desert.
7. With smiles the rising morn we greet.
8. Innumerable dismal stories we heard every day.
9. Homer surpasses all men in this quality.
10. Her time was filled by regular occupations.
11. I say this to you wholly in confidence.

CHAPTER 30
Analysis: Phrases as Modifiers

132. In analyzing sentences we have already seen that the subject may be modified by one or more adjectives, and the predicate by one or more adverbs (chapter 23).

We have since learned that a phrase may take the place of an adjective or an adverb. Obviously, therefore, among the **modifiers** of the subject there may occur **adjective phrases**, and among the modifiers of the predicate there may occur **adverbial phrases**. Thus,

A man of courage will not be overcome by trifling obstacles.

Here the complete subject is *a man of courage*; the complete predicate is *will not be overcome by trifling obstacles*. The simple subject is *man*, which is modified by the adjective phrase *of courage*; the simple predicate is the verb phrase *will be overcome*, which is modified

(1) by the negative adverb *not* and
(2) by the adverbial phrase *by trifling obstacles*.

Sentence Analysis

"Analysis" is a Greek word which means "the act of breaking up." Here is the basic method to use for analyzing sentences:

1. Divide each sentence by drawing a vertical line between the complete subject and the complete predicate.

2. Underline the simple subject once and the simple predicate twice.

3. Mention the modifiers of the subject and label them, whether adjectives or adjective phrases.

4. Mention the modifiers of the predicate and label them, whether adverbs or adverbial phrases.

Chapter 30 Exercises

I.

Analyze the sentences from chapter 29, Exercise III as follows:

    (1) Divide each sentence into the complete subject and the complete predicate.

    (2) Point out the simple subject and the simple predicate.

    (3) Mention the modifiers of the subject, whether adjectives or adjective phrases.

    (4) Mention the modifiers of the predicate, whether adverbs or adverbial phrases.

This is the usual order of analysis and may be used as a model.

II.

(1) In the following sentences pick out all the prepositional phrases and tell whether each is an adjective phrase or an adverbial phrase.

(2) In the former case mention the noun or pronoun to which the phrase belongs. In the latter case mention the verb, adjective, or adverb which it modifies.

1. A long journey lay before us.
2. The kitchen soon was all on fire.
3. The sea fowl is gone to her nest;
   The beast is laid down in his lair.
4. He was regarded as a merchant of great wealth.
5. The night was Winter in his roughest mood.
6. The chiming clocks to dinner call.
7. The blanket of night is drawn asunder for a moment.
8. Green pastures she views in the midst of the dale.
9. In this state of breathless agitation did I stand for some time.
10. The solution of this difficulty must come from you.
11. Grapevines here and there twine themselves round shrub and tree.
12. Our coach rattled out of the city.
13. La Fleur flew out of the room like lightning.
14. Graham came from his hiding place in the neighboring mountains.
15. Battles and skirmishes were fought on all sides.
16. The stone cannot be moved from its place by any force.
17. In silent horror o'er the boundless waste
    The driver Hassan with his camels passed.
18. They sat them down upon the yellow sand,
    Between the sun and moon upon the shore.
19. Large towns were founded in different parts of the kingdom.
20. My days now rolled on in a perfect dream of happiness.

Chapter 30 Additional Exercises

Identify the noun phrases, the verb phrases, the adjective phrases, and the adverbial phrases in each of the following sentences.

1. The British Parliament and the American Congress are lawmaking bodies.
2. The brave fireman had risked his life.
3. We were attacked on every side.
4. The gates of Amsterdam had been barred against him.
5. Birds of prey were wheeling about.
6. I have received a letter from my aunt.
7. The inn was beset by robbers.
8. The messenger was arrested and searched, and the letters from the enemy were found.
9. The roar of guns and the clang of bells lasted all night.
10. I have come here without an invitation.
11. Tom obeyed against his will.
12. In spite of his efforts the man could not swim against the tide.
13. A huge alligator was sunning himself on the bank.
14. An old dog cannot learn new tricks.
15. Speak in a loud, clear voice.

CHAPTER 31
Number

133. Study the following sentences:

> The *dog* was very hungry.
> The *dogs* were very hungry.

If we compare these two sentences, we see at once that the subject of the first (*dog*) denotes a **single** animal, whereas the subject of the second (*dogs*) denotes **two or more** animals.

This difference in the number of animals referred to is shown by a difference in the **form** of the noun. *Dogs* has an -*s* and *dog* has not.

Similarly, in the following sentences we can tell immediately, **from the form of each noun**, whether **one** person or thing is meant or **more than one**:

> The Arabs are mounted on horses trained to battle or
>   retreat.
> The hermit sat on a bench at the door.
> The shepherds gave the wanderer milk and fruits.
> These thoughts were often in his mind.

Again, in each of the following sentences we can tell **from the form of the pronoun** used as the subject whether **one** person or thing is meant or **more than one**:

> We stopped near a spring shaded with trees.
> They clambered up the side of the ravine.
> I understand you very well.
> Seldom we view the prospect fair.
> He dug a deep hole in the orchard.
> It is a rattlesnake.
> She sat spinning before the door of her cottage.

Accordingly, we have the following definitions:

134. **Number is that property of nouns and pronouns which shows whether they indicate one person or thing or more than one.**

135. **There are two numbers — the singular and the plural. The singular number denotes but one person or thing. The plural number denotes more than one person or thing.**

Singular: one person or thing

ꙮ

Plural: more than one person or thing

Thus, in the sentence, "The president was elected by a large majority," the noun *president* is in the **singular** number; in the sentence, "Presidents of the United States have great power," *presidents* is in the **plural** number.

Again, in the sentence, "He failed to win the game," the pronoun *he* is in the **singular** number, for it designates a single person. In "*They* failed to win," the pronoun *they* refers to two or more persons and is therefore in the **plural** number.

The change in the form of a noun or pronoun by which it passes from the singular number to the plural is an example of **inflection** (see Section 4).

136. **Most nouns form the plural number by adding -s or -es to the singular.**

SINGULAR	PLURAL	SINGULAR	PLURAL
dog	dogs	horse	horses
cat	cats	carriage	carriages
boy	boys	judge	judges
girl	girls	lass	lasses
teacher	teachers	compass	compasses
general	generals	dish	dishes
pupil	pupils	stitch	stitches

The -s of the plural often has the sound of z.

Chapter 31 Exercises

I.

In the following extracts find all the plural nouns. Give the singular of each.

1. The stranger who would form a correct opinion of the English character must not confine his observations to the metropolis. He must go forth into the country; he must sojourn in villages and hamlets; he must visit castles, villas, farmhouses, villages; he must wander through parks and gardens, along hedges and green lanes; he must loiter about country churches; attend wakes and fairs, and other rural festivals; and cope with the people in all their conditions and all their habits and humors. — Irving.

2. My raft was now strong enough to bear any reasonable weight. My next care was what to load it with, and how to preserve what I laid upon it from the surf of the sea. But I was not long considering this. I first laid all the plank or boards upon it that I could get; and, having

considered well what I most wanted, I first got three of the seamen's chests, which I had broken open and emptied, and lowered them down upon my raft. The first of these I filled with provisions, — bread, rice, three Dutch cheeses, five pieces of dried goat's flesh, which we lived much upon, and a little remainder of European corn which had been laid by for some fowls which we brought to sea with us; but the fowls were killed. There had been some barley and wheat together, but, to my great disappointment, I found afterwards that the rats had eaten or spoiled it all. — Defoe.

3. Weavers, nailers, rope makers, artisans of every degree and calling, thronged forward to join the procession from every gloomy and narrow street.

II.

Write a description of some farm, or piece of woods, or town, or village, that you know well.

Pick out all the nouns and adjectives.

Give the plural of every noun that you have used in the singular and the singular of every plural noun.

CHAPTER 32
Genitive or Possessive Case

The word **genitive** is rarely used in modern English grammar books. However, in the study of other languages you will encounter this word for **possessive case.**

≥▲

Nouns or pronouns expressing possession are called **possessive modifiers.**

137. If we wish to express, in the shortest possible way, the idea "a dog belonging to John" or "a dog possessed or owned by John," we can do it in two words:

> John's dog.

What is there in this phrase to express the idea of **ownership**? The answer is, of course, the ending *'s*, attached to the noun *John*. For, if we erase the ending *'s*, we have merely

> John dog,

which certainly does not express possession.

By adding *'s* to *John* we have not formed a new noun; we have simply **changed the form** of the noun *John* by adding an ending which denotes **possession**.

The form *John's* is said to be the **genitive case** of the noun *John* and the ending *'s* is called a **genitive ending**.

In like manner the first noun in each of the following phrases is in the genitive case.

the king's daughter	the man's dinner
the carpenter's shop	the horse's head
the girl's dolls	the fish's scales

In all these examples observe that the genitive case denotes possession. If the genitive ending is cut off, the idea of possession disappears.

The **genitive case** is also called the **possessive case**.

A noun may be modified by another noun or a pronoun expressing possession. Such nouns and pronouns are called **possessive modifiers.**

138. The genitive case of substantives[17] denotes possession.

---

[17] Remember that nouns and pronouns are substantives.

Chapter 32 Exercises

Fill each blank with a genitive (possessive modifier).

1. The _____ efforts were successful.
2. The _____ life was spared at the request of his comrades.
3. _____ brother lives in Kentucky.
4. The _____ paw was caught in the trap.
5. The _____ rifle went off by accident.
6. The _____ bravery saved the ship with all the passengers.
7. The _____ eyes shone with excitement.

CHAPTER 33
Forms of the Genitive

> Most
> **singular**
> **nouns** in the
> possessive
> case
> **end in 's.**
> &
> **Plural nouns**
> **ending in s**
> in the
> possessive
> case are
> *followed* by
> an
> **apostrophe.**
> &
> **Plural nouns**
> **not ending**
> **in s** in the
> possessive
> case
> **end in 's.**

139. The genitive case of most nouns has, in the singular number, the ending 's,

the *man's* hat	*Mary's* book
the *woman's* veil	the *horse's* head
the *dog's* bark	the *judge's* decision

140. Plural nouns ending in s take no further ending for the genitive. In writing, however, an apostrophe is put after the s to indicate the genitive case.

the *boys'* father (= the father of the *boys*)
the *girls'* mother (= the mother of the *girls*)
the *horses'* heads (= the heads of the *horses*)

Most plural nouns not ending in s take 's in the genitive.

the *men's* gloves (= the gloves of the *men*)
women's opinions (= the opinions of *women*)
the *children's* toys (= the toys belonging to the *children*)

The **apostrophe**, it should be observed, is **not an ending** and has no effect on pronunciation. In its use with the genitive it is merely a sign employed in written and printed speech to distinguish certain forms of the noun that would otherwise look exactly alike. These forms may be seen in the following sentences:

The *boys* were playing in the field.
[*Boys* is the subject.]

The *boy's* father called him.
[Genitive singular. Here *the boy's father* = the father of the *boy.*]

The *boys'* father called them.
[Genitive plural. Here *the boys' father* = the father of the *boys.*]

Chapter 33 Exercises

I.
Pick out all the genitives (possessive modifiers) and tell what each of them modifies.
1. The emperor's palace is in the center of the city, where the two great streets meet.

2. Oliver's education began when he was about three years old.
3. Caesar scorns the poet's lays.
4. The silver light, with quivering glance,
   Played on the water's still expanse.
5. Here on this beach a hundred years ago,
   Three children of three houses, Annie Lee,
   The prettiest little damsel in the port,
   And Philip Ray, the miller's only son,
   And Enoch Arden, a rough sailor's lad,
   Made orphan by a winter shipwreck, played
   Among the waste and lumber of the shore.
6. It is not the greatness of a man's means that makes him independent, so much as the smallness of his wants.
7. In faith and hope the world will disagree,
   But all mankind's concern is charity.
8. The jester's speech made the duke laugh.
9. A man's nature runs either to herbs or weeds.

II.
Write sentences containing the genitive singular of each of the following nouns:

> Boy, girl, dog, cat, John, Mary, Sarah, William, spider, frog, elephant, captain, sailor, soldier, chieftain, Shakespeare, Milton, Whittier, baker, manufacturer, chimney sweep.

III.
Write sentences containing the genitive of the names of twelve persons whom you know.

IV.
Pick out all the genitives and tell whether each is singular or plural. Give your reasons.

1. The monarch's wrath began to rise.
2. They err who imagine that this man's courage was ferocity.
3. Two years' travel in distant and barbarous countries has accustomed me to bear privations.
4. Hark! hark! the lark at heaven's gate sings.
5. Portia dressed herself and her maid in men's apparel.
6. He waved his huntsman's cap on high.
7. The Porters' visit was all but over.
8. The ladies' colds kept them at home all the evening.
9. The crags repeat the ravens' croak.
10. Farmer Grove's house is on fire!
11. The Major paced the terrace in front of the house for his two hours' constitutional walk.

V.

Write sentences containing the genitive plural of all the common nouns in Exercise II.

VI.

Insert the apostrophe in the proper place in every word that needs it.

1. The mans hair was black.
2. The mens courage was almost gone.
3. The spiders web was too weak to hold the flies.
4. The whole clan bewailed the warriors death.
5. The soldiers helmets were visible.
6. I gave him a months notice.
7. Six months time had elapsed.
8. Womens wages are lower than mens.
9. A womans wit has saved many a stupid man.
10. The chieftains sons are the most devoted of brothers.

CHAPTER 34
Genitive of Pronouns (Possessive Pronouns)

141. English **pronouns**, as we have seen, preserve more forms of inflection than English nouns. Hence we expect to find, in the **genitive case of pronouns**, more irregularities than in that of nouns.

142. The **nominative** and the **genitive** forms, singular and plural, of several important pronouns are as follows:

NOMINATIVE SINGULAR	GENITIVE SINGULAR	NOMINATIVE PLURAL	GENITIVE PLURAL
I	my *or* mine	we	our *or* ours
thou	thy *or* thine	you *or* ye	your *or* yours
he	his	they	their *or* theirs
she	her *or* hers	they	their *or* theirs
it	its	they	their *or* theirs

My book is torn.
Our dog ran away.
Thy ways are not our ways.
Your uncle is a merchant.

This box is *mine.*
The cat is *ours.*
Our hearts are *thine.*
The top is *yours.*

The genitive forms in the table above are often called **possessive pronouns**.

You, your, and *yours* are used in either a singular or a plural sense. In form, however, they are in the plural number.

The forms *mine, thine, ours, yours, hers, theirs,* are used in the **predicate**.

Make sentences containing all the forms of **pronouns** given in Section 142.

English pronouns change their form to show a change in case. This is **inflection.**

Pronouns in the nominative form are **subject pronouns.**

Pronouns in the genitive form are **possessive pronouns.**

You, your, and *yours* are used for singular or plural, but in form they are plural.

CHAPTER 35
Genitive Replaced by an *Of*-Phrase

143. Instead of using the genitive form to indicate possession we may often use the preposition *of*. Thus,

A **possessive** word can often be replaced with the preposition *of* and a noun.	GENITIVE	NOUN WITH *OF*
	Man's life is short.	The life *of man* is short.
	Mr. Smith's property is hardly safe.	The property *of Mr. Smith* is hardly safe.
	Shakespeare's plays are supreme.	The plays *of Shakespeare* are supreme.

In these sentences the noun that follows *of* is called its object, and is said to be in the objective case (see Section 104).

144. Possession may be expressed either by the genitive case or by a phrase consisting of the preposition *of* and its object.

Chapter 35 Exercises

I.

Make twenty sentences each containing a genitive. Let them express your own thoughts.

Replace each genitive by an *of*-phrase, and note the effect. Is the change an improvement or not?

II.

Make sentences containing either the genitive of each of the following nouns or an *of*-phrase replacing the genitive. Tell the grounds of your choice.

Boy, girl, mayor, boys, girls, men, man, Chicago, horse, horses, Charles, Mr. Williams, Boston, friendship, bandit, pirate, senator, Shakespeare, tree, Longfellow, house, wisdom, school, chimney, grocer, pansy, rose, lesson, century, bicycle, Julius.

CHAPTER 36
Analysis: Genitive and *Of*-Phrase

> **Genitive** (possessive) words and *of*-phrases are **adjective modifiers.**
>
> ❧
>
> When you see them in a sentence, identify them as **adjectives**.

145. A **genitive** or an **of-phrase** limits the substantive to which it is attached, as an adjective would do.

146. In analyzing a sentence, therefore, all **genitives** and most **of-phrases** are regarded as **adjective modifiers** of the substantives to which they belong. Thus,

> The patience *of Job* | is proverbial.
> *Joe's* strange panic | lasted for several days.

In the first sentence, *of Job* is an adjective modifier of *patience*, the subject of the sentence. It limits the noun by specifying exactly *whose patience* is referred to.

In the second sentence the subject *panic* has two adjective modifiers;

> (1) the genitive *Joe's*, and
> (2) the adjective *strange*.

Chapter 36 Exercise

Analyze the sentences below according to the plan in chapter 30.
Treat the genitives and *of*-phrases as adjective modifiers.

1. The chieftain's brow darkened.
2. Quickly sped the hours of that happy day.
3. Their friends have abandoned them.
4. Edison's great discovery was then announced.
5. The population of Chicago is increasing rapidly.
6. The captain of the steamer stood on the bridge.
7. The men's last hope had vanished.
8. Our distress was soon relieved.
9. The branches of the tree droop gracefully.
10. The bird's song rang out merrily.
11. A huntsman's life had always attracted me.

CHAPTER 37
Apposition

147. Examine the following sentence:

Thompson, the fireman, | saved the man's life.

The **complete subject** contains two nouns, *Thompson* and *fireman*, both referring to the same person. The second noun describes the person designated by the first. Compare:

> *Pontiac*, the Indian *chief*, | died in 1769.
> The *tree*, a great *elm*, | fell last night.

Similarly, in each of the following sentences, the **complete predicate** contains two nouns referring to the same person or thing:

> Crusoe | rescued *Friday*, a *savage*, from the cannibals.
> The officer | lost his only *weapon*, a *sword*.

In such sentences the second noun of the pair is said to be in **apposition** with the first, and is called an **appositive.**

148. The principle of apposition applies to pronouns as well as to nouns. Thus,

> *I*, the *king*, | command you.
> He | disobeys *me*, his *father*,

149. **When two substantives denoting the same person or thing stand in the same part of the sentence (subject or predicate), and the second describes the person or thing designated by the first, the second is said to be in apposition with the first and is called an appositive.**

> When **two nouns or pronouns** refer to the **same person or thing**, the second noun or pronoun is called an **appositive.**
> ❧
> When you see them in a sentence, identify them as **adjectives**.

Chapter 37 Exercises

I.
Fill the blanks with appositives.

1. Mr. Jones, the _____, is building a house for me.
2. Have you seen Rover, my _____, anywhere?
3. Animals of all kinds, _____, _____, _____, and _____, were exhibited in the menagerie.
4. Chapman, the _____ of the team, broke his collar bone.

5. My new kite, _____ from my uncle, is caught in the tree.
6. Washington, the _____ of the United States, is on the Potomac.
7. Who has met my young friend _____ today?
8. Charles I, _____ of England, was beheaded in 1649.
9. Washington, the _____ of his country, was born in 1732.
10. Tiger-hunting, a dangerous _____, was the sultan's chief delight.

II.

Pick out the appositives, and tell to what noun each is attached.

1. An Englishwoman, the wife of one of the officers, was sitting on the battlements with her child in her arms.
2. I went to visit Mr. Hobbes, the famous philosopher.
3. We were hopeful boys, all three of us.
4. Spring, the sweet Spring, is the year's pleasant king.
5. Then forth they all out of their baskets drew
   Great store of flowers, the honor of the field.
6. He was speedily summoned to the apartment of his captain, the Lord Crawford.
7. No rude sound shall reach thine ear,
   Armor's clang and war-steed champing.
8. And thus spake on that ancient man,
   The bright-eyed mariner.
9. There lived at no great distance from this stronghold a farmer, a bold and stout man, whose name was Binnock.

CHAPTER 38
Analysis: The Appositive

150. A **phrase** containing an appositive is called an **appositive phrase.**

> Stuart, *the dauntless explorer,* perished in the desert.

151. An appositive or appositive phrase is an adjective modifier of the noun to which it is attached.

> John, *the miller,* was doing a thriving business.

Here the appositive *miller* limits the subject *John* by defining what particular John is referred to. It is not John the carpenter, or John the mason, or John the machinist, but *John the miller,* that is meant.

An appositive, then, limits or describes a noun much as an adjective would do. Thus,

Appositive	Adjective
Smith, the *tanner,* is growing rich.	*Young* Smith is growing rich.
Jack, the *sailor,* saved the man from drowning.	*Brave* Jack saved the man from drowning.
Mr. Russell, the *banker,* sails for Europe on Friday.	*Rich* Mr. Russell sails for Europe on Friday.

152. In analyzing a sentence, therefore, any **appositive** or appositive phrase is counted as an **adjective modifier.**

153. We have now learned to recognize four kinds of adjective modifiers:

> **(1) an adjective,**
> **(2) an adjective phrase,**
> **(3) a genitive,**
> **(4) an appositive.**

Analyze the sentences in Section 151, and observe the similarity between the adjectives and the appositives.

When analyzing a sentence, **an appositive** phrase is identified as an **adjective modifier.**

૨૦

We have learned **four** kinds of adjective modifiers:

1. **adjectives**
2. **adjective phrases**
3. **genitives**
4. **appositives**

Chapter 38 Exercises

I.

Point out the appositives.

1. Stuart, the dauntless explorer, perished in the desert.
2. Spring, the sweet spring, is the year's pleasant king.
3. Quentin's captain, the Lord Crawford, summoned him.
4. The hiss of the serpent, a blood-curdling sound, was heard in the darkness.
5. The old sailor, a weather-beaten Scot, told a strange story.
6. The farmer, a bold, strong man, lived not far from the fort.
7. We, your oldest friends, will help you.
8. The castle, a battered ruin, stood by the river.
9. Ferguson, an earnest patriot, addressed the crowd.

II.

Analyze the sentences in Exercise I. Identify the complete subject, the complete predicate, the simple subject, the simple predicate, the appositive noun and its modifiers.

CHAPTER 39
Transitive and Intransitive Verbs — The Direct Object

154. Compare the verbs in the following sentences:

> The dog | *barked*.
> Brutus | *stabbed* Caesar.

We see at once that in the first the verb *barked* is not followed by any noun, but that in the second the verb *stabbed* is followed by the noun *Caesar*.

Further, we see that the verb *stabbed* really needs to be followed by some noun or pronoun if the sentence is to be complete. *Brutus stabbed* would at once seem to us unfinished, and would suggest the question, "Whom did he stab?" For it is impossible to stab without stabbing *somebody* or *something*.

On the other hand, the verb *barked* is complete in sense, and does not require the addition of a noun. In fact, if we were to add a noun to the sentence "The dog barked," we should make nonsense out of it. A dog does not *bark anybody* or *bark anything*.

Examining the noun that follows *stabbed* and **completes its sense**, we find that it is the name of the person (*Caesar*) to whom the act expressed by the verb was done, that is, **it designates the receiver of the action.**

155. Study the following sentences:

> God created the world.
> The smith made an anchor.
> We manufacture shovels.
> The earth produces grain.

Here the noun that follows each verb to complete its meaning designates rather **that which the action produces** than that to which the action is done.

156. **Some verbs that express action may be directly followed by a substantive designating either the receiver or the product of the action.**[18]

---

[18] Observe that we are speaking of the addition of a noun to the verb *directly*, without the insertion of a preposition between the verb and the noun. We may of course say "The dog barked *at John*"; but here the noun *John* does not immediately follow the verb *barked*, for *at* comes between. We cannot say "The dog *barked* John," as we could say "The dog *bit* John" or "Brutus *stabbed* Caesar."

Transitive verbs may be followed by a substantive which "receives" the action of the verb.

ə

A substantive that completes the meaning of a transitive verb by designating the receiver of the action is called the **direct object**.

ə

A **direct object** is called the **object complement**.

ə

Substantives that are direct objects are in the **objective case**.

ə

Intransitive verbs cannot have a direct object.

Such verbs are called transitive verbs.

All other verbs are called intransitive verbs.

A substantive that completes the meaning of a transitive verb by designating the receiver or the product of the action is called the direct object of the verb.

A direct object is said to be in the objective case.

An intransitive verb cannot have a direct object.

The **direct object** is often called the **object complement**.

These rules are illustrated below:

I. **Transitive verbs** with direct object (objective case):

> The fox *seized* the *goose* in his mouth.
> Marshall *discovered gold* in California.
> The King of England *assembled* a powerful *army.*
> He rushed on danger because he *loved it,* and on difficulties because he *despised them.*

II. **Intransitive verbs** (no object):

> Roses *bloom* in the garden.
> The boat *lies* at anchor.
> I *have fished* all day long.
> The messenger *was running* at the top of his speed.

157. A verb which is transitive in one of its senses may be intransitive in another.[19]

TRANSITIVE	INTRANSITIVE
The girl *filled* the *cup* with water.	The girl's eyes *filled* with tears.
The fireman *ran* the *locomotive.*	The horse *ran.*
The traveler *dried* his *coat.*	The water *dried* up.

158. A transitive verb may be used without an object expressed or even distinctly thought of.

Thus we may say—

---

[19] Sections 157-159 may be omitted till a review is made.

"The horse eats," as well as "The horse eats his grain";

"The soldier fires," as well as "The soldier fires his rifle";

"The man writes," as well as "The man writes a letter."

In such cases the transitive verb is said to be used **absolutely**.

159. Many transitive verbs may be used absolutely, — that is, merely to express action without any indication of the direct object.

It is easy to distinguish between a transitive verb used absolutely and a real intransitive verb. In the case of a transitive verb used absolutely, one can always add a noun or pronoun as the direct object; in the case of a real intransitive verb this is never possible.

Thus,

The man *eats*.	The man *laughs.*
We can add a direct object (like *an apple, his food, his dinner*) at will. *Eats*, then, in this sentence, is not an **intransitive** verb but a **transitive** verb used **absolutely.**	Here we cannot possibly add a noun or pronoun as the direct object. *Laughs*, then, is a real **intransitive** verb.

Chapter 39 Exercises

I.

In the following passages tell whether the verbs are transitive or intransitive and pick out the objects.

1. A small party of the musketeers followed me.
2. These, therefore, I can pity.
3. Through the darkness and the cold we flew.
4. Yet I insisted, yet you answered not.
5. The enemy made frequent and desperate sallies.
6. Fierce passions discompose the mind.
7. The gallant greyhounds swiftly ran.
8. The Scots killed the cattle of the English.
9. Down the ashes shower like rain.
10. While Spain built up her empire in the New World, the English seamen reaped a humbler harvest in the fisheries of New-Foundland.

II.

In several pronouns the objective case has a special form, different from that of the nominative. Thus,

I have a knife.   *He* is my friend.

You blame *me.*   I like *him.*

Fill the blanks with pronouns in the objective case.

1. They found _____ in the woods.
2. My friend asked _____ to dinner.
3. The savage dog bit _____ severely.
4. Our teacher has sent _____ home.
5. Their uncle visited _____ last week.
6. The rain drenched _____ in spite of my umbrella.
7. Mary's brother helped _____ with her lesson.
8. Arthur's book interests _____ very much.
9. The flood drove _____ from our farm.
10. A boat carried _____ across the river.

CHAPTER 40
Analysis: The Direct Object

> Direct objects are identified as **direct object** in sentence analysis. They are *not* considered to be a modifier.
>
> ঌ
>
> **Verbs** should be identified as **transitive** or **intransitive**.

160. You have already learned to analyze a sentence:

> (1) by dividing it into the **complete subject** and the **complete predicate**, and
> (2) by pointing out the **adjective modifiers** of the **subject** (adjectives, adjective phrases, genitives, or appositives) and the **adverbial modifiers** of the **predicate** (adverbs and adverbial phrases).

161. In the preceding chapter we have studied another element of the complete predicate, namely, the **direct object.** This is not, strictly speaking, a modifier of the predicate, for it does not change or modify the meaning of the verb; it **completes the sense** of the verb by naming the receiver or product of the action.

Accordingly, in analyzing a sentence that contains a direct object, the object is not mentioned among the modifiers, but is specially named by itself. Thus,

> The clever young mechanic earned money rapidly.

This is a declarative sentence. The complete subject is *the clever young mechanic*; the complete predicate is *earned money rapidly*. The simple subject is the noun *mechanic*; the simple predicate is the verb *earned. Mechanic* is modified by the adjectives *clever* and *young. Earned* is modified by the adverb *rapidly. Money* is the direct object of the transitive verb *earned.*

162. Analyze the following sentences according to the model:

> The strolling musician's monkey climbed the tree with agility.
> A good man loves his enemies.
> The swift runner won the race with ease.

Chapter 40 Exercises

I.
Analyze the following sentences according to the model given in the lesson. Identify these elements:

> (a) Whether the sentence is declarative, interrogative, imperative, or exclamatory
> (b) The complete subject

(c) The complete predicate

(d) The simple subject

(e) The simple predicate

(f) The adjective modifiers

(g) The adverb modifiers

(h) The direct object and the transitive verb

1. Jane wrote a hurried note.
2. The baron pardoned the young couple.
3. Every science has its undiscovered mysteries.
4. We heard the sound of music in the distance.
5. He turned away and strode off in the opposite direction.
6. The sheep and the cow have no cutting teeth in the upper jaw.
7. A tap on her door interrupted these musings.
8. Bessy's lip trembled and the color sprang to her face.
9. How had the gentle spirit of that good man sweetened our natures!

II.

Analyze the following sentences as you did in Exercise I.

1. How I envied the happy groups on the tops of the stagecoaches!
2. The carriage came on at a furious rate.
3. The Highlanders suddenly flung away their muskets, drew their broadswords, and rushed forward with a fearful yell.
4. I see the path of duty before me.
5. Nothing could resist their onset.
6. The fleet bombarded the town.
7. A crowd of children was following the piper about the streets.
8. Streams of lava rolled down the side of the mountain.
9. The anchor would not hold the ship.
10. The bomb exploded and scattered destruction.
11. The tide ebbed and left the boat on the bar.
12. A terrible earthquake has almost destroyed the city.
13. The flames poured out of the upper windows of the factory.
14. The conspirators attacked Caesar in the Senate-house. He resisted them for a time, but at last fell at the foot of Pompey's statue.

CHAPTER 41
Active and Passive Voice [20]

163. Compare the following sentences:

John struck Thomas.
Thomas was struck by John.

> In **active voice** the **subject** is **doing something.** The subject is the **doer.**
> ❧
> In **passive voice** the subject has something **done to it/ him.** The subject is the **receiver.**
> ❧
> The **verb** is identified as **active voice** or **passive voice**.

These sentences express the same idea. In both it is John who gave the blow and Thomas who received it. Yet the form of the sentences is quite different.

(1) In the first, *John* is the subject; in the second, the subject is *Thomas*.
(2) In the first, the subject *John* is represented as acting in some way, **as doing something**, and what he was doing is expressed by the verb *struck*. In the second, the subject *Thomas* is not represented as doing anything; the verb phrase *was struck* indicates, on the other hand, that **something was done to him** by somebody else.

There is, then, an essential difference of meaning between the predicate *struck* and the predicate verb phrase *was struck*, and this difference consists in the fact that *struck* represents its subject (*John*) as **acting** (as doing something), and *was struck* represents its subject (*Thomas*) as **acted upon**, that is, as **receiving** an action done by someone else.

This distinction of meaning between *struck* and *was struck* is called a distinction of **voice**. *Struck* is said to be in the **active voice**; *was struck*, in the **passive voice**.

164. Voice is that property of verbs which indicates whether the subject acts or is acted upon.

165. There are two voices: the active and the passive.

A verb is said to be in the active voice when it represents its subject as the doer of an act.

A verb is said to be in the passive voice when it represents its subject, not as the doer of an action, but as receiving an action.

---

[20] An elementary study of the passive is introduced here in order to complete the account of transitive verbs and to prepare for the predicate nominative.

166. Many languages have special forms of inflection for the passive voice. Thus, in Latin *amat* means "he loves" and *ama'tur* "he is loved." In English, however, there are no such verb forms, and the idea of the passive voice is therefore expressed by means of **verb phrases**.

Chapter 41 Exercises

I.

Find the passive verbs (verb phrases). Mention the subject of each sentence.

1. My command was promptly obeyed.
2. One of the men who robbed me was taken.
3. Now were the gates of the city broken down by General Monk.
4. Suddenly, while I gazed, the loud crash of a thousand cymbals was heard.
5. Judgment is forced upon us by experience.
6. Nature is often hidden, sometimes overcome, seldom extinguished.
7. Youth is always delighted with applause.
8. The hall was immediately cleared by the soldiery.
9. Just before midnight the castle was blown up.
10. My spirits were raised by the rapid motion of the journey.
11. A great council of war was held in the king's quarters.
12. Many consciences were awakened; many hard hearts were melted into tears; many a penitent confession was made.

II.

Change each verb from the active form to the passive.
Note that the object will become the subject.

> Example:　　　Her friends loved *her*.
> *She* was loved by her friends.

1. The sailor rescued the child.
2. Columbus discovered America.
3. The French settled Louisiana.
4. Intemperance wrecked the man's life.
5. Edward VII succeeded Victoria.
6. The Americans captured Major André.
7. Longfellow wrote "Hiawatha."
8. Robert Fulton invented the steamboat.
9. Exercises in analysis sharpen our wits.
10. An eclipse of the sun terrified the savages.

11. Julius Caesar twice invaded Britain.
12. Tom's clever play won the game.
13. A landslide buried the house.
14. Lightning struck the statue.
15. Her brother's unkindness grieved Jane.

CHAPTER 42
Predicate Adjective

167. An **adjective** may or may not stand in the same part of the sentence with the noun or pronoun to which it belongs. Thus, in

> The *black hat* hangs on the peg,

the adjective *black* and its noun are both in the **subject**; in

> The farmer shot the *mad dog*,

the adjective and its noun are both in the **predicate**. On the other hand, in

> The dog is *mad*,

the adjective *mad* is in the **predicate** and *dog*, the noun to which it belongs, is the **subject** of the sentence.

168. **An adjective in the predicate belonging to a noun or pronoun in the subject is called a predicate adjective.**

169. The number of verbs that may be followed by a predicate adjective is limited. The commonest are *is* (*was* and other forms of the copula), *become*, and *seem*.

Others are verbs closely resembling *become* or *seem* in sense: as, — *grow, turn, prove, appear, look*, etc.

EXAMPLES:

> Our notions upon this subject may perhaps appear *extravagant*.
> The weather proved extremely *bad* the whole day.
> He grew *careless* of life, and wished for death.
> The insolent airs of the stranger became every moment less *supportable*.

After *look, sound, taste, smell, feel*, an **adjective** is used to describe the subject. Thus,

She looks *beautiful*.	[NOT: looks beautifully]
The bells sound *harsh*.	[NOT: sound harshly]
My luncheon tastes *good*.	[NOT: tastes well]
The flowers smell *sweet*.	[NOT: smell sweetly]
Velvet feels *smooth*.	[NOT: feels smoothly]

An **adjective phrase** (chapter 28) may replace a predicate adjective.

Jane seemed in *good spirits*.	[Compare: Jane seemed *cheerful*.}

The **predicate adjective** is an adjective in the predicate that **modifies the subject** and is connected to the subject by a **linking verb (copula)**, such as *is* and its forms.

❧

Other verbs that connect **predicate adjectives** to the substantive:

become
seem
look
sound
taste
smell
feel

Chapter 42 Exercise

I.

Pick out the predicate adjectives. Show that each describes the subject of the sentence.

1. The river was now full of life and motion.
2. The sentiments of the hearers were various.
3. In the north the storm grew thick.
4. Soon his eyes grew brilliant.
5. Some fortifications still remained entire.
6. He lay prostrate on the ground.
7. The evening proved fine.
8. Alfred Burnham has become penitent.
9. How different the place looked now!
10. She seemed anxious to get away without speaking.
11. Their hearts are grown desperate.
12. The captain appeared impatient.
13. He began to look a little less stern and terrible.
14. Many houses were then left desolate.
15. Gertrude remained aghast and motionless.
16. He stood stubborn and rigid.
17. All my efforts were in vain.
18. These threats sounded alarming.
19. The same law holds good.
20. She seemed anxious and looked pale.
21. Such conduct is thought improper.
22. The air was fresh but balmy.
23. He lay for a long while motionless and silent.
24. A great part of the island is rather level.
25. Their conversation was gay and animated.
26. He had become sluggish and self-indulgent.
27. Martha was blunt and plain-spoken to a fault.
28. In the tall towers by the wayside the bells hung mute.
29. Lochiel was wise in council, eloquent in debate, ready in devising expedients, and skillful in managing the minds of men.
30. Captain Brown and Miss Jenkyns were not very cordial to each other.

II.

Fill each blank with a predicate adjective. Observe that each adjective completes the predicate but describes the subject.

1. The storm came on very suddenly. The whole landscape became _____.
2. The lake is _____ today.
3. Seals look _____, but are not dangerous.
4. The dog proved _____ to his master.
5. Washington was _____ in war and _____ in peace.
6. The leaves turn _____ in the autumn.
7. John has grown very _____ in the past year.
8. Every lesson seems _____ to the indolent.
9. Such conduct appears _____ to me.
10. Do not look so _____.
11. Why does Mary seem so _____?
12. Is the ice _____? It looks _____ enough.
13. You do not appear very _____.
14. The iron grew _____ in the fire.
15. Your affection for you friend has grown _____.
16. The weather has been _____ of late.
17. Be _____, and you will be _____.
18. Never be _____, for carelessness is stupidity.

CHAPTER 43
Predicate Nominative

The **predicate nominative** is a **substantive** (noun or pronoun) in the predicate that **describes or defines the subject** and is connected to the subject by a **linking verb (copula)**, such as *is* and its forms.

❧

Predicate nominatives are in the **nominative case.**

170. A **predicate adjective**, as we have just learned (Section 169), may be added to the **intransitive verbs** *is, seem, become,* and some others, to describe or define the **subject**. Thus,

The crag is *steep*.
The task seemed *difficult*.
The shouting mob became *silent*.

When thus added, such an adjective **completes the sense** of the **verb**. Omit the adjectives in the sentences above, and this will be clear to you.

171. In precisely the same way, the sense of such intransitive verbs as *is, seem,* and *become* may be completed by the addition of a **noun** or a **pronoun**. Thus,

William II is *emperor*.
Spartacus was *chief* of the gladiators.
Johnson became *governor*.
I am your *friend*.
It was *I*. You are *he*.

Each of the italicized substantives describes or defines the **subject**, much as the adjectives *steep, difficult,* and *silent* do in Section 170.

Such substantives are called **predicate nominatives**, because they stand in the predicate, and because, referring as they do to the same person or thing as the subject, they are of course in the **nominative case.**[21]

Chapter 43 Exercises

I.

Make seven sentences containing a predicate nominative after *am, is, are, was, were, has been,* or *had been*. Select the subjects of your sentences from the following list:

Thomas Jefferson, Columbus, elms, ash, carriage, sword, story, scissors, history, pencil, ships, Carlo, football, oranges, peace, lemons, war, kindness, verb, noun, pronoun.

---

[21] A predicate nominative or adjective is sometimes called an *attribute*.

II.

Fill each blank with a predicate nominative.

1. Thomas Smith is my _____.
2. My father's name is _____.
3. A noun is the _____ of a person, place, or thing.
4. A pronoun is a _____ used instead of a noun.
5. The banana is a delicious _____.
6. The boys are all _____.
7. Napoleon was _____ of France.
8. Albert has been your _____ for many years.
9. We had been _____ in England.
10. My birthday present will be a _____.
11. Fire is a good _____ but a bad _____.
12. Hunger is the best _____.
13. Our five senses are _____, _____, _____, _____, and _____.
14. My favorite flower has always been the _____.
15. A friend in need is a _____ indeed.
16. Virtue is its own _____.
17. My favorite game is _____.
18. Milton was an English _____.
19. "Hiawatha" is a _____ by Longfellow.
20. Benjamin Franklin was a _____.
21. John Adams was the second _____ of the United States.

CHAPTER 44
Direct Object and Predicate Nominative Distinguished

Be careful not to confuse **direct objects** with **predicate nominatives.**

᷎

Nouns or pronouns following an **intransitive** or **passive** verb are **predicate nominatives** in the **nominative case.**

172. The difference between the **direct object** of a **transitive** verb and a **predicate nominative** after an **intransitive** verb is very great; but the two constructions are often confused by beginners.

173. The only resemblance is that both the direct object and the predicate nominative serve to **complete the sense** of the verbs which they follow.

Study the following pair of sentences:

> Caesar conquers the general.
> Caesar becomes general.

These two sentences appear, at the first glance, to resemble each other very strongly in their make-up. In both *Caesar* is the subject, and in both the verb of the predicate is immediately followed by the noun *general*.

Closer examination, however, shows that the construction of *general* is by no means alike in the two sentences.

(1) In the first, the *general* and *Caesar* are **two different persons**. *Caesar*, the subject, is the person who conquers, and the *general* is the person whom Caesar conquers. *General*, then, is the **direct object** of the transitive verb *conquers* (see Section 156).

(2) In the second sentence, *Caesar*, the subject, does not do anything to the *general*. On the contrary, *Caesar* and the *general* are **one and the same person**. The verb *becomes*, then, is not a transitive verb, and *general* cannot be its object.

The difference between the two sentences may be stated as follows:

IN THE FIRST	IN THE SECOND
1. The noun in the predicate (*general*) refers to a person different from the subject (*Caesar*).	1. The noun in the predicate (*general*) refers to the same person as the subject (*Caesar*).
2. The verb of the predicate (*conquered*) is transitive.	2. The verb of the predicate (*became*) is intransitive.

129

3. The noun in the predicate (*general*) is the direct object of the verb (*conquered*). It names the person to whom the subject does something.

3. The noun in the predicate (*general*) is not an object of any verb, but is closely associated with the subject (*Caesar*). It defines or explains what the subject is or becomes.

A noun in the construction of *general* in the second sentence is called a **predicate nominative**.

174. Some **passive verbs** may be followed by a **predicate nominative**. Thus,

> Jackson was elected *president*.
> The boy was named *Philip*.
> The animals are called *kangaroos*.
> The Spaniard was chosen *ringleader*.
> He was proclaimed *dictator*.
> Phillips had been appointed *secretary*.

175. A noun or pronoun standing in the predicate after an intransitive or passive verb and referring to the same person or thing as the subject must, like the subject, be in the nominative case.

Such a noun or pronoun is called a predicate nominative.

Chapter 44 Exercises

I.

In the following sentences pick out:

> (1) the subjects,
> (2) the predicates,
> (3) the predicate nominatives.

1. He is an honest man and an honest writer.
2. The Malay has been a fearful enemy for months.
3. King Malcolm was a brave and wise prince.
4. You had been the great instrument of preserving your country from foreign and domestic ruin.
5. Still he continued an incorrigible rascal.
6. Dewdrops are the gems of morning,
   But the tears of mournful eve.

7. While still very young, she became the wife of a Greek adventurer.
8. Every instant now seemed an age.
9. Dr. Daniel Dove was a perfect doctor, and his horse Nobs was a perfect horse.
10. Francis the First stood before my mind the abstract and model of perfection and greatness.
11. The name of Francis Drake became the terror of the Spanish Indies.
12. Great barkers are no biters.
13. I hope she will prove a well-disposed girl.
14. He may prove a troublesome appendage to us.
15. His bridge was only loose planks laid upon large trestles.
16. I entered the town a candle-snuffer, and I quitted it a hero!
17. A very complaisant and agreeable companion may, and often does, prove a very improper and a very dangerous friend.
18. Real friendship is a slow grower.
19. He became a friend of Mrs. Wilberforce's.
20. My friends fall around me, and I shall be left a lonely tree before I am withered.

II.

Pick out the predicate nominatives and the direct objects. Explain the difference between the two constructions.

1. With how sad steps, O Moon, thou climb'st the sky!
2. The landscape was a forest wide and bare.
3. Here the Albanian proudly treads the ground.
4. Wing thy flight from hence on the morrow.
5. It was a wild and strange retreat
    As e'er was trod by outlaw's feet.
6. Honor is the subject of my story.
7. I alone became their prisoner.
8. A strange group we were.
9. The mountain mist took form and limb
    Of noontide hag or goblin grim.
10. The family specialties were health, good-humor, and vivacity.
11. The deep war-drum's sound announced the close of day.
12. You seem a sober ancient gentleman.
13. His house, his home, his heritage, his lands,
    He left without a sigh.
14. On the tenth day of June, 1703, a boy on the topmast discovered land.
15. Have you turned coward?
16. This goodly frame, the earth, seems to me a sterile promontory.
17. This southern tempest soon
    May change its quarter with the changing moon.
18. Mr. Bletson arose and paid his respects to Colonel Everard.

19. Escape seemed a desperate and impossible adventure.
20. Here I reign king.
21. She uttered a half-stifled shriek.
22. The sailors joined his prayer in silent thought.
23. We have been lamenting your absence.
24. This spark will prove a raging fire.

CHAPTER 45
Pronoun as Predicate Nominative

Pronouns which are **predicate nominatives** are in the **nominative case.**

᠊ᢞ᠊

Many English speakers incorrectly use objective pronouns for the predicate nominative. Be careful to use the right pronoun!

176. With **pronouns** the difference of construction between the **direct object** and the **predicate nominative** may often be seen clearly; for the **nominative form** of some pronouns differs greatly from the **objective**.

DIRECT OBJECT	PREDICATE NOMINATIVE
He loves *me*.	It is *I*.
Caesar killed *him*.	Caesar was *he*.
The teacher praise *us*.	It was *we*.
The general blamed *them*.	If ever there were happy men, the discharged soldiers were *they*.

Chapter 45 Exercise

Errors in the use of pronouns are common.

The pronouns in the following sentences are correctly used. Pick out the subjects and the predicate nominatives.

1. "Who's there?" "It's I!"
2. I wish to see Mr. Smith. Are you he?
3. "Do you know John Anson?" "Yes, that's he!"
4. See that poor fellow! I shouldn't like to be he.
5. "I asked to see your sons. Are these they?"
   "Yes, these are they. Shall I tell you their names?"
6. "It's she! There she is!" cried the children eagerly.
7. Yes, it was he, the famous admiral.
8. I wish it hadn't been I that broke the window.
9. If that is the rich Mrs. Blank, I shouldn't like to be she.
10. "Who's there?" "It's we." "Who are you?"
11. The best grammarians in the village are we four girls.

CHAPTER 46
Analysis: Predicate Nominative and Predicate Adjective

In analysis, identify **predicate nominatives** and **predicate adjectives** as such.

&

Predicate nominatives may have **adjective modifiers.**

&

Predicate adjectives may have **adverbial modifiers.**

177. In analyzing a sentence containing a **predicate nominative** or **predicate adjective**, the predicate nominative or adjective should, like the direct object (chapter 40), be mentioned by itself. Thus,

The injured man | grew rapidly stronger.

Here the complete predicate is *grew rapidly stronger*. It consists of

(1) the simple predicate *grew*,
(2) the predicate adjective *stronger*, and
(3) the adverbial modifier *rapidly*.

178. The predicate nominative being a substantive, may, like the subject, have adjective modifiers (see Section 153); the predicate adjective may be modified by an adverb or an adverbial phrase.

These modifiers should be designated in making an analysis of any sentence that contains them.

Chapter 46 Exercise

Analyze sentences from chapter 44, Exercise II, 1-4, 6-15 in accordance with the following plan:

(1) Divide each sentence into the complete subject and the complete predicate;
(2) mention the simple subject and predicate;
(3) mention the modifiers of the subject and of the predicate;
(4) mention the direct object, the predicate nominative, or the predicate adjective, if the sentence has any of these parts;
(5) mention the modifiers of the direct object, etc.

CHAPTER 47
Simple Subject and Compound Subject

179. Compare the following sentences:

> John | hunts bears.
> Old John | hunts bears.
> John of Oregon | hunts bears.
> John, the trapper, | hunts bears.

In each of these sentences the **subject** is *John*.

In the first sentence, *John* is unmodified and stands alone. In the second, *John* is modified by the adjective *old*; in the third, by the adjective phrase *of Oregon*; in the fourth, by the appositive noun *trapper*. But in all four the **simple subject**, the word which denotes the person referred to, is the **single noun** *John*.

180. Contrast, however, the following sentence:

> John and Thomas | hunt bears.

This sentence appears to have **two distinct subjects**, *John* and *Thomas*, connected by the conjunction *and*; for the assertion made by the verb *hunt* is just as true of Thomas as of John. The two nouns, then, stand in precisely the same relation to the predicate, and neither of them is a modifier of the other.

Similarly each of the following sentences appears to have two or more distinct subjects:

> My *brother* and *I* | meet every week.
> *Spears, pikes,* and *axes* | flash in air.
> A *crow, rook,* or *raven* | has built a nest in one of the young elm trees.

In such cases the various distinct subjects of the sentence, taken together, are regarded as making up a single **compound subject**.

181. **The subject of a sentence may be simple or compound.**

A simple subject consists of a single substantive.

A compound subject consists of two or more simple subjects, joined, when necessary, by conjunctions.

> Two **distinct subjects** connected by a conjunction form a **compound subject.**
>
> ❧
>
> A **simple subject** has one substantive.
>
> ❧
>
> A compound subject has **two or more simple subjects.**

135

182. The following conjunctions may be used to join the members of a compound subject: *and* (*both . . . and*), *or* (*either . . . or; whether . . . or*), *nor* {*neither . . . nor*).[22]

> You *and* I | are Americans.
> Captain *and* crew | were alike terrified.
> *Both* gold *and* silver | were found in the mine.
> *Either* you *or* Tom | broke this window.
> *Either* oranges *or* lemons | make up the cargo.
> *Neither* bird *nor* beast | was to be seen.

183. In **analysis**, a **compound subject** should be separated into the **simple subjects** of which it is made up, and the modifiers of each should be mentioned.

Chapter 47 Exercises

I.

Use the following substantives, in pairs, joined by conjunctions, as the compound subjects of sentences:

> Europe, Asia; boots, shoes; wood, iron; justice, mercy; fire, sword; goodness, truth; masons, carpenters; apples, oranges; books, pencil; father, mother; gulfs, bays; hills, plains; maple, cedar; thunder, lightning

II.

Divide the following sentences into their complete subjects and complete predicates.

Mention the several substantives that make up each compound subject, and tell by what conjunctions they are joined.

1. Sorrow and sadness sat upon every face.
2. These terrors and apprehensions of the people led them into a thousand weak, foolish, and wicked things.
3. Tears lie in him, and consuming fire.
4. Homer and Socrates and the Christian apostles belong to old days.
5. My childish years and his hasty departure prevented me from enjoying the full benefit of his lessons.
6. Everywhere new pleasures, new interests awaited me.
7. His integrity and benevolence are equal to his learning.
8. Both saw and axe were plied vigorously.

---

[22] *Either . . . or* and other conjunctions thus used in pairs are called *correlative conjunctions*.

9. Neither Turk nor Tartar can frighten him.
10. The duke and his senators left the court.
11. Either Rome or Carthage must perish.
12. Her varying color, her clouded brow, her thoughtful yet wandering eye, so different from the usual open, bland expression of her countenance, plainly indicated the state of her feelings.
13. Moss and clay and leaves combined
    To fence each crevice from the wind.
14. Tower and town and cottage
    Have heard the trumpet's blast.
15. The horsemen and the footmen
    Are pouring in amain
    From many a stately marketplace,
    From many a fruitful plain.
16. Groans and shrieks filled the air.
17. The walls and gates of the town were strongly guarded.
18. Chariots, horses, men, were huddled together.

CHAPTER 48
Simple Predicate and Compound Predicate

184. In the preceding chapter we learned the difference between a **simple subject** and a **compound subject**.

The **predicate** of a sentence may likewise be either **simple** or **compound**.

185. **A simple predicate contains but one verb.** Thus,

> Fire | *burns*.
> The soldiers | *charged* up the hill.
> The ship | *was driven* before the wind.
> Gunpowder | *was used* to demolish the castle.

186. **A compound predicate consists of two or more simple predicates, joined, when necessary, by conjunctions.** Thus,

> The dog | *ran* down the street and *disappeared* from sight.
> The captain | *addressed* his soldiers and *commended* their bravery.
> Washington | *was born* in 1732 and *died* in 1799.
> The lawyer | *rose, arranged* his papers, and *addressed* the jury.
> The prisoner | neither *spoke* nor *moved*.

187. The conjunctions mentioned in Section 182 may be used to join the members of a compound predicate. Thus,

> The wounded man | said nothing, *but* lay still with closed eyes.
> The messenger | *either* lost the money *or* spent it.
> The captive Indian | *neither* spoke *nor* moved.
> The man's carelessness | *both* disappointed *and* angered his friends.

188. A sentence may have both a compound subject and a compound predicate. Thus,

> The *American* and the *Englishman* | *met* and *discussed* the question.

Two **distinct verbs** connected by a conjunction form a **compound predicate.**

⋅&⋅

A **simple predicate** has one verb or verb phrase.

⋅&⋅

A **compound predicate** has two or more simple predicates.

Chapter 48 Exercises

I.

Divide the sentences into their complete subjects and complete predicates.

Mention the several verbs or verb phrases that make up each compound predicate and tell by what conjunctions they are joined.

1. The wakeful bloodhound rose, and shook his hide.
2. They clambered through the cavity, and began to go down on the other side.
3. During this time, I neither saw nor heard of Alethe.
4. The blackbird amid leafy trees,
   The lark above the hill,
   Let loose their carols when they please,
   Are quiet when they will.
5. She immediately scrambled across the fence and walked away.
6. John made no further reply, but left the room sullenly, whistling as he went.
7. I dressed myself, took my hat and gloves, and lingered a little in the room.
8. The sun had just risen and, from the summit of the Arabian hills, was pouring down his beams into that vast valley of waters.
9. They kept up the Christmas carol, sent true-love knots on Valentine morning, ate pancakes on Shrovetide, showed their wit on the first of April, and religiously cracked nuts on Michaelmas eve.

II.

Use the following verbs and verb phrases in pairs to make the compound predicate of sentences:

Seek, find; rose, spoke; wrote, sent; has fished, has caught; heard, told; tries, fails.

Additional Review Exercises

I.
Review chapter 25, Exercises II and III, and observe the compound subjects and predicates that you make.

II.
Analyze the following sentences, as in chapter 47. Divide each compound subject or predicate.

1. The wind was either too light or blew from the wrong quarter.
2. They obey their guide, and are happy.
3. The stranger neither spoke nor read English.
4. The water looked muddy and tasted brackish, but was eagerly drunk by the travelers.
5. The watchman was sleepy, but struggled against his drowsiness.
6. The fox was caught, but escaped.
7. The bear growled fiercely, but did not touch the boy.
8. The sails were drying, and flapped lazily against the mast.
9. The ladies and gentlemen were inclined to sneer, and were giggling audibly.
10. From the first, Miss Rice was interested in her servant, and encouraged her confidences.
11. He jumped into the gondola and was carried away through the silence of the night.
12. She grew pale herself and dropped his hand suddenly.
13. Reuben came in hurriedly and nodded a goodbye to all of us.
14. Gravely he greets each city sire,
    Commends each pageant's quaint attire,
    Gives to the dancers thanks aloud,
    And smiles and nods upon the crowd.
15. Flesh and blood could not endure such hardships.

CHAPTER 49
Clauses — Compound Sentences

189. Examine the following sentence:

> The horse reared and the rider was thrown.

This sentence consists of two distinct members,

> (1) *the horse reared,*
> (2) *the rider was thrown,*

each containing a subject and a predicate. These two members are called **clauses**. They are joined by means of the conjunction *and*.

190. **A clause is a group of words that forms part of a sentence and that contains a subject and a predicate.**

A **clause** differs from a **phrase** in that it contains a subject and a predicate, as a phrase does not.

191. Each of the following sentences consists, like the first example, of two distinct clauses, joined together by a conjunction.

> The dog barked | and | the burglar decamped. [Declarative]
> Shall I descend, | and | will you give me leave? [Interrogative]
> Listen carefully | and | take notes. [Imperative]

If we study the structure of these sentences, we observe that each consists of two **independent clauses**, that is, of two separate and distinct **assertions**, or **questions**, or **commands**, either of which might stand by itself as a complete sentence.[23]

Neither clause can be said to be more important than the other. Hence both are called **coordinate clauses**, that is, — clauses of the same "order" or rank.

A sentence made up of coordinate clauses is called a **compound sentence**.

192. The clauses of a compound sentence are not always connected by conjunctions. Thus,

> The whip cracked, | the coach started, | and we were on our way to Paris.

A **clause** is part of a sentence that contains its own **subject and predicate.**
❧
Two or more **clauses** linked together in one sentence are **coordinate clauses** in a **compound sentence.**
❧
Coordinate clauses are equal in importance.
❧
A **clause** which could **stand alone** as a complete sentence is called an **independent clause.**

---

[23] We may test this by omitting *and*: thus,

The dog barked.	The burglar decamped.
Shall I descend?	Will you give me leave?
Listen carefully.	Take notes.

193. **A compound sentence consists of two or more coordinate clauses, which may or may not be joined by means of conjunctions.**

194. The following conjunctions are used in forming compound sentences: *and (both . . . am), or (either . . . or), nor (neither . . . nor), but, for.*

Chapter 49 Exercise

Separate these compound sentences into the clauses of which they are composed. Mention the conjunctions that connect the clauses, if you find any.

1. The door opened, and the two men came out.
2. They seemed mere machines, and all their thoughts were employed in the care of their horses.
3. The neighbors stared and sighed, yet they blessed the lad.
4. Thy heart is sad, thy home is far away.
5. Days and weeks slide imperceptibly away; November is just at hand, and the half of it will soon be over.
6. Pass beneath the archway into the court, and the sixteenth century closes around you.
7. The ocean has its ebbings—so has grief.
8. Art thou here, or is it but a dream?
9. The robins are not good solo singers, but their chorus is unrivaled.
10. Summer was now coming on with hasty steps, and my seventeenth birthday was fast approaching.
11. The night had been heavy and lowering, but towards the morning it had changed to a slight frost, and the ground and the trees were now covered with rime.
12. The war-pipes ceased, but lake and hill
    Were busy with their echoes still.
13. St. Agnes' Eve — ah, bitter chill it was!
    The owl, for all his feathers, was a-cold;
    The hare limped trembling through the frozen grass,
    And silent was the flock in woolly fold.

CHAPTER 50
Complex Sentences — Adverbial Clauses

An **independent clause** may be modified by another clause. This modifying clause cannot stand alone and is a **dependent clause.**

&

Independent clauses are known as **main clauses** and dependent clauses are known as **subordinate clauses.**

&

Together they form a **complex sentence.**

195. Compare the following sentences:

> The chief arose *at daybreak.*
> The chief arose *when day dawned.*

These two sentences express precisely the same idea. They differ only in their way of expressing it.

In the first, the predicate *arose* is modified by the **adverbial phrase** *at daybreak*, which is equivalent to an **adverb of time**.

In the second, this adverbial modifier is replaced by *when day dawned*, — a group of words which we recognize as a **clause**, since it contains a **subject** (*day*) and a **predicate** (*dawned*).

The sentence then consists of **two clauses**. The first (*the chief arose*) is **independent**, that is, it could stand alone as a complete sentence. This is called the **main clause**, since it makes the main statement which the sentence is intended to express.

The second clause (*when day dawned*) is a mere adverbial modifier of the predicate of the main clause (*arose*), and cannot stand by itself as a complete sentence. Hence it is called a **dependent** or **subordinate clause**.

A sentence made up in this manner is called a **complex sentence**.

196. **A complex sentence consists of two or more clauses, at least one of which is subordinate.**

197. Separate each of the following complex sentences into the main clause and the subordinate clause:

> War was declared with Spain while McKinley was president.
> I will send you the money when I get my pay.
> Before the firemen arrived, the building fell.
> He sprang to his feet as he spoke.

In each of these sentences the **subordinate clause** is an **adverbial modifier** of the **predicate**. See if you can replace it by an **adverbial phrase**.

198. **A subordinate clause that serves as an adverbial modifier is called an adverbial clause.**

> A **subordinate clause** that serves as an **adverbial modifier** is called an **adverbial clause.**

199. Adverbial clauses may be introduced by adverbs of place, time, or manner: as, — *where, whither, whence, when, while, before, after, until, how, as.*

200. Adverbial clauses are often introduced by the conjunctions *because, though, although, if, that (in order that, so that)*, etc.

These are called **subordinate conjunctions** because they join the subordinate clause to the main clause.

Chapter 50 Exercise

I.

Separate each complex sentence into the main and the subordinate clause. Mention the adverbs or conjunctions that connect the clauses.

1. King Robert was silent when he heard this story.
2. He laughed till the tears ran down his face.
3. When the Arabs saw themselves out of danger, they slackened their pace.
4. We advance in freedom as we advance in years.
5. When I came back I resolved to settle in London.
6. As he approached the stream, his heart began to thump.
7. He struggled on, though he was very tired.
8. I consent because you wish it.
9. Dr. Acton came down while I was there.
10. We drove along through a beautiful country till at length we came to the brow of a steep hill.
11. As we grow old, our sense of the value of time becomes vivid.
12. Just when the oak leaves first looked reddish, the whole tribe of finches burst forth in songs from every bough.
13. Jason and the bull wrestled until the monster fell groveling on his knees.
14. If any dispute arises, they apply to him for the decision.
15. If this is no violent exercise, I am much mistaken.
16. Tell me the facts, since you know them.

II.

Analyze the sentences in Exercise I. Identify the following elements:
   (a) Main clause and subordinate clause (as in Exercise I)
   (b) Complete subject and complete predicate
   (c) Simple subject and simple predicate
   (d) Modifiers (adverbs, adjectives, adverbial clauses, adjective clauses)
   (e) Analyze the subordinate clause.

CHAPTER 51
Relative Pronouns

201. Examine the following **complex sentence**:

The officer shot the soldier who deserted.

The two **clauses** are:

1) the main statement, "The officer shot the soldier";
(2) the subordinate clause, "who deserted."

A **relative pronoun** connects a **dependent clause** to a **main clause** and also refers to a noun or pronoun in the main clause.

≈

Relative pronouns:
who
whose
whom
which
that

≈

A relative pronoun refers back to a **substantive in the main clause**; this substantive is called an **antecedent.**

If we examine this subordinate clause, we see that its subject *who* is a **pronoun**, for it serves to take the place of a noun; that is, it designates the soldier without naming him. The pronoun *who*, then, is the subject of the subordinate clause, and at the same time **connects** the subordinate with the main clause.

The method by which the pronoun *who* connects the subordinate clause with the main clause is by attaching itself directly in meaning to the noun *soldier*.

In other words, *who* is a pronoun which serves as the subject of a verb and which, at the same time, refers definitely back to a noun in another clause. On account of this referring backward, *who* is called a **relative pronoun**.

202. Relative pronouns connect dependent clauses with main clauses by referring directly to a substantive in the main clause.

The substantive to which a relative pronoun refers is called its antecedent.

203. Other **relative pronouns** are *whose, whom, which, that.*

Harry has lost a knife *which* belongs to me.
I have a friend *whose* name is Arthur.
The girl *whom* you saw is my sister.
Tell me the news *that* you have heard.

Chapter 51 Exercises

I.

Separate each sentence from Section 203 into the main and the subordinate clause, and give the subject and the predicate of each clause.

1. Harry has lost a knife *which* belongs to me.
2. I have a friend *whose* name is Arthur.
3. The girl *whom* you saw is my sister.
4. Tell me the news *that* you have heard.

In these sentences the relative pronoun is sometimes a subject, sometimes an object, and once a genitive. See if you can distinguish.

II.

Fill each blank with a relative pronoun, and mention its antecedent.

1. The house _____ stands yonder belongs to Colonel Carton.
2. Are you the man _____ saved my daughter from drowning?
3. The sailor's wife gazed at the stately ship _____ was taking her husband away from her.
4. A young farmer, _____ name was Judkins, was the first to enlist.
5. Nothing _____ you can do will help me.
6. The horses _____ belong to the squire are famous trotters.
7. James Adams is the strongest man _____ I have ever seen.
8. My friend, _____ we had overtaken on his way down town, greeted us cheerfully.
9. Behold the man _____ the king delighteth to honor!
10. That is the captain _____ ship was wrecked last December.

III.

Pick out each relative pronoun in the following sentences, and mention its antecedent.

Divide each sentence into its clauses, — main and subordinate, — and give the subject and the predicate of each clause.

1. A sharp rattle was heard on the window, which made the children jump.
2. The small torch that he held sent forth a radiance by which suddenly the whole surface of the desert was illuminated.
3. He that has most time has none to lose.
4. Gray rocks peeped from amidst the lichens and creeping plants which covered them as with a garment of many colors.

5. The enclosed fields, which were generally forty feet square, resembled so many beds of flowers.
6. They that reverence too much old times are but a scorn to the new.
7. The morning came which was to launch me into the world, and from which my whole succeeding life has, in many important points, taken its coloring.
8. Ten guineas, added to about two which I had remaining from my pocket money, seemed to me sufficient for an indefinite length of time.
9. He is the freeman whom the truth makes free.
10. There was one philosopher who chose to live in a tub.
11. Conquerors are a class of men with whom, for the most part, the world could well dispense.
12. The light came from a lamp that burned brightly on the table.
13. The sluggish stream through which we moved yielded sullenly to the oar.
14. The place from which the light proceeded was a small chapel.
15. The warriors went into battle clad in complete armor, which covered them from top to toe.
16. She seemed as happy as a wave
    That dances on the sea.
17. He sang out a long, loud, and canorous peal of laughter, that might have wakened the Seven Sleepers.
18. Thou hadst a voice whose sound was like the sea.
19. Many of Douglas's followers were slain in the battle in which he himself fell.

CHAPTER 52
Adjective Clauses

204. Examine the following sentences:

> A *courageous* man will not desert his friends.
> A man *of courage* will not desert his friends.
> A man *who has courage* will not desert his friends.

These three sentences express precisely the same idea, but in different ways.

In the first sentence we find the descriptive **adjective** *courageous*, belonging to the noun *man*.

In the second, the adjective *courageous* is replaced by the **adjective phrase** *of courage*, also belonging to *man*.

In the third, the adjective is replaced by *who has courage*. This group of words we recognize as a **clause** (not a phrase), since it consists of a subject (the relative pronoun *who*) and a predicate (*has courage*).

The clause *who has courage*, then, is closely attached to the noun *man* and has the force of an adjective. Such clauses are called **adjective clauses**.

205. The following examples illustrate the nature and use of **adjective clauses** and adjectives:

SIMPLE SENTENCE, WITH ADJECTIVE OR ADJECTIVE PHRASE	COMPLEX SENTENCE, WITH ADJECTIVE CLAUSE
A friend *in need* is a friend indeed.	A friend *who helps you in time of need* is a real friend.
A *sleeping* fox catches no poultry.	A fox *that does not keep awake* catches no poultry.
A *bad-tempered* man is a nuisance.	A man *who loses his temper continually* is a nuisance.

206. Most adjective clauses are **relative clauses**; that is, clauses introduced either by relative pronouns, or by relative adverbs of place or time (*where, when,* etc.).

> The men, *who were five in number*, skulked along in the shadow of the hedge.

The fire *which the boys had kindled* escaped from their control.
The hat *that lies on the floor* belongs to me.
The town *where this robbery occurred* was called Northampton.
The time *when this happened* was six o'clock.

207. The substantive described, limited, or defined by a clause introduced by a relative pronoun is always the **antecedent** of the pronoun.

Chapter 52 Exercises

I.
Find the adjective clauses.
What substantive does each describe or limit?

1. The careless messenger lost the letter which had been entrusted to him.
2. The merchant gave the sailor who rescued him a thousand dollars.
3. The officer selected seven men, veterans whose courage had often been tested.
4. My traveling companion was an old gentleman whom I had met in Paris.
5. The castle where I was born lies in ruins.
6. Alas! the spring which had watered this oasis was dried up.
7. The time that you have wasted would have made an industrious man rich.
8. A strange fish, which had wings, was this day captured by the seamen.
9. This happened at a time when prices were high.

II.
Analyze the sentences in Exercise I.

CHAPTER 53
Noun Clauses

208. A subordinate clause may be used as a substantive.

Compare the sentences that follow:

> Failure | is impossible.
> That we should fail | is impossible.

These two sentences express the same thought in different words.

In the first sentence the subject is the **noun** *failure*.

In the second, the noun *failure* is replaced by a group of words, *that we should fail*, which we recognize as a **clause**, since it contains a subject (*we*) and a predicate (*should fail*). This **clause** is now the subject of the sentence.

209. Compare the sentences in the columns below:

NOUN AS SUBJECT	CLAUSE AS SUBJECT
His ingratitude cut me to the heart.	That he should show such ingratitude cut me to the heart.
The yellowness of gold needs no proof.	That gold is yellow needs no proof.
His friendship for me shows itself in his actions.	That he is my friend shows itself in his actions.

210. Substantive clauses are very commonly introduced by *that*, which in this use is a **subordinate conjunction**.

They are used to express a variety of ideas, which will be particularly studied in later chapters.

211. Substantive clauses may be used in other noun constructions besides that of the subject.

Thus in examples 1 and 2 below, the noun clause is the **direct object** of a transitive verb; in 3 and 4 it is a **predicate nominative**; in 5 and 6 it is an **appositive**.

> 1. The sailor saw *that the ship was sinking*.
> 2. My father wished *that this tree should be cut down*.
> 3. My orders are *that we should set out at daybreak*.
> 4. My hope was *that some ship might be sighted*.

> A **noun clause**, which contains a subject and a predicate, can serve as a noun—either a **subject, direct object, predicate nominative,** or **appositive**.

5. The thought *that help was near* kept our spirits up.
6. The Council issued an order *that the troops should disband*.

Chapter 53 Exercises

I.
Make sentences showing the use of nouns as subjects, direct objects (chapter 39), predicate nominatives (chapter 43), and appositives (chapter 37).

II.
Find the noun clauses. Tell whether each is subject, direct object, predicate nominative, or appositive.

1. That some mistake had occurred was evident.
2. That republics are ungrateful is a common saying.
3. That fire bums is one of the first lessons of childhood.
4. That the fever was spreading became only too apparent.
5. I know that he has received a letter.
6. I wish that you would study harder.
7. From that moment I resolved that I would stay in the town.
8. Bassanio confessed to Portia that he had no fortune.
9. My opinion is that this story is false.
10. His decision was that the castle should be surrendered.
11. The saying that the third time never fails is old.
12. The lesson that work is necessary is learned early.

III.
Tell whether each sentence is compound or complex. Separate it into its clauses.
Point out the adjective, the adverbial, and the noun clauses.

1. All the birds began to sing when the sun rose.
2. The house stands where three roads meet.
3. He worked hard all his life that he might enjoy leisure in his old age.
4. The earth caved in upon the miner so that he was completely buried.
5. I will give you ten cents if you will hold my horse.
6. The wanderer trudged on, though he was very tired.
7. The only obstacle to our sailing was that we had not yet completed our complement of men.

8. Spring had come again, after a long, wet winter, and every orchard hollow blushed once more with apple blossoms.
9. A great stone that I happened to find by the seashore served me for an anchor.
10. If you will go over, I will follow you.
11. He would give the most unpalatable advice, if need were.
12. The first thing that made its appearance was an enormous ham.
13. As Pen followed his companion up the creaking old stair, his knees trembled under him.
14. Two old ladies in black came out of the old-fashioned garden; they walked towards a seat and sat down in the autumn landscape.
15. The brigand drew a stiletto and rushed upon his adversary. The man eluded the blow and defended himself with his pistol, which had a spring bayonet.
16. In the midst of this strait, and hard by a group of rocks called the Hen and Chickens, there lay the wreck of a vessel which had been entangled in the whirlpools and stranded during a storm.

CHAPTER 54
The Same Word As Different Parts of Speech

> The **same word** may be **different parts of speech.**
>
> ૪.
>
> Some words may be a **noun** *or* a **verb,** depending on the usage.

212. Words, as we learned at the outset, are merely signs of ideas: that is, **words stand for thoughts**. You have also learned into what **parts of speech** words are divided.

Naturally, the same word may stand for or express different kinds of thought under different circumstances.[24]

213. **The same word may be sometimes one part of speech, sometimes another.**

The meaning of a word in the sentence determines to what part of speech it belongs.

VERB	NOUN
We always *walk* to school.	Tom and I took a *walk*.
Tom and I *ride* almost every day.	The long *ride* was very tiresome.
You *attempt* to do too much.	The boy made a daring *attempt*.
Anchor the boat near the shore.	The *anchor* will not hold.
The farmer *ploughs* with a yoke of oxen.	The *ploughs* stood idle in the furrows.

The italicized words in the left-hand column are **verbs**; for they not only express action but also assert something.

The italicized words in the right-hand column make no assertion: they simply call the action or the implement by its name. They are therefore nouns.

214. **Verbs and nouns often have the same form in English; but they may always be distinguished by their different use.**

---

[24] In such cases the words are often different in origin though identical in form. This distinction, however, is not important for beginners.

Chapter 54 Exercises

I.

Tell whether each of the italicized words is a noun or a verb. Give your reasons.

1. We sit in the warm shade and feel right well
   How the sap creeps up and the blossoms *swell.*
2. Like the *swell* of some sweet tune
   Morning rises into noon,
   May glides onward into June.
3. Use your chances while they *last.*
4. Shoemaker, stick to your *last.*
5. Down came squirrel, eager for his fare,
   Down came bonny blackbird, I declare!
   Little Bell gave each his honest *share.*
6. Not what we give, but what we *share,*
   For the gift without the giver is bare.
7. Heaped in the hollows of the grove, the autumn leaves lie dead,
   They rustle to the eddying gust and to the rabbit's *tread.*
8. All that *tread* the globe
   Are but a handful to the tribes
   That slumber in its bosom.
9. But what shall I gain by young Arthur's *fall*?
10. The woods decay, the woods decay and *fall.*

II.

Use these words in sentences,
   (1) as nouns,
   (2) as verbs:

> Walk, use, order, alarm, match, fish, fall, fire, light, taste, faint, pity, row, crowd, wrong, rest, plant, reply, ink, frame, frown, dawn, studies, pastures, comforts, struggles.

CHAPTER 55
Nouns and Adjectives

> The **same word** may be **different parts of speech.**
>
> ❧
>
> Some words may be a **noun** *or* an **adjective,** depending on the usage.

215. The same word may often be used either as an **adjective** or as a **noun.**

The sense determines in every instance.

216. Compare the italicized words below:

NOUNS	ADJECTIVES
Iron will float in mercury.	An *iron* anchor will hold the ship.
The miner digs for *gold.*	My uncle gave me a *gold* watch.
Leather is made of the skins of animals.	The ancients commonly used *leather* bottles.
The street was paved with *stone.*	The beggar sat down on the *stone* floor.
A *brick* fell on the mason's head.	The boy fell down on the *brick* sidewalk.
Smith is a *millionaire.*	The *millionaire* banker built a splendid house.
Tom is going to *college.*	Tom's *college* studies are too hard for him.

The italicized **nouns** in the first column are used in the second column to describe objects, that is, as **adjectives.**

217. On the other hand, words that are usually **adjectives** may be used to name persons or things. They are then **nouns.** Thus,

ADJECTIVES	NOUNS
Old men can give advice.	The *old* should be our advisers.
Harry was a *cautious* rider.	The *cautious* are not always cowards.
Brave men are common.	Toll for the *brave*!

Chapter 55 Exercises

I.

Tell whether each of the italicized words is a noun or an adjective. Give your reasons.

1. God gives sleep to the *bad* in order that the *good* may be undisturbed.
2. Is thy news *good* or *bad*?
3. She shall be a high and *mighty* queen.
4. He hath put down the *mighty* from their seats.
5. Alexander was a *mighty* conqueror.
6. Give us some *gold*, good Timon! Hast thou more?
7. Man wants but *little* here below,
   "Nor wants that *little* long."
8. The fairy wore a *little* red cap.
9. I heard thee murmur tales of *iron* wars.
10. Strike now, or else the *iron* cools.
11. Without haste, without rest,
    Lifting *better* up to *best*.
12. You are a *better* scholar than I.
13. I stand before you a *free* man.
14. The Star Spangled Banner, O long may it wave
    O'er the land of the *free* and the home of the *brave*!
15. Nature ne'er deserts the *wise* and *pure*.

II.

Make sentences of your own, using each of the words studied above:
   (1) as a noun
   (2) as an adjective

III.

Make sentences, using each of the following words:
   (1) as a noun
   (2) as an adjective

> Silver, copper, wood, crystal, leather, tin, bold, cruel, savage, generous, evil, right, wrong, studious, inexperienced, young.

CHAPTER 56
Adjectives and Adverbs

218. A number of adverbs are identical in form with adjectives: *as, fast, quick, slow, right, wrong, straight, cheap, sound.*

ADJECTIVES	ADVERBS
John is a *fast* runner.	John runs *fast.*
That action is not *right.*	He cannot hit the ball *right.*
The child was in a *sound* sleep.	The dog sleeps *sound.*
This is a *cheap* pair of skates.	I bought them *cheap.*
Your voice is too *low.*	You speak too *low.*

> The **same word** may be **different parts of speech.**
>
> ❧
>
> Some words may be an **adjective** *or* an **adverb, depending on the usage.**

NOTE: In the oldest form of English many adverbs ended in -*e*, as if formed directly from adjectives by the addition of this ending. Thus, the adjective for *hot* was *hat,* side by side with which was an adverb *hate* (dissyllabic), meaning *hotly* or *in a hot manner.*

In the fourteenth century (in Chaucer, for example) this distinction was still kept up. Thus, Chaucer used not only the adjective *hot,* but also the dissyllabic adverb *hote* meaning *hotly.* Shortly after 1400 all weak final *e*'s disappeared from the language. In this way the adverb *hote,* for example, became simply *hot.* Thus these adverbs in -*e* lost everything which distinguished their form from that of the corresponding adjectives.

Hence in the time of Shakespeare there existed, in common use, not only the adjective *hot,* but also the adverb *hot* (identical in form with the adjective but really descended from the adverb *hote*). It was then possible to say not only "The fire is *hot*" (adjective), but "The fire burns *hot*" (adverb of manner).

The tendency in modern English has been to reduce the number of such adverbs by confining the form without ending to the adjective use and restricting the adverbial function to forms in -*ly.*

Thus, a writer of the present time would not say, in prose, "The fire burns *hot,*" but "The fire burns *hotly.*" A certain number of the old adverbs, identical in form with the corresponding adjectives, still remain in use, and students should take care not to regard these as erroneous.

In poetry, moreover, the language of which is usually more archaic than that of prose, adverbs of this kind are freely employed: as,

The boy like a gray goshawk stared *wild*. [In prose: stared *wildly*.]

219. Several English words are sometimes prepositions and sometimes adverbs.

PREPOSITIONS	ADVERBS
(Observe the object)	*(No object)*
The cat lay down *before* the fire.	You told me so *before*.
The brook runs *down* the mountain.	The horse fell *down* in the street.
The park lies *within* the city limits.	There is nobody *within*.
The cottage stands *by* the river.	Lay your book *by*. [That is, lay it *aside*.]

> Be careful! Sometimes a **preposition** is actually an **adverb**.
>
> **Prepositions** have **objects**, adverbs do not.

The **preposition** has an **object**, and thus may be easily distinguished from the **adverb**, which of course has none.

Chapter 56 Exercise

Study the italicized words and tell to what part of speech each belongs. Remember that the sense determines.

1. I must reach town *before* night.
2. I have met you *before*.
3. Is there anybody *within*?
4. *Within* this half hour will he be asleep.
5. The city stands on a hill *above* the harbor.
6. The sun shines *above*; the waves are dancing.
7. He went *by* the house at a great pace.
8. He passed *by* on the other side.
9. The horse was running *down* the road.
10. The lion lay *down* in his lair.
11. Come *quick*! We need your help at once.
12. Elton was a *quick* and skillful workman.
13. This remark cuts me to the *quick*.
14. *Hard* work cannot harm a healthy man.
15. A healthy man can work *hard*.
16. Jack rose *early*, for he meant to go a-fishing.

CHAPTER 57
Review: Structure of Sentences [25]

220. You have learned the main facts relating to the structure of sentences. These facts will now be summed up for reference and review.

The elements which make up a **sentence** are:

(1) **subject**,
(2) **predicate**,
(3) **modifiers**,
(4) the three **complementary elements**, predicate nominative, predicate adjective, object.

Out of these elements a single sentence of almost any length may be constructed.

221. The **simple subject** of a sentence is a noun or pronoun naming or designating the person, place, or thing that is spoken of (Sections 43, 48).

The **simple predicate** is a verb or verb phrase expressing, in whole or in part, that which is said of the subject (Sections 43, 48).

Two or more simple subjects, with or without modifiers, may be joined to make a single **compound subject** (Section 181).

Two or more simple predicates with or without modifiers may be joined to make a single **compound predicate** (Section 186).

Either the subject or the predicate or both of them may be compound (Section 188).

The simple or compound subject, with modifiers, makes up the **complete subject**. The simple or compound predicate, with modifiers or complementary elements, makes up the **complete predicate** (Section 186).

222. **Modifiers** are of two kinds:

(1) adjective modifiers and
(2) adverbial modifiers (Section 101).

---

[25] This chapter summarizes what the pupil has already learned of the structure of sentences. It should he used for the purpose of a thorough and systematic review of this subject. The Exercises appended to the several chapters furnish material for analysis.

223. **Adjective modifiers** are:

> (1) adjectives (Section 76-77),
> (2) genitives (Section 146),
> (3) appositives (Section 152),
> (4) adjective phrases (Section 122),
> (5) and adjective clauses (Section 204).

Any substantive in the sentence may take an adjective modifier.

224. **Adverbial modifiers** are of three kinds:

> (1) adverbs (Section 101),
> (2) adverbial phrases (Section 124), and
> (3) adverbial clauses (Section 198).

Any verb may take an adverbial modifier.

225. The **complementary elements** serve to complete the meaning of the simple predicate (verb or verb phrase).

They are the following:

> (1) **predicate nominative** (Section 171),
> (2) **predicate adjective** (Section 168), and
> (3) **object** (Section 156).

226. Certain expressions may be included in a sentence without being a part of its structure. Such are:

> (1) the **interjection** (Section 113),
> (2) the **vocative** (Section 71).

227. **Sentences** may be **simple, compound**, or **complex** (Sections 193, 196).

A **simple sentence** consists of a single statement, question, command (entreaty), or exclamation.

228. A **compound sentence** consists of two or more simple statements, questions, etc., which may or may not be joined by **coordinate conjunctions** (*and, or*, etc.)

Each of these statements, questions, etc., is a **clause** of equal rank in the sentence.

A **compound sentence**, then, consists of two or more **coordinate clauses** (Section 191).

229. A **complex sentence** consists of

> (1) a **main clause**, and
> (2) one or more **subordinate clauses** used as modifiers or as substantives (Section 196).

Subordinate clauses are also called **dependent clauses**.

A **subordinate clause** may be an

> (1) **adjective clause** (Section 204),
> (2) an **adverbial clause** (Section 198),
> (3) or a **noun clause** (Section 208).

Noun clauses are also called **substantive clauses**.

A **noun clause** may be

> (1) the subject of a sentence,
> (2) an appositive, or
> (3) a complementary element, — predicate nominative or object (Section 211).

230. A **clause** is made up of the same elements that compose a sentence,

> (1) **subject,**
> (2) **predicate,**
> (3) **modifiers**, and
> (4) **complementary elements.**

Two or more **clauses** may be joined to make one **compound clause**, just as two or more sentences may be joined to make one compound sentence.

231. There is in theory no limit to the length of a sentence.

> (1) Since any noun or verb may be modified by a clause, a complex sentence may become very long and intricate. For example, the predicate of a subordinate clause may be modified by another subordinate clause, and so on.
> (2) A sentence may be both **compound** and **complex**.

Such a sentence may be made by joining together two or more complex sentences by means of a coordinate conjunction. It is called a **compound complex sentence**.

Every sentence, however long and complicated, may be resolved into the simple elements described in the preceding sections.

This process of resolving a sentence into its elements is called **analysis**.

A formula for analysis is given in chapter 58 (next page).

CHAPTER 58
Form of Analysis [26]

232. In analyzing a **simple sentence,** the following order may be followed:

(1) **Divide** the sentence into the **complete subject and the complete predicate**;

(2) **mention the simple subject and the simple predicate**;

(3) **mention the modifiers** of the subject and of the predicate, and describe each modifier;

(4) **mention the complementary elements,** — predicate nominative, predicate adjective, object;

(5) **mention by themselves all interjections or vocatives,** since these have nothing to do with the structure of the sentence.

233. In analyzing a **compound sentence:**

(1) **Divide the sentence into its clauses,** and mention the conjunctions that connect them.

(2) **Analyze each clause** as if it were a simple sentence (see above).

234. In analyzing a **complex sentence:**

(1) **Divide it into its clauses,** and tell which is the main and which is the subordinate clause.

(2) **Analyze the main clause,** mentioning the subordinate clause in its proper place as a modifier or as a substantive.

(3) Analyze the subordinate clause.

(4) If the sentence is both compound and complex, **divide it into the several complex sentences** of which it is composed, and analyze each of these as above.

---

[26] The exercises which precede afford abundant opportunity for practice in the analysis of sentences of various kinds. At this stage of his studies, the pupil should not be required always to analyze sentences to their very dregs, nor should he be expected to analyze any sentence that is so complicated as to be puzzling.
Editor's note: The teacher may wish to select sentences from chapters 1-57 exercises for extra analysis practice.

CHAPTER 59
Inflection

> Change in word **form** is called **inflection.**
>
> ❧
>
> **Inflection** indicates a **change in the meaning** of the word.

235. At the very outset we learned that words may change their form to indicate some change in the sense.

Thus the nouns *George, John, Smith, dog, carpenter, farmer,* may change their form to the genitive by the addition of 's. The verbs *walk, tell, recite* may change their form to *walks, tells, recites,* or *walked, told, recited.*

Such a change of form is called **inflection**, and a word is said to be **inflected** when it changes its form to indicate some change in its meaning.

Inflectional change always indicates some change in meaning.

236. We have already studied[27] a considerable number of the inflectional changes which words undergo in the expression of thought. (See the chapters on the plural of nouns and pronouns and those on the genitive of nouns and pronouns.)

We must now consider systematically the various **inflections** of English words, and with this study the chapters that immediately follow will be chiefly occupied.

---

[27] At this point the teacher may find it useful to make a systematic review of chapters 31-34 and 39 with special attention to the nature of inflection as illustrated by the singular and plural, by the genitive, and by the case-forms of pronouns. The extent and thoroughness of the review will naturally depend on the needs of the pupils, but some such recapitulation of what has already been learned about inflections will usually be found worth while.

CHAPTER 60
Summary of Inflections [28]

This summary gives an overview of the concepts taught in the coming chapters.

Inflection of a noun: **declension.**

❧

Inflection of a verb: **conjugation.**

❧

Inflection of number in nouns and pronouns **indicate singular and plural.**

❧

Pronouns have **inflection of gender.**

❧

Nouns and **pronouns** have **inflection of case.**

237. Before studying inflection in detail, we must consider the various kinds of inflectional change of which English words are capable.

In many languages the forms of inflection are numerous and difficult.

Thus a Roman schoolboy had to learn more than a dozen different forms for every adjective, and children in ancient Greece had to know as many different forms not only of the adjective, but even of the definite article.

A thousand years ago our own language also abounded in inflections, but in the course of time most of these have disappeared, so that modern English is one of the least inflected of languages.

238. The inflection of a **substantive** is called its **declension**; that of a **verb**, its **conjugation**.

239. **Nouns** and **pronouns** have inflections of **number** which show whether they refer to one person or thing or more than one.

There are two numbers, the **singular** and the **plural**.

240. **Pronouns** have inflections of **gender** to show the sex of the objects which they designate.[29]

There are three genders:

> (1) the **masculine**
> (2) the **feminine**
> (3) the **neuter** (See chapter 61)

241. **Nouns** and **pronouns** have inflection of **case** to show their relations to verbs or prepositions, and sometimes to other nouns.

---

[28] This chapter, like chapter 2 (on the parts of speech) is intended for reading and reference. It should not be committed to memory at this point. It may also be used as a summary when the subject of inflection is reviewed. See chapters 89, 119, footnotes.

[29] Strictly speaking some of the pronominal forms for different genders are in fact distinct words, not inflectional variations. These words, however, are so associated with each other in our minds that they may be conveniently treated as inflections. See chapter 68, footnote.

English has three cases:

> (1) the **nominative** (or subject case),
> (2) the **objective** (or object case), and
> (3) the **genitive** (or possessive case).

The nominative and objective of nouns are always the same, but some pronouns show a difference of form between these two cases. (See chapter 68.)

242. Many **adjectives** have inflections of **comparison** which show in what degree of intensity the quality that they designate exists.

There are three degrees of comparison: the **positive**, the **comparative**, and the **superlative**. (See chapter 76)

Many **adverbs** also have inflections of **comparison**.

243. Verbs have inflections of **tense** to show the **time** of the action or state which they assert. (See chapter 90)

There are two inflectional tenses:

> (1) the **present** (for present time)
> (2) the **preterite** (for past time)

Future time and certain varieties of past time are indicated by verb phrases.

244. **Verbs** have inflections of **mood** to indicate the manner in which they express action.

There are three moods:

> (1) the **indicative** (which is used in most sentences),
> (2) the **imperative** (which expresses a command or entreaty), and
> (3) the **subjunctive** (which has certain special uses).

Other varieties of action are expressed by verb phrases.

245. The **voice** of a verb (**active** or **passive**, see chapter 109) is distinguished in English by means of verb phrases.

Adjectives and **adverbs** have **inflection of comparison: positive, comparative, superlative.**

Verbs have inflection of **tense: present and preterite (past).**

Verbs have inflection of **mood: indicative, imperative, subjunctive.**

Other changes in verb meaning are expressed by **verb phrases.**

CHAPTER 61
Gender

Gender is the distinction of male, female, or "neither" (things without animal life).

≈

English **nouns** have no *inflection* of gender, but some English words are definitely masculine, feminine, or neuter (see examples in text.)

≈

English **pronouns** do have inflection of gender.

246. Gender is distinction according to sex.

> Male beings, whether men or animals, are of the **masculine gender**;
> Female beings are of the **feminine gender;**
> Things without animal life are of the **neuter gender**.

Neuter is a Latin word for "neither." Things without animal life are of the neuter gender because they are *neither* masculine nor feminine.

247. In accordance with the definitions just given, **English nouns and pronouns are said to be of the masculine, the feminine, or the neuter gender.**

1. **A noun or pronoun denoting a male being is of the masculine gender.**

    EXAMPLES: man, bull, ram, Charles, John, bishop, governor, general, actor, carpenter, mason.

2. **A noun or pronoun denoting a female being is of the feminine gender.**

    EXAMPLES: woman, cow, ewe, Mary, Harriet, lady, seamstress, governess.

3. **A noun or pronoun denoting a thing without animal life is of the neuter gender.**

    EXAMPLES: rock, tree, house, money, book, wood, machine, castle, mountain, glass.

A noun or pronoun that may be either masculine or feminine is sometimes said to be of **common gender**.

    EXAMPLES: cat, puppy, goat, sheep, nurse, physician, friend, companion.

248. The rules in Section 247 are important in one particular only: with regard to the form and meaning of **pronouns**, for English nouns have no inflection of gender. If we hear the sentence

> John lost *his* dog,

A **pronoun** must be the same gender as the noun for which it stands.

≈

Masculine pronouns: *he, his, him*

≈

Feminine pronouns: *she, her, hers*

≈

Neuter pronouns: *it, its, which*

≈

Masculine *or* Feminine (but not neuter): *who, whom, whose*

≈

Pronouns of any gender: *I; you; they, their, them; either, neither.*

we know that the pronoun *his* refers to *John*, for both *John* and *his* are of the masculine gender.

Again, in the sentence

John helped Mary find *her* dog,

the pronoun *her* refers, of course, to *Mary*, and not to *John*; for both *Mary* and *her* are feminine, and *John* is masculine.

Accordingly, we have the following important general rule for the gender of pronouns:

249. A pronoun must be in the same gender as the noun for which it stands or to which it refers.

250. The only pronouns that indicate **difference of gender** are the following:

> Masculine: *he, his, him*
> Feminine: *she, her, hers*
> Neuter: *it, its, which*
> Masculine or Feminine: *who, whom, whose*

All other pronouns may refer to nouns of any gender.

Such are: *I; you; they, their, them; either, neither.*

> I like *Charles* and *John*, because *they* are polite. [Masculine]
> I like *Mary* and *Katie* because *they* are polite. [Feminine]
> I like *Charles* and *Mary* because *they* are polite. [Masculine and Feminine]
> I like *apples* and *pears* because *they* are juicy. [Neuter]
> I do not like *Charles* and *Mary* because *neither of them* is agreeable. [Masculine and Feminine]

Chapter 61 Exercises

I.

In the following sentences point out all the pronouns; tell the gender of each, and mention the noun to which each refers.

1. The horse was injured in one of his hind legs.
2. Esther was going to see if she could get some fresh eggs for her mistress's breakfast before the shops closed.
3. All speech, even the commonest speech, has something of song in it.
4. Sam ran out to hold his father's horse.
5. "Now, Doctor," cried the boys, "do tell us your adventures!"
6. Our English archers bent their bows,"
   Their hearts were good and true,
   At the first flight of arrows sent,
   Full fourscore Scots they slew.
7. The bridegroom stood dangling his bonnet and plume.
8. Emma was sitting in the midst of the children, telling them a story; and she came smiling towards Erne, holding out her hand.

II.

Fill each blank with a noun or a pronoun. Tell its gender, and give your reason

1. The poet had written _____ last song.
2. _____ swept the hearth and mended the fire.
3. The old farmer sat in _____ arm chair.
4. Tom lost _____ knife; but Philip found _____.
5. Arthur and Kate studied _____ lessons together.
6. The Indian picked up a stone and threw _____ at the bird.
7. The tracks were so faint that _____ could not be followed.
8. My aunt has sold _____ horse to _____ cousin.

CHAPTER 62
Special Rules of Gender, Part 1: Personification

251. Many nouns ordinarily of the neuter gender may become masculine or feminine.

> **Personification** applies human qualities to lifeless objects or animals or qualities.
>
> ❧
>
> Nouns which are normally neuter become **masculine or feminine** when they are **personified.**

1. Any **lifeless object** may be regarded as a **person** capable of thought, speech, and action. Thus,

    > *Mont Blanc* is the monarch of mountains;
    >   They crowned *him* long ago
    > On a throne of rocks, in a robe of clouds,
    >   With a diadem of snow.

    >   My mother Earth!
    > And thou fresh breaking Day, and you, ye Mountains,
    > Why are ye beautiful? I cannot love ye.

2. One of the **lower animals** may be represented as thinking and speaking. So in fables.

3. Human **qualities, emotions**, and the like, are often regarded as persons. Thus,

    > *Hope* enchanted smiled, and waved *her* golden hair.
    >   *Revenge* impatient rose:
    > *He* threw *his* blood-stain'd sword, in thunder, down.

252. The usage described in Section 251 is called **personification**, and the things, animals, or qualities thus treated are said to be **personified.**[30]

253. The name of a personified quality or emotion is regarded as a **proper noun** and begins with a capital letter. So, often, in the case of a thing or animal that is personified. Thus,

    > Haste thee, nymph, and bring with thee
    > *Jest* and youthful *Jollity,*
    > *Sport*, that wrinkled *Care* derides,
    > And *Laughter*, holding both his sides.

---

[30] The personification of lifeless objects is a natural tendency of the human mind, as may be seen from the talk of young children. The personification of abstract ideas is common in poetry and is the basis of all allegory. The personification of animals is perhaps a survival of a very early stage of culture when animals were regarded as capable of thought and speech.

254. In referring to a **ship** or other vessel the pronouns *she* and *her* (not *it* and *its*) are regularly used.

Hence the nouns *ship, barque, brig, schooner*, and the like, may be regarded as of the **feminine** gender.

Thus, Admiral Byron, in describing the loss of the ship "Wager," writes as follows:

> In the morning, about four o'clock, the ship struck. The shock we received upon this occasion, though very great, being not unlike a blow of a heavy sea, such as in the series of preceding storms we had often experienced, was taken for the same; but we were soon undeceived by her striking again more violently than before, which laid her upon her beam ends, the sea making a fair breach over her. In this dreadful situation she lay for some little time, every soul on board looking upon the present minute as his last; for there was nothing to be seen but breakers all around us. However, a mountainous sea hove her off from thence; but she presently struck again, and broke her tiller.

> A **ship** or other vessel uses the feminine pronouns *she* and *her*.

Chapter 62 Exercises

Find examples of personification in your reader. An excerpt from Richard Henry Dana's *Two Years Before the Mast* is given in *The Mother Tongue Student Workbook 1* for your convenience. Why are some objects and qualities regarded as masculine and others as feminine?

CHAPTER 63
Special Rules of Gender, Part 2: Pronouns for Animals[31]

255. The names of the **lower animals** (as, *dog, horse, sheep, cat, butterfly, ant*) are variously treated with regard to their **gender**.

When it is necessary to distinguish the sex of animals (for example, in a treatise on natural history), care is taken to refer to them by means of the pronoun *he* or *she* according as the animal is male or female.

In ordinary speech, on the other hand, most large animals are referred to by means of the pronoun *he*, most insects and small animals by means of the pronoun *it*.

If, however, we wish to emphasize the fact that we are talking of **living beings**, we may use the pronoun *he* of any creature however small. So especially in fables.

256. In the use of the pronouns *who* and *which* with reference to the **lower animals**, there is considerable difference of usage. The general rule is to use *which*; but *who* is not uncommon, especially when an animal is thought of as an intelligent being.

Thus, one would always say "The *horse which* I bought yesterday is not very valuable"; even if one immediately added "*He* is not worth more than one hundred dollars."

But the hunter in Scott's "Lady of the Lake," when addressing his gallant gray who had fallen exhausted after the stag hunt, might well have said "You, my gallant gray, *who* have carried me safely through so many perils, must now die in this lonely spot."

Such questions as this can never be settled by mere rules of grammar. The feeling of the speaker must decide in each case.

Thought gives laws to grammar; grammar does not govern thought.

257. *It* and *its* are often used in referring to very young children. Thus,

> The baby fell and hurt *its* head.

258. In older English the pronoun *his* was neuter as well as masculine. Hence in Shakespeare, for example, *his* will often be found where in modern English *its* would be used. Thus,

---

> There is a variety of usage when applying pronouns to animals.
>
> ❧
>
> Choosing *who* or *which* in reference to animals can depend on the usage.
>
> ❧
>
> Thought gives laws to grammar; grammar does not govern thought.

---

[31] This chapter is meant for reading and conversation. It is not to be committed to memory.

My life has run *his* compass.
That same eye did lose *his* luster.

Chapter 63 Exercise

Make sentences illustrating the gender of nouns and pronouns as follows:

1. Use *he, she,* and *it* so that each shall refer to some noun in the proper gender.
2. Use the genitives *his, her, its* in the same way.
3. Use *they* to refer to two masculine nouns; to two feminine nouns; to two neuter nouns; to two nouns of different gender.
4. Use *I, my, thou, you* in sentences, and see if you can tell their gender.
5. Use, in properly constructed sentences, *who, whose,* and *whom* to refer to persons; *which* to refer to animals; *which* to refer to things.

CHAPTER 64
Plural of Nouns [32]

259. Substantives have inflection of **number.**

260. Most nouns form the plural number by adding *-s* or *-es* to the singular.

> Nouns have a singular and plural form. This is the **inflection of number.**
> ❧
> **Most nouns** form the plural simply by **adding *-s* or *-es.***
> ❧
> **In some nouns,** the **base word changes** before adding the plural ending.

EXAMPLES:

SINGULAR	PLURAL
crow	crows
flower	flowers
class	classes

261. Sometimes the last letter of the singular form is changed before the ending *-s* or *-es* of the plural.

EXAMPLES:

SINGULAR	PLURAL
fly	flies
ally	allies
remedy	remedies

In a very few words this change of letter indicates a change of sound.

EXAMPLES:

SINGULAR	PLURAL
calf	calves
half	halves
loaf	loaves
knife	knives

---

[32] At this point chapter 31 should be reviewed.

Chapter 64 Exercises

Write in parallel columns the singular and the plural of:

a. Boy, girl, field, street, paper, book, pencil, brick, bell, door, hat, lesson, president, governor.
b. Fly, cry, reply, supply, ally, remedy, subsidy.
c. Toy, play, alley, donkey, ray, dray, survey, essay.
d. Calf, half, loaf, knife, wife, life.

Compare your four lists, and see if you can frame a rule for the plural of:
   (1) nouns that end in -*y* after a consonant,
   (2) nouns that end in -*y* after a vowel,
   (3) nouns like *calf* and *knife*.

CHAPTER 65
Irregular Plurals, Part 1

A few nouns
form the
plural by
adding -en.

A few nouns
form the
plural by
**changing the
medial
(middle)
vowel.**

A few nouns
do not change
their form
when changed
to plural.

262. A few nouns form an irregular plural in **-en**.

These are: ox, *plural* oxen; brother, *plural* brethren (more commonly, brothers); child, *plural* children.

In older English there were many more *n*-plurals than at present; as—*eyen* (later spelled *eyne*), eyes; *ashen* ashes; *daughtren,* daughters; *sistren* sisters; *hosen,* hose.

263. A few nouns form the plural number not by adding a termination to the singular, but by a **change of vowel** in the word itself. These are:

SINGULAR	PLURAL		SINGULAR	PLURAL
man	men		tooth	teeth
woman	women		goose	geese
merman	mermen		mouse	mice
foot	feet		louse	lice

Compound nouns of which the second part is *man* or *woman* belong to this class.

EXAMPLES:

SINGULAR	PLURAL
horseman	horsemen
washerwoman	washerwomen

So, Englishman, Frenchman, Dutchman.
Norman, however, has the plural *Normans.*[33]

264. A few nouns have the *same form* in both singular and plural.

EXAMPLES: deer, sheep, swine, neat (i.e. cattle).
My pet *deer* is dead.
The hunter saw a great herd of *deer.*
There are a hundred *sheep* in this flock.

---

[33] *German, Mussulman, Ottoman, dragoman, firman* are not compounds of *man*. Hence they make their plural in -s: *Mussulmans, Ottomans,* etc.

265. A few nouns have **two plurals**. Thus,

Singular	Plural
brother	brothers *or* brethren
penny	pennies (single coins) pence (collectively)
fish	fishes (singly) fish (collectively)
horse	horses (animals) horse (cavalry)
cloth	cloths (pieces of cloth) clothes (garments)
die	dies (for stamping) dice (for gaming)

In such cases there is always some difference in the meaning or the use of the two forms. *Brethren*, for example, is applied not to one's real *brothers*, but to one's associates in religion or some fraternal organization.

For full information as to particular words, a large dictionary should be consulted.

> The four *pennies* rolled along the floor.
> The price of this thing is *fourpence*.
> Mr. Thomas owns six *horses*.
> The troop consisted of sixty *horse*.

266. Some **foreign words** that have been taken into English keep their **foreign plurals**. Many of them also make a plural by adding *-s* or *-es* after the English fashion.[34]

> **Examples:**
>
> | Singular | Plural |
> |----------|--------|
> | erratum | errata |
> | memorandum | memoranda or memorandums |
> | thesis | theses |
> | parenthesis | parentheses |
> | appendix | appendices *or* appendixes |
> | fungus | fungi *or* funguses. |

A few nouns have **two plural** forms. See the examples in the text.

ॐ

Be careful! Some English words taken from foreign languages keep the plural form of that language. Others use the English form of adding *-s* or *-es*.

---

[34] The dictionary should be consulted for such words.

CHAPTER 66
Irregular Plurals, Part 2 [35]

The plural of letters, numbers, and signs or symbols is formed by adding an **apostrophe and *s*.**

෨

Modern punctuation emphasizes simplicity and the apostrophe after numerals is often omitted. *e.g. The 1800s, etc.*

෨

Compound nouns form their plural in various ways. Study the list in the text.

267. **Letters** of the alphabet, **figures** indicating number, and other **signs** add -**'s** in the plural.

> You make your *u's* and your *n's* too much alike.
> Dot your *i's* and cross your *t's*.
> Mind your *p's* and *q's*.
> Cross out all the *3's* and *4's*.
> What queer looking *&'s*!
> Be careful about your *+'s* and *×'s*.

So also words when regarded merely as **things** spoken or written. Thus,

> You have omitted all the *and's*.
> He writes all his *John's* with small *j's*.

268. A noun consisting of two or more words united into one is called a *compound noun*.

> EXAMPLES: bookcase, teacup, railroad, window-pane, box-cover, handkerchief, commander-in-chief, father-in-law.

Such nouns make their plurals in various ways.

Sometimes only the first part of the compound is put into the plural form; sometimes only the last part; sometimes both parts are made plural.

SINGULAR	PLURAL
hatband	hatbands
bookcase	bookcases
snowbird	snowbirds
spoonful	spoonfuls
mother-in-law	mothers-in-law
man-of-war	men-of-war
general-in-chief	generals-in-chief
man-servant	men-servants
woman-servant	women-servants

---

[35] For study and reference.

269. The parts of a compound noun are sometimes connected by a hyphen (as in *box-cover*) sometimes written together without a hyphen (as in *teacup*), and sometimes written as separate words (as in *boat club*).

These differences are matters of custom, and usage varies much in different words of the same kind and sometimes in the same word. In cases of doubt the pupil should consult a good dictionary.

270. Some nouns are seldom or never used in the plural number.

> Such are many names,
>
> —of qualities (as *perseverance, indignation, wrath, satisfaction*),
> —of sciences (as *astronomy, biology*),
> —of forces (as *gravitation, electricity*), etc.

Many other nouns are confined to the singular in their general sense, but in some special meaning may take a plural. Thus,

> *Iron* (a metal), plural *irons* (fetters);
> *brass*, plural *brasses* (brass tablets);
> *glass*, plural *glasses* (drinking vessels, spectacles, etc.).

271. Some nouns are used in the plural number only.

> Such are: *scissors, pincers, tongs, lees, dregs, trousers, annals, billiards, proceeds.*

272. A few nouns are plural in form, but singular in sense.

> Such are: *news, gallows, measles, small-pox* (for *small pocks*), and some names of sciences (as *mathematics, physics*).
>
> No *news* is good news.
> The *measles* is a disease of children.

Most of these nouns were formerly plural in sense as well as in form. *News*, for example, originally meant "new things," and it was customary to write not "this news," but "these news."

In some words usage varies. Thus, *bellows* is sometimes regarded as a singular and sometimes as a plural.

CHAPTER 67
Irregular Plurals, Part 3

273. With regard to the plural of proper names with the titles *Mr., Mrs, Miss*, and *Master* usage is as follows:

Mr. Smith
Messrs. Smith
ॐ
Mrs. Smith
Mrs. Smiths
ॐ
Miss Smith
Misses Smith *or*
  Miss Smiths
ॐ
Master Smith
The Masters
  Smith

1. The plural of *Mr.* (*Mister*) is *Messrs.* (pronounced *Messers*). With this title the name itself remains in the singular. Thus,

   Mr. Smith, plural *Messrs.* (or *the Messrs.*) *Smith.*

2. The title *Mrs.* cannot be put into the plural. Hence the name itself receives the plural form. Thus,

   Mrs. Thompson, plural *the Mrs. Thompsons*

3. In the case of *Miss*, sometimes the title is put in the plural, sometimes the name. Thus,

   Miss Smith, plural *the Misses Smith* or *the Miss Smiths.*

4. In the case of *Master* the title is put in the plural, the name itself remaining in the singular. Thus,

   Master Prescott, plural *the Masters Prescott.*

Chapter 67 Exercises

I.

Use in sentences the plurals of these nouns:
1. Man, fisherman, deer, sheep, child, ox, penny, Miss Clark, Mr. Ray, Mrs. Ray, cattle, horseman, tooth, German, mouse.
2. Foot, brother (*both plurals*), Master Wilson, Miss Atkins, handful, son-in-law, man-of-war, bluebird, handkerchief.

Explain all the forms that you have used.

II.

Pick out the plural nouns, and give the singular when you can.
Mention any peculiar plurals that you find.

1. Riches do many things.
2. Tears and lamentations were seen in almost every house.
3. The skipper boasted of his catch of fish.

4. With figs and plums and Persian dates they fed me.
5. The rest of my goods were returned me.
6. The sheep were browsing quietly on the low hills.
7. The Messrs. Bertram were very fine young men.
8. The admiration which the Misses Thomas felt for Mrs. Crawford was rapturous.
9. He drew out the nail with a pair of pincers.
10. His majesty marches northwards with a body of four thousand horse.
11. Flights of doves and lapwings were fluttering among the leaves.
12. Down fell the lady's thimble and scissors into the brook.
13. The Miss Blacks lived, according to the worldly phrase, out of the world.
14. The day after came the unfortunate news of the queen's death.
15. No person dined with the queen but the two princesses royal.
16. I cannot guess at the number of ships, but I think there must be several hundreds of sail.
17. The Miss Bertrams continued to exercise their memories.
18. Weavers, nailers, rope makers, artisans of every degree and calling, thronged forward to join the procession from every gloomy and narrow street.
19. Now all the youth of England are on fire.
20. Charles has some talent for writing verses.

CHAPTER 68
Personal Pronouns, Part 1

274. Each of the following sentences has a **pronoun** for its subject:

> I walk.
> Thou walkest.
> He walks.

If we examine the sentences, we see at once that their subjects (the pronouns *I thou, he*) do not all refer to the same person. *I* denotes the person who **speaks** the sentence; *thou* denotes the person who is **spoken to**; *he* denotes neither the speaker nor the person spoken to, but some third person, whom we may call the person **spoken of**.

Hence these pronouns are called **personal pronouns**.

275. The personal pronouns serve to distinguish

> **(1) the speaker,**
> **(2) the person spoken to, and**
> **(3) the person or thing spoken of.**

276. The personal pronouns are divided into three classes, as follows:

> Pronouns of the **first person** (denoting the **speaker**): *I*; plural, *we*.
>
> Pronouns of the **second person** (denoting the person **spoken to**): *thou*[36]; plural, *you* (or *ye*).
>
> Pronouns of the **third person** (denoting the person or thing **spoken of**): masculine, *he*; feminine, *she*; neuter, *it*; plural (masculine, feminine, and neuter), *they*.

PERSON	SINGULAR	PLURAL
1st	I	we
2nd	thou	you/ye
3rd	he/she/it	they

277. The several personal pronouns take various forms, according to their relation to other words in the sentence, that is, according to their **construction**.

Personal pronouns are divided into three classes: **first person, second person, third person.**

In modern English, the second person singular *thou* is no longer used. The **second person plural form** *you* is used for **both singular** and **plural second person**. (See chapter 69.)

---

[36] Although "thou" and "ye" are now archaic and used only in poetry. See chapter 69 for a fuller explanation on these pronouns.

We have already seen most or all of these forms in the preceding lessons. We will now collect them and arrange them in order; in other words, we will study the **inflection** or **declension**[37] of the personal pronouns.

278. The personal pronouns are inflected as follows:[38]

THE PRONOUN OF THE FIRST PERSON: *I*

	SINGULAR	PLURAL
Nominative	I	we
Genitive	my *or* mine	our *or* ours
Objective	me	us

THE PRONOUN OF THE SECOND PERSON: *thou*[39]

	SINGULAR	PLURAL
Nominative	thou	you *or* ye
Genitive	thy *or* thine	your *or* yours
Objective	thee	you *or* ye

THE PRONOUNS OF THE THIRD PERSON: *he, she, it.*

	SINGULAR			PLURAL
	Masculine	*Feminine*	*Neuter*	*Masculine, Feminine, and Neuter*
Nominative	he	she	it	they
Genitive	his	her *or* hers	its	their *or* theirs
Objective	him	her	it	them

---

[37] Editor's Note: The declension of nouns or pronouns shows how the word changes form according to its case. This is "inflection." Remember that nominative case means that the noun or pronoun is either the subject or the predicate nominative; genitive case means the noun or pronoun is possessive; objective case means the noun or pronoun is the object of the preposition, the direct object, or the indirect object. See chapter 70.

[38] What we regard as different forms of the same pronoun are sometimes distinct words (see chapter 60, second footnote). Thus, in the first person we have four distinct words: (1) *I*, (2) *my, mine, me*, (3) *we* (4) *our, us*; in the second person, the plural is a different word from the singular. In the third person, all the singular forms except *she* belong together (*it* being for an older *hit*), but the plural is a distinct word.

[39] Editor's Note: See chapter 69

CHAPTER 69
Personal Pronouns, Part 2

279. The pronouns of the first and second persons (*I* and *thou*) are of **common gender**; that is, they may be used for either male or female beings.

In the pronouns of the third person there is a distinction of **gender** in the **singular** (*he, she, it*); in the **plural**, however, the single form *they* serves for all three genders.

> **Third person singular pronouns** make a distinction of **gender:** *he, she, it*
>
> ଌ
>
> *You, your,* and *yours* are used for singular number as well as plural.

280. The forms *thou, thy, thine, thee,* and *ye* are seldom used except in poetry and in solemn language like that of prayer.

Members of the Society of Friends (commonly called Quakers) and of some other religious bodies use *thee* and *thy* in their ordinary conversation.

281. Except in poetry and in solemn language, *you, your,* and *yours* do duty for the **singular** number as well as for the **plural**. Thus,

> *You* are the best scholars in the class. [Plural]
> *You* are the best scholar in the class. [Singular in sense]

When the forms *you* and *your* (or *yours*) are used in a singular sense, they are often said to be in the singular number. Yet *you*, whether singular or plural in sense, always takes the verb forms that are used with plural subjects. Thus,

> *You were* my friend. *You were* my friends.

Such a form as *you was* is a gross error. It is best, therefore, to describe *you* as always **plural** in **form**, but as **singular** in **sense** when it refers to a single person or thing.

Chapter 69 Exercises

I.

Pick out the personal pronouns. Tell whether each is of the first, the second, or the third person. Mention the gender and number of each.

1. He was my friend, faithful and just to me.
2. Mahomet accompanied his uncle on trading journeys.
3. Our Clifford was a happy youth.

4. And now, child, what art thou doing?
5. I think I can guess what you mean.
6. Then boast no more your mighty deeds!
7. Round him night resistless closes fast.
8. I was in the utmost astonishment, and roared so loud that they all ran back in fright.
9. She listens, but she cannot hear
   The foot of horse, the voice of man.
10. He hollowed a boat of the birchen bark,
    Which carried him off from shore.
11. At dead of night their sails were filled.
12. Men at some time are masters of their fates.
13. Here is a sick man that would speak with you.
14. Why should we yet our sail unfurl?
15. I once more thought of attempting to break my bonds.
16. Our fortune and fame had departed.
17. The Hawbucks came in their family coach, with the blood-red hand emblazoned all over it.
18. The spoken word cannot be recalled. It must go on its way for good or evil.
19. He saw the lake, and a meteor bright
    Quick over its surface played.
20. I have endeavored to solve this difficulty another way.
21. The military part of his life has furnished him with many adventures.
22. He ambled alongside the footpath on which they were walking, showing his discomfort by a twist of his neck every few seconds.
23. Our provisions held out well, our ship was stanch, and our crew all in good health; but we lay in the utmost distress for water.
24. Sweet day, so cool, so calm, so bright —
    The bridal of the earth and sky—
    The dew shall weep thy fall tonight,
    For thou must die.
25. Lend me thy cloak, Sir Thomas.
26. Captain Fluellen, you must come presently to the mines. The Duke of Gloucester would speak with you.
27. Madam, what should we do?
28. Worthy Macbeth, we stay upon your leisure.
29. Fair and noble hostess,
    We are your guest tonight.

II.
Mention the case of each personal pronoun under I, above. Give your reasons.

III.

In these sentences from chapter 4 Exercise I, tell the person, number, and gender of each pronoun; then give its case with your reasons.

This exercise is called "parsing" words.

1. A number of young people were assembled in the music room.
2. He leads towards Rome a band of warlike Goths.
3. By ten o'clock the whole party were assembled at the Park.
4. Have I not reason to look pale and dead?
5. People were terrified by the force of their own imagination.
6. The Senate has letters from the general.
7. You misuse the reverence of your place.
8. There is hardly any place, or any company, where you may not gain knowledge if you please.
9. Here comes another troop to seek for you.
10. Their mastiffs are of unmatchable courage.
11. Our family dined in the field, and we sat, or rather reclined, round a temperate repast.
12. Our society will not break up, but we shall settle in some other place.
13. Let nobody blame him; his scorn I approve.
14. The Senate have concluded
    To give this day a crown to mighty Caesar.
15. He is banished, as enemy to the people and his country.
16. Society has been called the happiness of life.
17. His army is a ragged multitude
    Of hinds and peasants, rude and merciless.
18. There is a great difference between knowledge and wisdom.
19. All the country in a general voice cried hate upon him.
20. The king hath called his Parliament.
21. Let all the number of the stars give light to thy fair way!

IV.

Use these personal pronouns in sentences of your own:

> Me, he, you (objective), him, she, us, ye, thou, my, mine, thee, its, yours, our, I, ours, their, it (nominative), thine, his, her (objective), it (objective), theirs, her (genitive), we, thy, your, you (nominative), hers, they, them.

CHAPTER 70
Nominative and Objective Case

282. Nouns and pronouns, as we have already learned, may change their form to indicate some of their relations to other words in the sentence.

Thus, the noun *man* has one form (*man*) when it is the **subject** or the **object** of a verb, another form when it indicates **possession.**

> The *man* rides well. [Subject]
> The horse kicked the *man.* [Object]
> The *man's* name is Jones. [Possession]

Such changes of form are said to indicate the **case** of the substantive.

283. **Substantives have inflections of case to indicate their grammatical relations to verbs, to prepositions, or to other substantives.**

284. English grammar distinguishes three cases,

> the **nominative** (or subject case),
> the **objective** (or object case), and
> the **genitive** (or possessive case).

285. **A substantive that is the subject of a verb is in the nominative case.**

> *I* am your son.   The *bear* growled.
> *Thou* art the man.   The *horse* gallops.
> *We* are Americans.   The *iron* sank.

286. **A substantive that is the object of a verb or preposition is in the objective case.**

> He wrongs *me.*   Smith gave *him money.*
> The laws protect *us.*   Ye call *me chief.*
> You sent *me* to *him.*   John has torn his *coat.*

287. There is no difference of form between the nominative and the objective case of nouns. Several pronouns, however, show such a difference.

See the table on the following page.

Subjects are in the **nominative case.**

❧

Objects are in the **objective case.**

❧

In English, **nouns** in nominative and objective case have the same **form.**

❧

Nominative case pronouns are different in form from **objective case pronouns.**

	SINGULAR		PLURAL	
NOMINATIVE	OBJECTIVE	NOMINATIVE	OBJECTIVE
I	me	we	us
thou	thee	ye (*or* you)	you (*or* ye)
he	him		
she	her	they	them
it	it		
who	whom	who	whom

Chapter 70 Exercise

In the following sentences pick out the subjects and objects and tell the case of each. Give your reasons.

1. Forth on his fiery steed betimes he rode.
2. A thick forest lay near the city.
3. When they met, they made a surly stand.
4. It is true, hundreds, yea thousands of families fled away at this last plague.
5. Some of these rambles led me to great distances.
6. When the moonlight nights returned, we used to venture into the desert.
7. He loaded a great wagon with hay.
8. With her two brothers this fair lady dwelt.
9. The lord of the castle in wrath arose.
10. The fair breeze blew, the white foam flew,
    The furrow followed free;
    We were the first that ever burst
    Into that silent sea.
11. A dense fog shrouded the landscape.
12. How he blessed this little Polish lady!

CHAPTER 71
Predicate Nominative [40]

The **predicate nominative** is in the **nominative case.**

ᨠ

A **pronoun** as a **predicate nominative** must be in the **nominative case.**

ᨠ

Nominative pronouns and **objective pronouns** take different forms.

ᨠ

Be careful! Always use **nominative pronouns** as **predicate nominative.**

288. An important **nominative** construction is the **predicate nominative**, already studied in chapters 41-46.

289. A substantive standing in the predicate after an intransitive or passive verb and referring to the same person or thing as the subject is in the nominative case.

Such a substantive is called a predicate nominative.

290. This rule is very important in dealing with **pronouns**. With nouns it is of less practical value, since nouns have the same form for both nominative and objective.

RIGHT	WRONG
It is *I*. [Nominative]	It is *me*. [Objective]
Are you *he?*	Are you *him?*
It is *we* who call.	It is *us* who call.
That is *he.*	That is *him.*
It is *they.*	It is *them.*

291. The number of intransitive verbs that may be directly followed by a predicate nominative is not large. The commonest are *is* (*was*, and other forms of the copula), *become*, and *seem*.

Others are verbs or phrases closely resembling *become* or *seem* in sense: as, *grow, turn, prove, turn out, appear, look.*

> This may appear a very simple *principle.*
> The new mare proved a *treasure.*
> He seems a very genteel, steady young *man.*

292. **Pronouns** are seldom found in the predicate nominative except after *is*, *was*, or some other form of the copula. The subject is commonly the neuter pronoun *it.* Thus,

> It was I.   [NOT: It was me.]
> It is they. [NOT: It is them.]
> It is we.   [NOT: It is us.]

---

[40] Here chapters 42-46 should be reviewed.

The **predicate nominative** after a passive verb is sometimes preceded by *as*.

❧

Predicate nominatives often follow *to be* or *to become*.

293. Certain transitive verbs in the **passive voice** may be followed by a predicate nominative. Thus,

> John was chosen *umpire*.
> Washington was elected *president*.
> This experienced soldier was appointed *general-in-chief*.

These are mostly verbs of *choosing, calling*, and the like.

294. The predicate nominative after passive verbs is sometimes preceded by the adverb *as*. Thus,

> He was regarded *as a hermit*.
> Adams was selected *as arbitrator*.

295. After the phrases *to be* and *to become* the predicate nominative is very common. Thus,

> How should you like to be *I*?
> I like best to be *myself*. I don't wish to be *you* or *he* or *she* or *anybody* else.
> This hunter seemed to be an *Indian*.
> The boy wishes to become a *sailor*.
> This constant noise began to be a great *annoyance*.
> Philip was thought to be an honest *lad*.

Chapter 71 Exercise

Review the Exercises from chapters 43-46.

CHAPTER 72
Nominative in Exclamations

296. **A noun or pronoun** may be used as an **exclamation** without a verb. Thus,

> Poor *John*! what can he do?
> Poor, unfortunate *I*! whither shall I turn?
> A *horse*! a *horse*! my kingdom for a horse!
> *Bananas! bananas!* ripe *bananas*!
> *Nonsense*! I don't believe a word of it.
> *Courage*, my friends! Help is at hand.

Such nouns and pronouns are called **exclamatory nominatives**.[41]

297. The nominative case may be used in an exclamation without a verb.

298. The exclamatory nominative should be carefully distinguished from the vocative, or nominative of direct address (chapter 15).[42]

> *Poor John!* What can you do? [Vocative]
> *Poor John!* What can he do? [Exclamatory Nominative]

In the first sentence, the speaker is directly addressing John; hence *John* is in the **vocative** construction.

In the second sentence, the speaker is talking about John, not addressing him; hence *John* is an **exclamatory nominative**.

> **Exclamatory nominatives** are nouns or pronouns used in exclamation without a verb.

---

[41] Some of these exclamatory nouns are really fragments of sentences. Thus, in the last sentence, "Courage!" may be regarded as the remnant of "Have courage! " or "Take courage!" No one, however, has a complete sentence in mind in using such exclamations. It is best, therefore, to regard the substantives as standing by themselves, and to treat them as exclamatory nominatives. See chapter 84 footnote.

[42] Here chapter 15 on the vocative should be reviewed.

Chapter 72 Exercises

I.

Review chapter 15, Exercise II.

II.

Pick out all the vocatives and all the exclamatory nominatives. Give your reasons in each case.

1. Roll on, thou deep and dark-blue ocean, roll!
2. Weapons! Arms! What's the matter here?
3. Tartar, and Saphi, and Turcoman,
   Strike your tents and throng to the van.
4. Awake! what ho, Brabantio! thieves! thieves! thieves!
5. She, poor wretch! for grief can speak no more.
6. Fair daffodils, we weep to see
   You haste away so soon.
7. Weep no more, woeful shepherds, weep no more.
8. O father! I am young and very happy.
9. O wonder! how many goodly creatures are there here!
10. Milton! thou should'st be living at this hour.
11. Liberty! freedom! Tyranny is dead!
12. Farewell, ye dungeons dark and strong.

III.

Write sentences containing the following nouns:
> (1) as vocatives,
> (2) as exclamatory nominatives.

Use an adjective with each noun.

> Mary, boy, hunter, Rover, Scott, woman, friend, comrades, king, sailor, Harry, winter, rain, father, brother.

IV.

Analyze the sentences in II. (In analyzing, a vocative or an exclamatory nominative should be mentioned by itself, and not treated as a modifier.)

Additional Review Exercises

Identify the nominatives in the following sentences. Parse them by telling the nominative class to which it belongs (subject, predicate nominative, vocative, exclamatory, appositive, nominative absolute[43]), the gender (masculine, feminine, or neuter), and number (singular or plural).

1. The moonbeams streamed on the tall tower of St. Mark.
2. Their parents were respectable farmers.
3. A cold chill ran through Sam's veins.
4. The crowd was dispersed, and several of the rioters were slain.
5. Howling Winter fled afar.
6. Poor Cinderella! Her life was very hard.
7. Captain Brown and his two daughters lived in a small house on the outskirts of the village.
8. O ye wild groves, O, where is now your bloom?
9. Auspicious Hope, in thy sweet garden grow
   Wreaths for each toil, a charm for every woe.
10. The haymakers were at work in the fields, and the perfume of the new-mown hay brought with it the recollection of my home.
11. My uncle listened with inward impatience while the little marquis descanted, with his usual fire and vivacity, on the achievements of his ancestors, whose portraits hung along the wall.
12. Every visitor who arrived after nightfall was challenged from a loophole or from a barricaded window.
13. The Romans were, in their origin, banditti.
14. Her father dwelt where yonder castle shines
    O'er clust'ring trees and terrace-mantling vines.
15. Delay not, Caesar. Read it instantly.

Parsing a Word

To **parse** a word is to describe its **grammatical form** and to give its **construction.** In parsing a substantive, we mention the class to which it belongs (*e.g.* common or proper?), give its gender (masculine, feminine, neuter?), number (singular or plural?), and case (nominative, genitive, objective?), and tell why it is in that case.

---

[43] Editor's note: The nominative absolute will not be studied until chapter 116.

CHAPTER 73 [44]
Genitive or Possessive Case

Possessive case is formed by **adding 's** to the singular noun or plural noun which does not end in *s*.

❧

Possessive case is formed by **adding '** to the plural noun which ends in *s*.

❧

Interesting fact: Old English formed the possessive by adding an *-es* or *-is* ending. Forming the possessive with an apostrophe *s* was based on an incorrect understanding of old English.

299. The genitive case of substantives denotes possession.

300. The meaning and the common forms of the **genitive case** have already been studied (chapters 33-34).

301. The genitive case of most nouns has, in the singular number, the ending 's.

> EXAMPLES: the lion's head, the cat's paw, the horse's mane, the pirate's cave, George's book, Mary's father.

302. Plural nouns ending in *s* take no further ending for the genitive. In writing, however, an apostrophe is put after the *s* to indicate the genitive case.

> EXAMPLES: the lions' heads, the cats' paws, the boys' fathers, the horses' manes, the pirates' cave.

303. Plural nouns not ending in *s* take 's in the genitive.[45]

> EXAMPLES: the women's gloves, the children's lessons, the men's swords, fishermen's luck.

In older English the genitive of most nouns was written as well as pronounced with the ending *-es* or *-is*. Thus, in Chaucer, the genitive of *child* is *childes* or *childis*; that of *king* is *kinges* or *kingis*; that of *John* is *Johnes* or *Johnis*. The use of an apostrophe in the genitive is a comparatively modern device, and is due to a misunderstanding of the real nature of the genitive termination. Scholars at one time thought that the *s* of the genitive was a fragment of the pronoun *his*: that is, they took such a phrase as *George's book* for an abbreviated form of *George his book*. Hence they used the apostrophe before *s* to signify the supposed omission of part of the word *his*. Similarly, in the genitive plural, there was thought to be an omission of a final *es*: that is, such a phrase *as the horses' heads* was thought to be a shortened form of the *horseses* heads. Both these errors have long been exploded.

304. Nouns like *sheep, deer,* which have the same form in the plural as in the singular, ordinarily take 's in the genitive plural. Thus,

---

[44] Here chapters 33-35 should be reviewed

[45] With some of these nouns (as *geese, oxen*) the *of*-phrase is commonly used.

The *sheep's* food consisted of turnips. [Singular]
The *sheep's* food consisted of turnips. [Plural]
The *deer's* horns were long and branched. [Singular]
The *deer's* horns were long and branched. [Plural]

> **Singular nouns** ending in *s* or with an *s*-sound form the genitive in different ways.
>
> ❧
>
> Single syllable words ending in *s* form the possessive by adding *'s*.
>
> ❧
>
> Nouns of two or more syllables have various possessive forms. Study the text carefully for these differences.

305. In **sound** the genitive plural is almost always the same as the genitive singular. The use of the *s'* forms may, therefore, render our meaning doubtful. We should avoid them except when the connection makes the sense clear. An *of*-phrase may be used instead.

306. With regard to the genitive singular of nouns which end in *s* or an *s*-sound (such as *Jones, Julius, Midas, conscience*, etc.), there is much difference of usage both in speech and writing.

By the rule already given (Section 301), the genitive of these words would end in *'s*. Thus,

Jones's house.   *Midas's* golden touch.
Julius's victory over Pompey.   For *conscience's* sake.

In practice, however, good writers and speakers do not always add *'s* in making the genitive of these *s*-words. The following statements agree with the best modern usage:

1. **Monosyllabic** nouns ending in *s* make their genitive singular in the regular way; that is, by adding *'s*. Thus,

   Jones's house.   Mr. *Briggs's* name.

   Watts's great invention, the steam engine.

Most of the nouns that come under this rule are proper names, for English has many monosyllabic family names ending in *-s*.

2. Nouns of **two or more syllables**, not accented on the last syllable, may make their genitive singular either in the regular way (by adding *'s*) or may take no ending in the genitive.

In the latter case the sound of the genitive form does not differ from the sound of the word itself, but, in writing, an **apostrophe** is added to indicate the genitive case. Thus,

Mr. *Sturgis's* horse,   or Mr. *Sturgis'* horse;
Midas's golden touch,   or *Midas'* golden touch;
Julius's victory,   or *Julius'* victory;
Aeneas's wanderings,   or *Aeneas'* wanderings;
For *conscience's* sake,   or for *conscience'* sake.
Felix's sister,   or *Felix'* sister.

This rule applies to many English surnames as well as to a very large number of Greek and Latin proper names common in English writers.

3.   Nouns of **two or more syllables**, when accented on the last syllable, follow the rule for monosyllables. Thus,

> *Laplace's* mathematics, NOT *Laplace'* mathematics.
> *Alphonse's* father, NOT *Alphonse'* father.

NOTE: When the word following the genitive begins with *s* or an *s*-sound, the genitive loses its ending more easily than under other circumstances. Thus one is more likely to say *Julius' sister* than *Julius' brother*.

The use of an *of*-phrase enables one to avoid, at will, most of the difficulties that beset the genitive of *s*-nouns.

Thus, instead of balancing between *Julius's victory* and *Julius' victory*, we may say *the victory of Julius*.

307. Nouns that do not denote living beings are seldom used in the genitive. They commonly replace this form by a phrase with a preposition (usually *of*).

> **Nouns** that name **non-living beings,** such as *door, book, Rome,* or *power,* seldom form the genitive case. Instead, an *of-***phrase** is used.

In accordance with this rule we should say:

> the handle *of the door*, NOT the *door's* handle;
> the cover *of the book*, NOT the *book's* cover;
> the siege *of Rome*, NOT *Rome's* siege;
> the great fire *in Chicago*, NOT *Chicago's* great fire;
> the abuse *of power*, NOT *power's* abuse.

308.   The *of*-phrase is often used, even with words that denote living beings, to avoid a harsh-sounding genitive.

Thus, "the horns *of the oxen*," "the wings *of the geese*," are preferred to "the *oxen's* horns," "the *geese's* wings."

309.   In many cases either the genitive or the *of*-phrase may be used at will. In such instances the choice is a question of style, not of grammar.[46]

> EXAMPLE: The two phrases "Shakespeare's style" and "the style of Shakespeare" are both perfectly good English, and one is as agreeable in sound as the other.

The rule in Section 307 is far from absolute. It is merely a brief statement of the tendency that appears to prevail among the best modern writers

---

[46] Compare the remarks in the Introduction, on the distinction between questions of grammar and questions of style.

and speakers, and it is subject to frequent exceptions. The use of the genitive was formerly much more extensive than now, and many phrases like *at swords' points, at my fingers' ends, from year's end to year's end, for mercy's sake* (and other phrases with *sake*), still survive in good use. Besides, usage is not yet uniform. Some writers go much farther than others in retaining the genitive, and it often happens that the choice between the two forms of expression is a matter of taste. There can, however, be no hesitation in condemning such expressions as "New York's population has increased rapidly," "Chicago's new mayor," or "Boston's Public Library," as in very bad taste. All this applies to prose only; the poets still use the genitive with perfect freedom.

Chapter 73 Exercises

I.
Attach a noun to the genitive of each of these names.
Thus,

Smith Smith's stable

Jones, Thomas, Gibbs, Cyrus, Charles, Caesar, Julius, Mr. Converse, Mr. Conners, Mrs. Ross, Charles Foss, Antonius, Brutus, Cassius, Mr. Anthony Brooks, J. T. Fields, Romulus, Remus, Mr. Strangways, Mrs. Smithers, Matthew, John Matthews, Dr. Morris, Maurice, Lord Douglas, Dr. Ellis, James, Francis, Frances, Eunice, Felix, Rose.

II.
Use in sentences the phrases that you have made in Exercise I.

III.
Review chapter 35, Exercise II.

IV.
Attach a noun to the genitive, singular and plural, of each of these words (as in I, above):

Horse, man, woman, child, fish, gentleman, deer, sheep, bird, wolf, calf, tiger, snake, badger, fly, spy, turkey, donkey, ally.

V.
In the sentences from chapter 33, Exercises I and IV, reproduced below, pick out all the genitives and all the *of*-phrases and tell to what noun or pronoun each belongs.
(Chapter 33, I)
1. The emperor's palace is in the center of the city, where the two great streets meet.

2. Oliver's education began when he was about three years old.
3. Caesar scorns the poet's lays.
4. The silver light, with quivering glance,
   Played on the water's still expanse.
5. Here on this beach a hundred years ago,
   Three children of three houses, Annie Lee,
   The prettiest little damsel in the port,
   And Philip Ray, the miller's only son,
   And Enoch Arden, a rough sailor's lad,
   Made orphan by a winter shipwreck, played
   Among the waste and lumber of the shore.
6. It is not the greatness of a man's means that makes him independent, so much as the smallness of his wants.
7. In faith and hope the world will disagree,
   But all mankind's concern is charity.
8. The jester's speech made the duke laugh.
9. A man's nature runs either to herbs or weeds.

(Chapter 33, IV)
1. The monarch's wrath began to rise.
2. They err who imagine that this man's courage was ferocity.
3. Two years' travel in distant and barbarous countries has accustomed me to bear privations.
4. Hark! hark! the lark at heaven's gate sings.
5. Portia dressed herself and her maid in men's apparel.
6. He waved his huntsman's cap on high.
7. The Porters' visit was all but over.
8. The ladies' colds kept them at home all the evening.
9. The crags repeat the ravens' croak.
10. Farmer Grove's house is on fire!
11. The Major paced the terrace in front of the house for his two hours' constitutional walk.

VI.

In each sentence in Exercises I and IV, chapter 33, substitute, orally, an *of*-phrase for a genitive or a genitive for an *of*-phrase, as the case may be, and tell whether the sentence as thus changed is good or bad English.[47]

———————————

[47] In some of the sentences either form is permissible.

CHAPTER 74 [48]
Case of Appositives

310. An appositive is in the same case as the substantive which it limits or defines.

Thus, an appositive limiting either the subject or a predicate nominative is in the **nominative case**; an appositive limiting an object is in the **objective case**.

311. What is the **case** of the **appositive** in each of the following sentences?

1. Our friends *the Indians* left us at this point.
2. We, the *people*, protest against this injustice.
3. I, your *chief*, bid you disperse.
4. Philip Smith, a young *boatman*, was drowned yesterday.
5. Three members of the club, *John and Charles* and *I*, refused to vote for the admission of Joe Dalling.
6. We sat in the firelight, *you* and *I*.
7. My friend, *he* who had stood by me in a thousand dangers, was no more.
8. We drove off the enemy, *horsemen* and *footmen*.
9. This rule applies to three of us, — *you* and *Jack* and *me*.
10. Nobody misses us, *you* and *me*.

> **Appositives** take the same case as the **substantive which they define.**
>
> ❦
>
> This is most significant for **pronouns**, which change their form as they change their case.

As these examples show, the rule for the case of appositives is important with respect to **pronouns**.

312. An apparent exception to the rule for the agreement of the appositive is seen in such sentences as follow:

> *Smith* the *grocer's* dog bit me. [Not: *Smith's* the grocer's *dog*.]
> My *friend William's* boat is stove.
> Our *daughter Mary's* hair is brown.

Here the genitive ending is added to the appositive only, and not to each noun. In other words, the whole phrase (*Smith the grocer, my friend William, our daughter Mary*) is treated as if it were a single noun.

313. A phrase ending with an appositive may be put into the genitive by adding the genitive ending to the appositive.

---

[48] Here chapters 37-39 should be reviewed.

Chapter 74 Exercises

I.

Review the exercises from chapter 37, reprinted below. Explain the case of each appositive.

Chapter 37, I:

1. Mr. Jones, the _____, is building a house for me.
2. Have you seen Rover, my _____, anywhere?
3. We saw animals of all kinds in the menagerie, _____, _____,
   and _____.
4. Chapman, the _____ of the team, broke his collar bone.
5. My new kite, _____ from my uncle, is caught in the tree.
6. Washington, the _____ of the United States, is on the Potomac.
7. Who has met my young friend _____ today?
8. Charles I, _____ of England, was beheaded in 1649.
9. Washington, the _____ of his country, was born in 1732.
10. The sultan was fond of tiger-hunting, a dangerous _____.

Chapter 37, II:

1. An Englishwoman, the wife of one of the officers, was sitting on the battlements with her child in her arms.
2. I went to visit Mr. Hobbes, the famous philosopher.
3. We were hopeful boys, all three of us.
4. Spring, the sweet Spring, is the year's pleasant king.
5. Then forth they all out of their baskets drew
   Great store of flowers, the honor of the field.
6. He was speedily summoned to the apartment of his captain, the Lord Crawford.
7. No rude sound shall reach thine ear,
   Armor's clang and war-steed champing.
8. And thus spake on that ancient man,
   The bright-eyed mariner.
9. There lived at no great distance from this stronghold a farmer, a bold and stout man, whose name was Binnock.

II.

Pick out the appositives.
Explain the case of each.

1. I visited my old friend and fellow-traveler, Mr. Henshaw.
2. At length the day dawned, — that dreadful day.
3. 'Twas where the madcap duke his uncle kept.

4. So off they scampered, man and horse.
5. The north wind, that welcome visitor, freshened the air.
6. I see him yet, the princely boy!
7. His prayer he saith, this patient, holy man.
8. The vices of authority are chiefly four: delays, corruption, roughness, and facility.
9. 'T is past, that melancholy dream!
10. Campley, a friend of mine, came by.
11. The mayor, an aged man, made an address.
12. He lent me his only weapon, a sword.
13. Captain William Robinson, a Cornishman, commander of the "Hopewell," a stout ship of three hundred tons, came to my house.

Analyze each of the sentences above (see chapter 38).

CHAPTER 75
Indirect Object

314. Examine the following sentence:

> John sent a letter.

Here the transitive verb *sent* is followed by its **direct object**, *letter*.

If we wish, however, to mention the **person to whom** John sent the letter, we can do so by inserting a noun or pronoun immediately after the verb. Thus,

> John sent *Mary* a letter.

The transitive verb *sent* will then have **two objects**:

> (1) its **direct object**, *letter*;
> (2) an **indirect object**, *Mary,* denoting the **person to whom** John sent the letter, — that is, the person toward whom is directed the action expressed by the rest of the predicate.

Other examples of verbs with (1) a **direct object** only, and (2) both a **direct** and an **indirect object**, may be seen in the following sentences:

DIRECT OBJECT ONLY	DIRECT OBJECT AND INDIRECT OBJECT
My father gave money.	My father gave the *sailor* money.
I sent a message.	I sent *him* a message.
Thomas lent his knife.	Thomas lent *Albert* his knife.

> The **indirect object** indicates the person toward which the action is directed.
>
> ❧
>
> **Indirect objects** are nouns or pronouns in the **objective case.**

315. **Some transitive verbs, from the nature of their meaning, may take two objects, a direct object and an indirect object.**

The indirect object denotes the person or thing toward whom or toward which is directed the action expressed by the rest of the predicate.

316. The verbs that take an indirect object are, for the most part, those of *telling, giving, refusing*, and the like.

Such are: allot, assign, assure, bequeath, bring, deny, ensure, fetch, forbid, forgive, furnish, give, grant, guarantee, leave, lend, loan, pardon, pay, refund, refuse, remit, sell, show, spare, tell, vouchsafe, warrant.

317. The position of the indirect object is immediately after the verb. Thus,

> The merchant sold *him* the goods.
> [NOT: The merchant sold the goods *him*.]

> The banker refused my *friend* credit.
> [NOT: The banker refused credit my *friend*.]

318. The indirect object is in the objective case.[49]

The force of this rule may be seen when a **pronoun** is an indirect object.

319. The indirect object may be recognized by the following test:

> **It is always possible to insert the preposition to before the indirect object without changing the sense.**

320. The indirect object is sometimes used without a direct object expressed. Thus,

> He told *John*.

Here *John* may be recognized as the indirect object by the test already given (Section 319, above): we may insert *to* before it without destroying the sense.

Chapter 75 Exercises

I.
Fill each blank with an indirect object (noun or pronoun).

1. My sister gave _____ a book.
2. A deserter brought _____ news of the battle.
3. The king granted _____ a pension of a hundred pounds.
4. Fred will show _____ his collection of postage stamps.
5. The governor paid _____ the reward.

[49] In many languages the indirect object has a special form of inflection, called the *dative case,* which distinguishes it from the direct object. This was once true of English also; but, in the present poverty of inflection which marks our tongue, there is no distinction between the two except in sense.

6. The prisoner told _____ the whole story.
7. De Quincey's father left _____ a large sum of money.
8. Our teacher granted _____ our request.
9. Can such conduct give _____ any satisfaction?
10. His indulgent father forgave _____ his many faults.
11. The grocer refused _____ credit.
12. The surly porter refused _____ permission to enter the building.
13. Poor little Fido gave _____ a piteous look.
14. I can spare _____ ten dollars.

II.

In the following sentences pick out all the direct objects, and all the phrases in which the idea of the indirect object is expressed by means of *to*.

1. He by will bequeathed his lands to me.
2. To Mortimer will I declare these tidings.
3. He has told all his troubles to you.
4. Entrust your message to her.
5. Do you give attention to my words?
6. The judges awarded the prize to Oliver.
7. Do you ascribe this drama to Shakespeare?
8. Show the drawing to your teacher.
9. The scout made his report to the officer.

III.

Make ten sentences containing the following verbs, each with both a direct and an indirect object:

Sold, told, pays, sends, will bring, have brought, had shown, fetches, denied, lent.

IV.

In the following sentences find (1) the subjects, (2) the predicates, (3) the direct objects, (4) the indirect objects.

1. I shall assign you the post of danger and of renown.
2. The king ordered him a small present and dismissed him.
3. The thoughts of the day gave my mind employment for the whole night.
4. Miss Pratt gave Uncle Adam a jog on the elbow.
5. The king made me a present.
6. I will bring you certain news from Shrewsbury.
7. I will deny thee nothing.

8. Fetch me the hat and rapier in my cell.
9. Forgive us our sins!
10. My father gave him welcome.
11. I will not lend thee a penny.
12. The mayor in courtesy showed me the castle.
13. I shall tell you a pretty tale.
14. Vouchsafe me one fair look.
15. The reading of those volumes afforded me much amusement.
16. I have occasioned her some confusion, and, for the moment, a little resentment.
17. He'll make her two or three fine speeches, and then she'll be perfectly contented.
18. Voltaire, who was then in England, sent him a letter of consolation.
19. The evening had afforded Edmund little pleasure.
20. Mrs. St. Clair here wished the happy pair good morning.

CHAPTER 76
Comparison of Adjectives, Part 1

321. Examine the following sentences:

> John is *tall*.
> Thomas is *taller* than John.
> James is the *tallest* boy in the school.

In these sentences we observe that the same adjective appears in three different forms, — *tall, taller, tallest*. The sense, too, changes as we add to the simple form *tall* the endings -*er* (making *tall-er*) and -*est* (making *tall-est*). Yet this variation of meaning does not affect the essential meaning of the adjective: John and Thomas and James are all three *tall*.

The difference, then, is not one of **kind** but one of **degree**.

In the first sentence we simply assert that John is *tall*, and we make no **comparison** of his tallness with the stature of anybody else.

In the second sentence we not only assert that Thomas is tall, but we **compare** his height with that of another person, asserting that he is *taller* than John.

In the third sentence we go still farther. We do not merely assert that James is tall, nor do we content ourselves with saying that he is *taller* than some other person, but we use the strongest form known to us to express his tallness: we say that he is the *tallest*.

These three forms which adjectives may assume are known as **degrees of comparison**; and they are called, respectively,

> the **positive**,
> the **comparative**, and
> the **superlative** degree.

Inflection of adjectives show **degrees of comparison.**

❧

Degrees of comparison are called: **positive, comparative, superlative.**

322. **The degrees of comparison of an adjective indicate by their form in what degree of intensity the quality described by the adjective exists.**

323. **There are three degrees of comparison: the positive, the comparative, and the superlative.**

324. **The positive degree is the simplest form of the adjective and has no special ending.**

It simply describes the quality without suggesting a comparison between the person or thing possessing it and any other person or thing.

Thus, the positive degree of the adjective *tall* is *tall*.

325. The comparative degree of an adjective is formed by adding the termination *-er* to the positive degree.

It indicates that the quality exists in the person or thing described in a higher degree than in some other person or thing.

Thus, the comparative degree of the adjective *tall* is *taller*.

326. The superlative degree is formed by adding *-est* to the positive degree.

It indicates that the quality exists in the highest degree in the person or thing described.

Thus, the superlative degree of the adjective *tall* is *tallest*.

327. Other examples of the **comparison of adjectives** are:

POSITIVE DEGREE	COMPARATIVE DEGREE	SUPERLATIVE DEGREE
strong	stronger	strongest
fair	fairer	fairest
quick	quicker	quickest
clear	clearer	clearest

> **The positive degree** is the simplest form of the adjective.
>
> The **comparative degree** is formed by adding *-er*.
>
> The **superlative degree** is formed by adding *-est*.

CHAPTER 77 [50]
Comparison of Adjectives, Part 2

328. In forming the **comparative** and **superlative** degrees by means of the endings -*er* and -*est*, the following rules of spelling should be observed:

1. Adjectives ending in silent -*e* drop this letter before the comparative ending -*er* and the superlative ending -*est*. Thus,

> Study the **spelling rules** for the inflection of adjectives.

POSITIVE DEGREE	COMPARATIVE DEGREE	SUPERLATIVE DEGREE
fine	finer (*not* fine-er)	finest (*not* fine-est)
rare	rarer	rarest
rude	ruder	rudest
blithe	blither	blithest
polite	politer	politest

2. Most adjectives ending in -*y* change *y* to *i* before the endings -*er* and -*est* Thus,

POSITIVE DEGREE	COMPARATIVE DEGREE	SUPERLATIVE DEGREE
dry	drier	driest
holy	holier	holiest
worthy	worthier	worthiest
merry	merrier	merriest

3. Adjectives having a short vowel and ending in a single consonant double this before the endings -*er* and -*est* Thus,

POSITIVE DEGREE	COMPARATIVE DEGREE	SUPERLATIVE DEGREE
fat	fatter	fattest
thin	thinner	thinnest
hot	hotter	hottest

---

[50] This chapter is for reference only.

Chapter 77 Exercises

I.

Write in three columns the following adjectives in the three degrees of comparison:

> Bright, lowly, tall, smooth, rough, quick, nimble, fierce, black, able, subtle, crazy, mad, sane, muddy, wet, dry, red, sad, humble.

II.

Pick out such adjectives as are in the comparative or the superlative degree. Give the positive degree of each. Mention the substantive to which each belongs.

1. He was a bigger boy than I.
2. They were some of the choicest troops of his whole army.
3. The town is one of the neatest in England.
4. Life is dearer than the golden ore.
5. Byron was, at his death, but a year younger than Burns.
6. On the highest part of the mountain is an old fortress.
7. The storm of passion insensibly subsided into calmer melancholy.
8. The sternest sum total of all worldly misfortunes is death.
9. Her astonishment now was greater than ever.
10. The air grew colder and colder; the mist became thicker and thicker; the shrieks of the sea fowl louder and louder.

III.

Make sentences containing the following adjectives,
   (1) in the positive degree;
   (2) in the comparative degree;
   (3) in the superlative degree:

> Fast, pure, low, clumsy, high, large, brown, ragged, cross, deep, cheery, merry, short, hungry, quiet, green, manly, noble, severe, handsome, lovely.

CHAPTER 78
Comparison of Adjectives, Part 3

329. Many adjectives are compared, not by means of the endings *-er* and *-est*, but by prefixing the adverbs *more* and *most* to the positive degree.

He is a *more honorable* man than his neighbor.
[NOT: He is an *honorabler* man than his neighbor.]

He is the *most honorable* man in the company.
[NOT: He is the *honorablest* man in the company.]

Examples of comparison by means of *more* and *most* are the following:

POSITIVE DEGREE	COMPARATIVE DEGREE	SUPERLATIVE DEGREE
difficult	more difficult	most difficult
splendid	more splendid	most splendid
horrible	more horrible	most horrible
capacious	more capacious	most capacious
magnificent	more magnificent	most magnificent

> Comparison of adjectives by means of adding *-er* and *-est* is called **inflectional comparison.**
>
> ❧
>
> Comparison of adjectives by a means of *more* and *most* is called **analytical comparison.**

In this method of comparison, *more* and *most* are adverbs modifying the adjective before which they stand.

330. Comparison by means of *-er* and *-est* is called **inflectional** comparison.

Comparison by means of *more* and *most* is called **analytical** comparison.

331. Some adjectives may be compared in two ways: (1) by means of the endings *-er* and *-est*, and (2) by means of the adverbs *more* and *most*.

EXAMPLES: worthy, worthier, worthiest; OR, worthy, more worthy, most worthy.

Most adjectives, however, can be compared in only one way. It is usually short adjectives that are compared by means of *-er* and *-est*. Many adjectives of two syllables and most adjectives of three or more syllables admit only of comparison by means of *more* and *most*.

NOTE: Comparison by means of *-er* and *-est* was formerly much more common than now. Thus, such forms as *famouser, famousest, honorabler, honorablest, difficulter,* and *difficultest*, which would not be allowable in modern English, occur in old writers.

The present tendency of our language is to decrease the use of inflectional and to increase the use of analytical comparison. It is well, however, to hold to such cases of -*er* and -*est* as are still in good use.

Chapter 78 Exercise

Find the comparatives and the superlatives.

1. The evening was more calm and lovely than any that yet had smiled upon our voyage.
2. The environs are most beautiful, and the village itself is one of the prettiest I ever saw.
3. Example is always more efficacious than precept.
4. The Edinburgh scholars of that period were more noted for clearness of head than for warmth of heart.
5. Nothing could be more bleak and saddening than the appearance of this lake.
6. The country became rougher, and the people more savage.
7. He sat down with a most gloomy countenance.
8. The Caliph remained in the most violent agitation.
9. A more extraordinary incident has seldom happened.
10. The wind was even more boisterous than usual.
11. The most elaborate preparations had been made.
12. The garret windows and housetops were so crowded with spectators that I thought in all my travels I had not seen a more populous place.

CHAPTER 79
Comparison of Adjectives, Part 4

332. Several very common adjectives have irregular forms of comparison.

The most important of these **irregular adjectives** are:

POSITIVE DEGREE	COMPARATIVE DEGREE	SUPERLATIVE DEGREE
bad (evil, ill)	worse	worst
far	farther	farthest
—	further	furthest
good	better	best
late	later, latter	latest, last
well (in health)	better	—
little	less, lesser	least
much, many	more	most

> Some common adjectives have **irregular forms of comparison.**
>
> ❧
>
> Study and master these irregular forms and be sure to use them correctly in your speech and writing.

In some of these cases the comparative and superlative are different words from the positive, but they have been so long associated with it in the minds of all speakers and writers that they are felt to belong to it almost as much as if they were simply modifications of its form.

333. The adjective *old* has two forms (*older* and *elder*) for the comparative, and two (*oldest* and *eldest*) for the superlative.

The forms *elder* and *eldest* are used only with reference to the age of persons. They are further restricted

(1) to certain nouns signifying relationship and
(2) to the phrases *the elder* and *the eldest*. Thus,

My *elder* brother is named Charles.

John is *older* than I.

She has an *elder* sister.

The dog is *older* than his young master.

Frank is the *eldest* of the cousins.

The *oldest* book may be the best.

Elder is sometimes a noun. Thus,

Children should respect their *elders*.
The *elders* of the people took counsel.

211

334. *Next* is in form an old superlative of *nigh*, but it is used only in the special sense of "the very nearest," "immediately adjacent." Thus,

> My friend lives in the *next* house.
> The landing of the troops took place on the *next* day.
> Our lesson in geography comes *next*.

335. A few superlatives ending in *-most* are in more or less common use. With these, one or both of the other degrees are commonly wanting.

POSITIVE DEGREE	COMPARATIVE DEGREE	SUPERLATIVE DEGREE
—	(former)	foremost
hind	hinder	hindmost
—	inner	inmost, innermost
(out, *adverb*)	outer	outmost, outermost
	(utter)	utmost, uttermost
(up, *adverb*)	upper	uppermost
—	—	endmost
—	nether	nethermost
top	—	topmost
—	—	furthermost
north	—	northmost
northern	(more northern)	northernmost
south	—	southmost
southern	(more southern)	southernmost
east, eastern	(more eastern)	easternmost
west, western	(more western)	westernmost

NOTE: The ending *-most* is not the adverb *most*. It is a very old superlative ending *-mest* changed under the influence of the adverb *most*.

Chapter 79 Exercise

Find the comparatives and the superlatives.

1. He walked off without further ceremony.
2. A friend in the court is better than a penny in purse.
3. Caesar has been called the foremost man of all this world.
4. The inquisitive prince passed most of his nights on the summit of his tower.
5. I must confess your offer is the best.
6. The worst minds have often something of good principle in them.
7. So doth the greater glory dim the less.
8. This island was at a greater distance than I expected, and I did not reach it in less than five hours.
9. There are two or three more pens in the box.
10. I ne'er had worse luck in my life!
11. Lead the way without any more talking.
12. He grows worse and worse.
13. I said an elder soldier, not a better.
14. Orlando approached the man and found it was his brother, his elder brother.
15. Present fears are less than horrible imaginings.
16. That is Antonio, the duke's eldest son.
17. A sad tale's best for winter.
18. To fear the worst oft cures the worse.
19. The bird is perched on the topmost bough.
20. My title's good, and better far than his.
21. I have three daughters; the eldest is eleven.
22. To weep is to make less the depth of grief.
23. He has his health, and ampler strength, indeed,
    Than most have of his age.
24. I will use my utmost skill in his recovery.
25. Brutus' love to Caesar was no less than his.
26. My utmost efforts were fruitless.
27. We cannot defend the outer fortifications.

CHAPTER 80
Comparison of Adjectives, Part 5

336. Some adjectives are, from their meaning, **incapable of comparison**. Thus, we can say:

> The figure is *three-cornered*.

But it would be absurd to say:

> That figure is *more three-cornered* than the other.
> This is the *most three-cornered* of several figures.

Some adjectives are not capable of comparison.

For, if what we are describing is three-cornered at all, that is the end of it: there can be no degrees of triangularity. In general, then:

Adjectives which denote an absolute degree of a quality do not admit of comparison.

NOTE 1: To this class are commonly said to belong such words as *perfect, straight, exact*, and the like; but such a statement is not quite accurate. If *perfect* is used in its strict sense, that is, to denote **absolute perfection**, it is, of course, impossible to compare it; for a thing which is perfect is perfect, and cannot be spoken of as *more perfect* or *most perfect*. But *perfect* has also another sense, namely, "partaking in a higher or lower degree of the qualities which make up absolute perfection," so that it is possible to describe one statue as **more perfect** than another, or one of three statues as the **most perfect** of them all. In this use, which is entirely unobjectionable, we simply admit that there is nothing in the world **absolutely** faultless or flawless, and assert that the three statues commented on **approach ideal perfection** in various degrees.

NOTE 2: The question what adjectives are capable of comparison and what are incapable of comparison is not, strictly speaking, a question of grammar at all. It is a question either of logic (common sense) or of style. If, therefore, we say "This is the most three-cornered figure that I ever saw," we are, to be sure, talking nonsense, but our nonsense is quite grammatical, for no rule of grammar is violated. If, on the other hand we say "This is the three-corneredest figure that I have ever seen," we are both talking nonsense and violating a rule of grammar, since the word *three-corneredest* is not properly formed.

CHAPTER 81
Comparison of Adverbs

337. Adverbs, like adjectives, have three degrees of comparison:

the positive,
the comparative, and
the superlative.

338. Most adverbs are compared by means of *more* and *most*. Thus,

The wind blows *violently*. [Positive]
The wind blows *more violently* than ever. [Comparative]
The wind blows *most violently* in the winter. [Superlative]

339. A few adverbs are compared by means of the endings *-er* and *-est*: Thus,

POSITIVE DEGREE	COMPARATIVE DEGREE	SUPERLATIVE DEGREE
cheap	cheaper	cheapest
dear	dearer	dearest
early	earlier	earliest
fast	faster	fastest
hard	harder	hardest
high	higher	highest
long	longer	longest
loud	louder	loudest
near	nearer	nearest
often (oft)	oftener	oftenest
quick	quicker	quickest
slow	slower	slowest
soon	sooner	soonest
sound (of sleeping)	sounder	soundest

Many comparatives and superlatives in *-er* and *-est* that are no longer allowable in prose are still used in poetry.

Adverbs have **three degrees of comparison: positive, comparative, superlative.**

ક

Most adverbs are compared by using the words *more* and *most*.

ક

Some adverbs form their comparison by adding *-er* and *-est*. Study the list and use these words properly.

CHAPTER 82
Irregular Comparison of Adverbs

340. Several very common adverbs have irregular forms of comparison.

POSITIVE DEGREE	COMPARATIVE DEGREE	SUPERLATIVE DEGREE
far	farther	farthest
forth	further	furthest
ill (evil)	worse	worst
badly		
nigh	nigher	nighest
		next
well	better	best
late	later	latest
		last
little	less	least
much	more	most

Some common adverbs have **irregular forms of comparison.**

❧

Study and master these irregular forms and be sure to use them correctly in your speech and writing.

❧

Good and *bad* are **never** adverbs.

❧

Many adverbs are incapable of comparison.

These adverbs are in the main identical in form with the adjectives discussed in Section 332, above.

Note, however:

> (1) that *good* and *bad* are never adverbs;
> (2) that *ill* and *well, better* and *best, worse* and *worst,* may be either adverbs or adjectives.

341. Some adverbs admit of either inflectional or analytical comparison.

342. Many adverbs are, from their meaning, incapable of comparison. Such are:

> (1) *here, there, then, so, now,* and the like;
> (2) adverbs derived from adjectives that express a quality as absolute or complete (see chapter 80 and notes).

Chapter 82 Exercise

In the following sentences select all the adverbs and tell what each modifies.

If the adverb is capable of comparison, give its **three degrees**. If its meaning makes it incapable of comparison, state that fact and give your reasons.

1. Youth seldom thinks of dangers.
2. To every man upon this earth
   Death cometh soon or late.
3. So the days passed peacefully away.
4. It would ill become me to boast of anything.
5. Delvile eagerly called to the coachman to drive up to the house, and anxiously begged Cecilia to sit still.
6. They came again and again, and were every time more welcome than before.
7. Perhaps this awkwardness will wear off hereafter.
8. And he, God wot, was forced to stand
   Oft for his right with blade in hand.
9. He heard a laugh full musical aloft.
10. The following morning Gertrude arose early.
11. She walks too fast, and speaks too fast.
12. The seamen spied a rock within half a cable's length of the ship, but the wind was so strong that we were driven directly upon it, and immediately split.
13. Was that the king that spurred his horse so hard?
14. "We know each other well."
    "We do, and long to know each other worse."
15. He came too late; the ship was under sail.
16. How slow this old moon wanes!
17. Your judgment is absolutely correct.
18. The tide rose higher and higher.
19. He swims energetically but slowly.
20. The courtiers were all most magnificently clad.

CHAPTER 83
Use of Comparative and Superlative

343. It is a common mistake to use the **superlative** degree of adjectives and adverbs for the **comparative**.

In the following sentences the two degrees are correctly employed:

> Smith is *the better* of the two men.
> Jones is *the best* of the three men.

In the first sentence **two** persons are compared, and the **comparative** degree is used; in the second, **more than two** persons are compared, and the **superlative** is used.

We should never think of saying "He is the *better* of the *three* men." It is, however, a common error to say "He is the *best* of the *two* men"; that is, to use the superlative when only two persons are spoken of, and when, therefore, the comparative is the proper form.

344. The comparative degree, not the superlative, is used in comparing two persons or things.

The superlative is used in comparing one person or thing with two or more persons or things.

345. In a few idiomatic phrases the rule given in Section 344 is not observed. Thus we say,

> "He puts his **best** foot foremost," not,
> "He puts his **better** foot foremost,"

although a man has but two feet.[51]

NOTE: In older English the superlative was often used instead of the comparative.

346. It is an error to use *more* and *most* before adjectives or adverbs that are already in the comparative or the superlative degree. Thus, such expressions as *more better, most best, the most proudest* are incorrect.

NOTE: Double comparison was allowed in older English, but is not now in good use.

347. An adjective phrase may sometimes be compared by prefixing *more* and *most* to it. Thus,

---

> **Be careful!**
> Use **comparative degree** to compare two persons or things.
>
> ❧
>
> Use **superlative degree** to compare one person or thing with two or more persons or things.

---

[51] Compare "the *first* of the two men."

Your hat is *more in fashion* than mine.

[*More in fashion = more fashionable.*]

The eldest son was *most in favor* with his father.

This plan is *more to my mind* than the other.

Usually, however, the effect of the comparative or the superlative degree is produced by inserting a comparative or superlative adjective with the noun of the adjective phrase. Thus,

A person of respectability told me the story.

A person of still *higher* respectability told me this.

A person of *the highest* respectability told me this.

Chapter 83 Exercises

I.

Make sentences in which you use the following adjectives and adverbs correctly:

Better, best, sooner, most agreeable, nimbler, nimblest, most, more, quicker, quickest, smallest, smaller, most interesting, slower, slowest, more accurate, most accurate.

II.

Analyze the sentences that you have made.

III.

Fill the blanks with adjectives or adverbs in the comparative or the superlative degree as the meaning requires.

Give the grounds of your choice in each case.

1. Tom and I are friends. Indeed he is the _____ friend I have.
2. Which is the (more or most?) _____ studious of your two sisters?
3. Both generals are brave, but the old_____ is of course the (more or most?) _____ experienced of the two.
4. Of all the men in our company I think the very brave_____ was Corporal Jackson.
5. Texas is the large_____ of the United States.
6. Which is large_____ , Chicago or Philadelphia?
7. Mention the large_____ city in the world.
8. I don't know which I like (better or best?) _____, history or arithmetic.
9. Which do you like (better or best?) _____, history, arithmetic, or reading?

10. I like history _____ than anything else.
11. Of all my studies I like history _____.
12. Which is the heavi_____, a pound of feathers or a pound of gold?
13. Which is the heavi_____, a pound of feathers, a pound of lead, or a pound of gold?
14. Jane is the tall_____ of the family.

IV.
Compare the following adverbs:

Soon, often, badly, well, noisily, merrily, far, much, furiously.

V.
Use the superlative of each adverb in IV in a sentence of your own.

CHAPTER 84
Demonstrative Pronouns and Adjectives

348. Each of the following sentences has a **pronoun** for its subject:

This is a good knife.   That is a tall man.

The words *this* and *that*, the subjects of these sentences, are obviously **pronouns**, for they **designate** some person or thing but do not give it a **name** (Section 25).

In their use in these sentences *this* and *that* resemble the personal pronouns of the third person. For *this* might be replaced by *it*, and *that* by *he*, without any very great change in the meaning. Thus,

It is a good knife.   He is a tall man.

This and *that*, however, are stronger and more definite than *it* and *he* would be.

The difference is that *this* and *that* appear to **point out** somebody or something. We can easily imagine the speaker as actually pointing with the finger as he utters the word.

For this reason *this* and *that* are called **demonstratives**, that is, *"pointing"* words (for *demonstrate* comes from a Latin word which means "to point out").

349. **The demonstratives are *this* (plural, *these*) and *that* (plural, *those*). They are used to point out or designate persons or things for special attention.**

This is a red apple.	*These* are tall buildings.
That is a Spanish soldier.	*Those* were excellent oranges.
I do not like *that*.	He is angry at *this*.

> **Demonstrative pronouns** designate some person or thing without naming it.
>
> ❧
>
> *This* and *that*, *these* and *those*, are **demonstrative pronouns.**
>
> ❧
>
> **Demonstrative pronouns** are often the subject of a sentence or clause.

350. In the examples given above, the demonstratives are used **substantively** as subjects or objects.[52] But the same words may also be used to **limit** a noun.

<table>
<tr><td>This man is guilty of theft.</td><td>These books are shabby.</td></tr>
<tr><td>That river runs rapidly.</td><td>Those birds fly high.</td></tr>
</table>

> **Demonstrative pronouns** can also be used as an **adjective** to limit a noun.

In these sentences the demonstratives *this, these, that, those* are **adjectives**.

351. The demonstratives may be used either as pronouns or as adjectives.

Other examples of **demonstrative adjectives** are:

That picture is by Sir Godfrey Kneller.
Under *this* tree sat the sprightly old lady with her knitting needles.
This brave duke came early to his grave.
Then turn your forces from *this* paltry siege.
That judge hath made me guardian to *this* boy.

Chapter 84 Exercises

Write twenty sentences, each containing a demonstrative (*this, that, these,* or *those*).

Examine each sentence, and tell whether you have used the demonstrative as a pronoun (substantively) or as a limiting adjective (adjectively).

---

[52] The pupil should not be directed to "supply nouns" in such sentences as those in Sections 348, 349. For example, it is unscientific to expand the first sentence in Section 349 to "*This* (*apple*) is a red apple," and then to "parse" *this* as an adjective. It is even more objectionable to expand the third sentence by inserting *thing* (or the like) after *that*. The plan of "supplying" unexpressed words (as being "understood") tends to confuse real distinctions of language, and should never be resorted to when it can be avoided.

CHAPTER 85
Inflection of Demonstratives

352. Demonstrative pronouns and adjectives have only the inflection of number.

The nominative and objective cases are alike; the genitive is wanting and is replaced by *of* with the objective.

<table>
<tr><td></td><td></td><td>SINGULAR</td><td>PLURAL</td></tr>
<tr><td rowspan="11">Demonstrative pronouns change their inflection (form) only when changing from singular to plural.</td><td></td><td></td><td></td></tr>
<tr><td>Nominative</td><td>this</td><td>these</td></tr>
<tr><td>Objective</td><td>this</td><td>these</td></tr>
<tr><td>Genitive</td><td>[of this]</td><td>[of these]</td></tr>
<tr><td></td><td></td><td></td></tr>
<tr><td>Nominative</td><td>that</td><td>those</td></tr>
<tr><td>Objective</td><td>that</td><td>those</td></tr>
<tr><td>Genitive</td><td>[of that]</td><td>[of those]</td></tr>
</table>

353. Demonstratives have the same form for all three genders. Thus,

That man; *that* woman; *that* tree.
This gentleman; *this* lady; *this* axe.
These boys; *these* girls; *these* hammers.
Those lords; *those* ladies; *those* castles.

Chapter 85 Exercises

I.

Tell whether each demonstrative below is a pronoun or an adjective. Mention its number and case.

1. This is the whole truth.
2. This apple is sour.
3. These men are brave.
4. That is a strange fish.
5. That story is false.
6. Are you sure of that?
7. John told me this.
8. These are facts.

II.

Pick out the demonstratives below. Tell whether each is used substantively (as a pronoun) or adjectively (as a limiting adjective).

1. These thoughts did not hinder him from sleeping soundly.
2. These are Clan-Alpine's warriors true.
3. Loth as they were, these gentlemen had nothing for it but to obey.
4. "Major Buckley," I said, "what horse is that?"
5. Nor yet for this, even as a spy,
   Hadst thou, unheard, been doomed to die.
6. Ill with King James's mood that day
   Suited gay feast and minstrel lay.
7. That horse's history would be worth writing.
8. All this was meant to be as irritating as possible.
9. These fertile plains, that softened vale,
   Were once the birthright of the Gael.
10. Many hundred large volumes have been published upon this controversy.
11. What a good old man that is!
12. That absolves me from any responsibility.
13. Jim will be sorry to hear of this.
14. To hear this beautiful voice after so long a silence — to find those calm, dark, friendly eyes regarding him — bewildered him, or gave him courage, he knew not which.
15. This murderous chief, this ruthless man,
    This head of a rebellious clan,
    Hath led thee safe, through watch and ward,
    Far past Clan-Alpine's outmost guard.
16. Those are terrible questions.
17. These were the strong points in his favor.
18. I'll fill these dogged spies with false reports.
19. These soldiers are Danes, those are Swedes.
20. Can you hesitate long between this and that?

CHAPTER 86 [53]
Indefinite Pronouns and Adjectives

354. A number of words that resemble the **demonstratives** in their use are called **indefinites**.

> EXAMPLES: each, every, either, both, neither, some, any, such, none, other, another, each other, one another.

Their use may be seen in the following sentences:

> *Each* of us has his own faults.
> *Every* soldier carried a pike.
> I do not dislike *either* of you.
> He gave money to *both.*
> *Some* birds cannot fly.
> Give me *some* of that gold.
> *Such* a villain is unfit to live.

From these examples it is clear that the indefinite pronouns and adjectives point out or designate objects, but less clearly or definitely than demonstratives do.

355. Most of the **indefinites** may be either **pronouns** or **adjectives**. But *none* is always a substantive in modern use, and *every* is always an adjective.

356. *Each other* and *one another* may be regarded as compound pronouns. They designate persons or things that stand in some kind of mutual relation. Thus,

> The children love *each other.*
> They all fought with *one another.*

There is no real distinction between *each other* and *one another.* The rules sometimes given for such a distinction are not supported by the best usage and may be disregarded.

357. *One* (genitive *one's*) is often used as a kind of indefinite personal pronoun; as,

> *One* does not like *one's* motives to be doubted.

All, several, few, many, and similar words are often counted among indefinites. They may be used as adjectives or as substantives.

Everybody, everything, anybody, anything, etc., may be called indefinite nouns.

Indefinite pronouns and **adjectives** point out objects, but less clearly than demonstratives.

❧

None is always a **substantive.**

❧

Every is always an **adjective.**

❧

One is often used as an **indefinite pronoun.**

❧

Other indefinites *all, several, few, many* may be used as adjectives or substantives.

---

[53] This chapter is for reference.

Chapter 86 Exercise

Parse the indefinite pronouns, nouns, and adjectives. See chapter 72, additional review exercises, for instructions on how to parse a word.

1. They talked about each other's books for hours.
2. Some war, some plague, some famine they foresee.
3. The two armies encountered one another at Towton Field, near Tadcaster. No such battle had been seen in England since the fight of Senlac.
4. The morning was raw, and a dense fog was over everything.
5. Some wild young colts were let out of the stockyard.
6. They tell one another all they know, and often more too.
7. Bate me some and I will pay you some.
8. I do not wish any companion in the world but you.
9. The big round tears coursed one another down his innocent nose.
10. Grace and remembrance be to you both.
11. I know it pleaseth neither of us well.
12. Each hurries toward his home.
13. Gentlemen both, you will mistake each other.
14. No such apology is necessary.
15. Does either of you care for this?
16. Mine honor is my life. Both grow in one.
17. The parcels contained some letters and verses.
18. Think you there was ever such a man?
19. A black day will it be to somebody.
20. Friend, we understand not one another.

CHAPTER 87
The Self-Pronouns

358. The English language possesses a number of **compound personal pronouns** of which the first part is one of the personal pronouns in some form, and the second part is the word *self.*

These are: myself, *plural* ourselves; thyself, yourself , *plural* yourselves; himself, herself, itself, *plural* themselves.

To these may be added *oneself*, more commonly written as two words, *one's self.*

Observe that *yourself* is singular, and *yourselves* plural.

Hisself and *theirselves* are incorrect forms.

359. The **self-pronouns** have two distinct uses which may be seen in the following sentences:

> The captain *himself* replied to my question.
> He *himself* was present.

> The defeated general killed *himself* in despair.
> He betrayed *himself* by his folly.

In the first two of the sentences *himself* simply makes more emphatic the noun or pronoun to which it is attached. In this use the self-pronouns are called **intensive pronouns**, because they serve merely to **intensify** or strengthen the meaning of some substantive.

In the third and fourth sentences the use of *himself* is quite different. In each, *himself* is the direct object of a transitive verb (*killed, betrayed*); yet *himself* refers to the same person denoted by the subject of the sentence (*general, he*). In other words, the **subject** (*general, he*) is represented as **doing something to itself.**

The difference between such an object as *himself* and an ordinary object may be seen by comparing the following sentences:

> The man shot the burglar.

[Here the subject (*man*) and the object (*burglar*) are obviously **different persons**. The subject is described as acting on some other person.]

> The man shot himself.

[Here the subject (*man*) the object (*himself*) are obviously one and the **same person**. The subject is described as acting on himself.]

Compound personal pronouns formed with the suffix *self* are known as **self-pronouns.**
❧
Self-pronouns intensify the meaning of a substantive *or* **self-pronouns** serve as the **direct object** of a transitive verb, when the subject is the same person as the object.

227

In this use the self-pronouns are called **reflexive pronouns**.

The word *reflexive* means "bending back." It is applied to the pronouns because, in this use, we must **refer back** to the **subject** of the sentence in order to know *who* or *what* is the person or thing designated by the object.

These two uses of the self-pronouns are easily confused, though quite distinct.

> Self-pronouns which intensify a substantive are called **intensive pronouns.**
>
> 🙤
>
> Self-pronouns which are used as objects are called **reflexive pronouns.**

360. The compound personal pronouns ending in -*self* may be used to emphasize substantives.

In this use they are called intensive pronouns.

361. An intensive pronoun may be regarded as in apposition with the substantive to which it is attached.

362. The compound personal pronouns ending in -*self* may be used as the objects of transitive verbs or of prepositions when the object denotes the same person or thing as the subject of the sentence or clause.

In this use they are called the reflexive pronouns.

A reflexive pronoun may be the indirect object of a verb whose meaning allows. Thus,

> He gave *himself* a blow.
> [He gave a blow to *himself*].

Chapter 87 Exercise

In the following sentences point out all the intensive pronouns and tell with what noun or pronoun each is in apposition.

Point out all the reflexive pronouns, mention the verb or preposition of which each is the object, and tell to what noun or pronoun each refers back.

1. The people abandoned themselves to despair.
2. Jack sat by himself in a corner.
3. They have talked themselves hoarse.
4. The men themselves carried no provisions except a bag of oatmeal.
5. Envy shoots at others, and wounds herself.
6. We ourselves were wrapped up in our furs.

7. Clifford wrapped himself in an old cloak.
8. I myself am to blame for this.
9. I shall hardly know myself in a blue dress.
10. I have not words to express the poor man's thankfulness, neither could he express it himself.
11. Every guilty deed holds in itself the seed of retribution.
12. Jane herself opened the door.
13. She amused herself with walking and reading.
14. The story itself was scarcely credible.
15. The lieutenant was presented to Washington himself.
16. Nobody save myself so much as turned to look after him.
17. One seldom dislikes one's self.
18. The guides themselves had lost the path.
19. The prisoner threw himself into the sea and swam for the shore.
20. The old clock itself looked weary.
21. Guard thyself from false friends.
22. You must prepare yourself for the worst.
23. You cannot protect yourselves from wrong.

CHAPTER 88
Special Uses of the Self-Pronouns

363. The adjective *own* is sometimes inserted between the first and the second part of the **self-pronouns** for emphasis. These forms may be regarded as compound pronouns.

> EXAMPLES: my own self, your own self, his own self, your own selves, their own selves.

364. The **intensive pronouns** are sometimes used idiomatically without being immediately preceded by a noun or pronoun. Thus,

> It is *myself.*

Here *myself* is equivalent to *I myself.*

365. In older English and in poetry intensive pronouns often stand by themselves in constructions in which ordinary English would require the use of a simple personal pronoun before the intensive. Thus,

> *Myself* am king.
> [Instead of: *I myself* am king.]

This use should be avoided in prose.

366. In older English and in poetry the simple personal pronouns are often used in a reflexive sense instead of the *self*-pronouns. Thus,

> He laid *him* down.
> [Instead of: He laid *himself* down.]

In colloquial language this old construction is often retained, but only in a few expressions, such as *I hurt me* (instead of *I hurt myself*). It should be avoided in writing and in careful speech.

CHAPTER 89
Numerals

367. In expressing our thoughts it is often necessary to indicate exactly **how many** persons or things we are thinking of, or **how many times** an action takes place. For these purposes language employs certain peculiar words called **numerals**, that is, "words of number."

Examples may be seen in the following sentences:

> *Three* merry companions once set out on a journey to Spain.

> *Thirty* days hath September,
> April, June, and November;
> All the rest have *thirty-one,*
> Excepting February alone,
> Which has just *eight* and a *score,*
> Till Leap-year gives it *one* day more.

The *first* prize was won by Edwards.
The *second* house in the street belongs to me.
The *thirteenth* day of next month will be Tuesday.
Seven of my friends met me at the station.
Did you ring the bell *once* or *twice?*
I *thrice* presented him a kingly crown.

368. Numerals are adjectives, nouns, or adverbs.

In the preceding examples most of the numerals are **adjectives**, because they limit substantives. *Score*, however, is a **noun**, and so is *seven* in the last example but two. *Once, twice,* and *thrice* are **adverbs**, since they modify verbs by telling how many times the action took place.

369. Numeral adjectives limit substantives by defining the exact number of persons or things thought of.

370. The most important classes of numeral adjectives are called **cardinals** and **ordinals**.

371. Cardinal numeral adjectives (*one, two, three, four*, etc.) are used in counting, and answer the question "How many?" Thus,

> *Three* wise men of Gotham
> Went to sea in a bowl.

> *Thirty* days hath September.

> That man is *seventy-nine* years old.

Numerals are **adjectives, nouns,** or **adverbs.**

☙

Cardinal numeral adjectives are counting numbers: *one, two, three*, etc.

☙

Ordinal numeral adjectives are position numbers: *first, second, third,* etc.

☙

For example: In expressions like "The boy was *sixteen,*" the numeral may be regarded as a predicate adjective limiting *boy*. It is unnecessary to say "sixteen years old."

372. Ordinal numeral adjectives (*first*, *second*, *third*, etc.) denote the position or order of a person or thing in a series.

> Monday is the *first* day of the week.
> February is the *second* month.
> The child was in the *third* year of his age.

373. All the cardinal numerals may be used as nouns.

> *One* of my friends told me this.
> A *million* is a great number.
> *Eighty-one* of the enemy were killed in this skirmish.

374. The cardinals, in some of their uses as nouns, may receive a plural ending. Thus,

> The boy can count by *threes*.
> My friends came up in *threes* and *fours*.
> Five *tens* are fifty.
> Many *hundreds* fell in this battle.
> *Thousands* of dollars were spent in this experiment.

Note: *Hundred, thousand, million* were originally nouns, but are now equally common in the adjective construction.

375. Certain numeral adjectives (*single, double, triple*, etc.) indicate how many times a thing is taken or of how many like parts it consists. Thus,

> The pavement consisted of a *double* layer of bricks.
> A *threefold* cord is not easily broken.

Some of these words may be used as adverbs.

> His labor was repaid *threefold*.

376. Certain numeral adverbs and adverbial phrases indicate how many times an action takes place.

> I hit the ball *once*.
> John knocked *twice* at the door.
> *Thrice* the bell tolled.
> The sharpshooter fired *eleven times* before he was killed.

The only adverbs of this kind in common use are *once* and *twice*. For larger numbers a phrase consisting of a cardinal with the noun *times* is regularly used. *Thrice*, however, is still common (instead of *three times*) in poetry and the solemn style.

Cardinal numerals may also be **nouns.**

❧

Numeral adverbs and **adverbial phrases** indicate how many times an action takes place. Such as *once, twice, thrice, eleven times,* etc.

Chapter 89 Exercise

Tell whether each numeral is an adjective (cardinal, ordinal, or other), a noun, or an adverb.

1. Twice through the hall the chieftain strode.
2. Hundreds in this little town are upon the point of starving.
3. I have paid you fourfold.
4. The third time never fails.
6. The English lie within fifteen hundred paces of your tents.
6. Methought I saw a thousand fearful wrecks.
7. The threefold shield protected him.
8. They shouted thrice; what was the last cry for?
9. Yet thousands still desire to journey on.
10. Byron died in the thirty-seventh year of his age.
11. This note doth tell me of ten thousand French
    That in the field lie slain: of princes, in this number,
    And nobles bearing banners, there lie dead
    One hundred twenty-six: added to these,
    Of knights, esquires, and gallant gentlemen,
    Eight thousand and four hundred.

Review Exercise[54]

Explain the forms and constructions of the substantives, adjectives, and adverbs.

1. Will you shake hands with me now?
2. Delay not, Caesar! Read it instantly!
3. Do you not know that every hard, cold word you use is one stone on a great pyramid of useless remorse?
4. Lay thy finger on thy lips.
5. Have you ever had your house burnt down?
6. Did you take me for Roger Bacon?
7. What, has this thing appeared again tonight?
8. Our neighbor's big black mastiff sprang over the fence.
9. Theodore's cousin has just returned from Asia.

---

[54] Here the inflection of nouns, pronouns, adjectives, and adverbs (chapters 61-89) should be reviewed. Sections 237-242 will serve as a summary, and should accordingly be studied at this point. The miscellaneous sentences on this page give examples of various forms and constructions and may be used for practice in parsing and analysis at the close of the review.

10. The jay's noisy chatter silenced our talk.
11. The old pilot's skill saved the ship from destruction.
12. I owe you much already.
13. They shall fetch thee jewels from the deep.
14. I sell thee poison; thou hast sold me none.
15. Sing high the praise of Denmark's host.
16. Pen never told his mother a falsehood.
17. Last night the very gods showed me a vision.
18. He strode down the creaking stair.
19. The ruling passion conquers reason still.
20. Four seasons fill the measure of the year.
21. He feels the anxieties of life.
22. The long carpets rose along the gusty floor.
23. The needle plies its busy task.
24. I spent some time in Holland.
25. Great offices will have great talents.

CHAPTER 90
Inflection of Verbs — Tense

377. Compare the following sentences:

> Queen Victoria *rules* over England.
> Queen Elizabeth *ruled* over England.

(1) *Rules* and *ruled* are really the same verb with different **endings**.

(2) *Rules* refers to the **present** time and *ruled* refers to **past** time.

In other words, the difference between *rules* and *ruled* is a difference in **ending** that indicates a difference in the **time of the action**.

Similarly, we can distinguish between the time referred to by each of the verbs in the following pairs:

come, came	bind, bound	kill, killed
dwell, dwelt	walk, walked	fill, filled

This distinction of **time** in verbs is called **tense**.

The word *tense* is simply an English form of the French word for *time*.

378. Every action, of course, must take place at the present time, in past time, or in future time.

379. **Verbs have distinction of tense to indicate present, past, or future time.**

> **A verb in the present tense refers to present time.**
> **A verb in the preterite tense refers to past time.**[55]
> **A verb in the future tense refers to future time.**

*Preterite is from the Latin, and means simply "gone by," "past." *Preterite* is a better name for the tense than *past*, for both the perfect and the pluperfect tenses refer to past time as well as the preterite.

Preterite means "gone by," or "past." The preterite tense is usually called the **"past tense,"** but remember that the perfect and pluperfect tenses also refer to past time.

---

[55] Editor's Note: Modern grammar texts no longer use the term "preterite" for the past tense. While this word is now out of use, it is helpful for students to learn that this is the former name for past tense. *Preterite* is still used in the study of some other languages.

CHAPTER 91
Preterite (Past) Tense[56]

380. The **present** and the **preterite** tense have special forms of inflection.

For the moment we will consider, in both of these tenses, the form which the verb has when its subject is the first personal pronoun *I*.

381. In the present tense the verb appears in its simplest form, without any inflectional ending.

I *walk* along the street.	I *dwell* in this world.
I *answer* all questions.	I *drink* water.

382. If we change the verbs in the foregoing sentences (Section 381) so that they shall express **past** instead of **present** time, the sentences will read as follows:

I *walked* along the street.	I *dwelt* in this world.
I *answered* all questions.	I *drank* water.

All these forms, *walked, answered, dwelt, drank*, are then in the **preterite tense**.

PRESENT TENSE	PRETERITE TENSE
walk	walked
answer	answered
dwell	dwelt
drink	drank

(1) The verbs *walk* and *answer* form their preterite tense by adding -*ed* to the present.
(2) The verb *dwell* forms its preterite tense by adding -*t* to the present (omitting one *l*).
(3) The verb *drink* forms its preterite tense by changing the vowel *i* of the present to *a*, and adds no ending.

383. The preterite tense is formed in one of two ways:

   (1) By adding to the present tense the ending -*ed*, -*d*, or -*t*;

> Many verbs form the **preterite (past) tense** by adding -*ed*, -*d*, or -*t*. These verbs are known as **weak verbs.**
>
> ❧
>
> Many other verbs form the **preterite (past) tense** by changing the medial vowel of the present-tense form. These verbs are known as **strong verbs.**

---

[56] Editor's note: Modern texts generally call the preterite tense the "past tense." We keep the term here because it is helpful to understand the foundation of English grammar. It is also useful for students who study other languages and encounter "preterite" tense.

(2) By changing the vowel of the present tense without the addition of an ending.

According as verbs form their preterite tense in one or the other of these two ways, they are called **(1) weak verbs**, or **(2) strong verbs**.

384. **Weak verbs** form the preterite tense by adding *-ed*, *-d*, or *-t* to the present.

> EXAMPLES: fill, filled; stay, stayed; bless, blessed; dwell, dwelt; defend, defended; select, selected; compare, compared.

> Weak verbs are also called **regular verbs.**
>
> ॰
>
> **Strong** verbs are also called **irregular verbs.**

385. **Strong verbs** form the preterite tense by changing the vowel of the present, without the addition of an ending.

> EXAMPLES: sing, sang; spin, spun; win, won; fall, fell; ride, rode; shine, shone; bear, bore; tear, tore.[57]

Weak verbs are sometimes called **regular**, and strong verbs **irregular verbs**.[58]

386. The terms **strong** and **weak** were first applied to verbs for a somewhat fanciful reason. The strong verbs were so called because they seemed to form the preterite tense out of their own resources, without calling to their assistance any ending. The weak verbs were so called because they were incapable of forming their preterites without the aid of the ending *-ed*, *-d*, or *-t*.

Chapter 91 Exercise

Change all the presents to preterites. Tell whether each preterite that you have made is weak or strong.

1. I ride to Hyde Park.
2. The country becomes disturbed, and nightly meetings of the peasantry take place.
3. Many of the boldest sink beneath the fear of betrayal.

---

[57] *Silent *-e* in *bore*, *tore* etc., is not counted as an ending.

[58] A strong verb is really just as regular as a weak verb: that is to say, all strong verbs form their preterites in accordance with definite rules and not in obedience to mere chance. To ascertain these rules, however, requires a long study, not merely of the English language, but of several other languages, like German and the Scandinavian tongues, with which English is closely related. The student who is beginning the study of English grammar, therefore, must learn the forms of the strong verbs as separate facts, without much regard to the reasons for their existence.

4. When Calabressa calls at the house in Curzon Street he is at once admitted.

5. He walks on, his heart full of an audacious joy.

6. Returning to the cottage, he proceeds to sweep the hearth and make up the fire.

7. Where the remote Bermudas ride
   In the Ocean's bosom unespied,
   From a small boat that rows along,
   The listening winds receive this song.

8. Many fresh streams run to one salt sea.

9. The camels from their keepers break;
   The distant steer forsakes the yoke.

10. Lady Evelyn is a tall, somewhat good-looking, elderly lady, who wears her silver-white hair in old-fashioned curls.

11. His faded yellow hair begins to grow thin, and his thread-bare frock coat hangs limp from sloping shoulders.

12. I wander lonely as a cloud.

13. The next morning he comes down to the breakfast room earlier than is his custom, and salutes everybody there with great cordiality.

14. To the belfry, one by one, haste the ringers.

15. No haughty feat of arms I tell.

16. The senators mean to establish Caesar as a king.

17. I rest two or three minutes, and then give the boat another shove, and so on, till the sea is no higher than my armpits.

18. His heart jumps with pleasure as the famous university comes in view.

CHAPTER 92
Preterite (Past) Tense of Strong (Irregular) Verbs

387. The definition of a strong verb has already been given in Section 385.

Strong verbs form the preterite tense by changing the vowel of the present, without the addition of an ending.

> **Strong verbs,** sometimes called irregular verbs, actually come to us from old English (Anglo-Saxon) and change tense according to the rules of the old language.
>
> ❧
>
> **Strong verbs** change to preterite tense by changing the *vowel*, not the ending.

> sing, *pret.* sang;
> drink, *pret.* drank;
> write, *pret.* wrote;
> bear, *pret.* bore.[59]

388. The **strong verbs** are an exceedingly important element in our language. Many of the weak verbs might disappear without being missed, but there are very few of the strong verbs that we could conveniently spare. For these verbs express, for the most part, simple and fundamental ideas with which the language of everyday life is constantly occupied.

Thus, among the strong verbs are such essential words as:

eat, drink, stand, rise, fall, ride, find, break.

389. The strong preterites, which appear so irregular and accidental to us, were originally formed in accordance with definite principles of language, and in the oldest English (Anglo-Saxon) it is easy to classify them. In the course of time, however, the old classes have become confused so that the strong verbs seem no longer to follow any rules.

A full list of the strong verbs is given in Appendix B for reference.

---

[59] Some strong verbs have in the preterite a silent final *e* which does not appear in the present, but this is not properly an ending. Thus: *break, broke; wear, wore; bear, bore; tear, tore.*

CHAPTER 93
Weak Preterites (Regular Past Tense) in *-ed* or *-d*

390. Most weak verbs form their preterite in -ed.

> act, acted;
> mend, mended;
> jump, jumped;
> confess, confessed;
> regard, regarded;
> attend, attended.

Weak verbs, form their preterite tense by **adding *-ed* or *-d.***

Although *-ed* is added, the *e* **is usually silent.**

If *-ed* is added to a verb ending in *-t* or *-d,* the *-ed* **is fully pronounced.**

A few verbs add the *-ed* or *-d* suffix *and* change the vowel. Study the list of these verbs.

In modern English, *e* in the ending *-ed*, though written, is silent unless preceded by *d* or *t*.

Thus, we write *filled*, but pronounce *fill'd*; we write *knocked*, but pronounce *knockt*.

If, however, the present ends in *-t* or *-d* (as in *request, command*), the preterite ending *-ed* is fully pronounced (*requested, commanded*).

Otherwise the preterite would not differ in pronunciation from the present, for we cannot pronounce *request'd* or *command'd* so as to distinguish it from *request* or *command*.

391. A few verbs add *-d* (not *-ed*) in the preterite and also show a change of vowel.

> sell, sold;
> tell, told;
> flee, fled;
> shoe, shod;
> hear, heard (pronounced *herd*);
> say, said.

392. *Make* has *made* in the preterite, and *have* has *had*.

Chapter 93 Exercise

Make sentences containing the preterites of the following weak verbs:

Act, govern, rush, knock, fish, tend, tell, rattle, carry, delay, flee, try, address, pitch, talk, experiment, describe, rebel.

CHAPTER 94
Weak Preterites (Past Tense) in -*t*

393. Many weak verbs form the preterite tense in -*t*.[60]

dwell, dwelt;   keep, kept;
feel, felt;   leave, left.

Most verbs of this *t*-class show special irregularities.

394. Some verbs that have a long vowel sound in the present have in the preterite a short vowel sound before the ending -*t*.[61]

creep, crept;   feel, felt;
keep, kept;   deal, dealt (pronounced *delt*);
sleep, slept;   mean, meant (pronounced *ment*);
sweep, swept;   lose, lost;
weep, wept;   leave, left.

395. Some verbs in -*nd* and -*ld* form their preterite tense by changing this -*d* to -*t*.

bend, bent;   rend, rent;
send, sent;   spend, spent;
lend, lent;   build, built.

396. A few weak verbs not only add -*t* in the preterite, but also change the vowel of the present and show other irregularities. These are:

bring, brought   beseech, besought
buy, bought   teach, taught
catch, caught   think, thought
seek, sought   methinks, methought

Work has an old preterite tense *wrought*, common in poetry; its usual preterite is *worked*. For *must, would*, etc., see Appendix B.

> Many **weak** verbs form the past tense by adding -*t* rather than -*ed*.
>
> ❧
>
> Some verbs ending in -*nd* form the past tense by changing the *d* to *t*.
>
> ❧
>
> A few verbs form the past tense by adding *t* and changing the vowel.

---

[60] As we have seen, the ending -*ed* often stands for the sound of -*t*; as *passed*, pronounced *past*. In such forms the ending, from the point of view of the spoken language, is of course -*t*.

[61] In *leave* and *bereave* observe also the difference of sound between *v* and *f*. For the irregular weak verbs, see Appendix B.

CHAPTER 95
Weak Preterites Without Ending

397. Some weak verbs in -*d* or -*t* preceded by a long vowel sound have a short vowel in the preterite but add no ending.

bleed, bled	read (pronounced *reed*), read (pronounced *red*)
breed, bred	meat, met
feed, fed	shoot, shot
speed, sped	light, lit (*also* lighted)
lead, led	

Some **weak** verbs form the past tense by **changing the vowel** rather than adding an ending.

๛

Some **weak** verbs **keep the same form** in present and past tense.

398. Some weak verbs in -*d* or -*t* have in the preterite the same form as in the present.

PRESENT	PRETERITE (PAST)
shed	shed
spread	spread
bet	bet
hit	hit
set	set
spit	spit
put	put
shut	shut
cut	cut
hurt	hurt
cast	cast

Note: The verbs described in Sections 397 and 398 might at first appear to be strong verbs, since they have no ending in the preterite and change the vowel. They are, however, all weak verbs. Their lack of ending is due to the fact that the *d* or *t* of the termination has been absorbed in the final *d* or *t* of the verb itself. Thus, the preterite *set* was originally *settë* (dissyllabic), and this form, after the loss of -*ë*, became indistinguishable in sound from *set*, the present.

Chapter 95 Exercises

I.

Make sentences containing the preterite tense of the following verbs, some of which are weak and some strong.

> Bend, sell, act, review, try, spin, drink, eat, carry, lose, compel, read, lead, tread, leave, work, spend, know, set, sit, lie, lay, rend, bring, rear, arise, ring, break, bind, copy, spare, multiply, catch, divide, subtract, telegraph, strike, run, wrestle, blow, burst, climb, sing, begin, stand, understand, go, change, teach, reach, split.

II.

Pick out all the preterites, and tell whether they are weak or strong. Give the present tense in each case.

When midnight drew near, and when the robbers from afar saw that no light was burning and that everything appeared quiet, their captain said to them that he thought that they had run away without reason, telling one of them to go and reconnoitre. So one of them went, and found everything quite quiet. He went into the kitchen to strike a light, and, taking the glowing fiery eyes of the cat for burning coals, he held a match to them in order to kindle it. But the cat, not seeing the joke, flew into his face, spitting and scratching.

III.

Fill each blank with a preterite. Tell whether each preterite is weak or strong.

1. The hunter took careful aim and _____; but the deer _____ away unharmed.
2. A portrait of Mr. Gilbert _____ on the wall.
3. I _____ my companion to lend me his knife.
4. In the distance _____ the lights of the village.
5. The sailor _____ into the sea and _____ to the rescue.
6. The boy _____ on the burning deck.
7. The kite _____ majestically into the air.
8. A puff of wind _____ off the boy's cap and it _____ along the ground. He _____ after it as fast as he could. The faster he _____, the faster the cap _____.
9. The mischievous fellow _____ three leaves out of my book.
10. The maid _____ the bucket with water and _____ it to the thirsty wayfarers.
11. Tom _____ on a rock, fishing patiently.
12. The miser _____ a hole to conceal his treasure.
13. Joe _____ the tree to get some apples.

CHAPTER 96
Singular and Plural Verbs

399. Nouns and pronouns, as we have seen, may be of either the **singular** or the **plural** number. The same is true of **verbs**. Thus, in

> The officer *encourages* his men;
> He *speaks* good German,

the verbs *encourages* and *speaks* are, like their subjects *officer* and *he*, in the **singular number**.

But if we change the subjects of these sentences to the **plural** number, we find ourselves obliged to change the form of the verbs also.

> The officers *encourage* their men.
> They *speak* good German.

Here the **verbs**, as well as the **subjects**, are in the **plural**.

400. A verb must agree with its subject in number.

> A **verb** must agree with its **subject** in number.

The importance of this rule may be seen from the bad results of breaking it. We immediately recognize the following sentences as ungrammatical:

All the *men* | *goes* to church.　　　The *child* | *are* sick.
He | *are* a good fellow.　　　　　　*They* | *is* all feeble.
The *soldiers* | *marches*.　　　　　The *soldier* | *march*.

All these sentences strike us at once as very bad.

The reason is that in none of them does the verb **agree with its subject in number.** We can correct the sentence in each case by changing the **number** of the verb from singular to plural or from plural to singular.

Chapter 96 Exercises

I.

Fill the blanks with a singular or a plural verb in the present tense.

Tell which number you have used in each sentence.

1. I _____ sorry to hear of your misfortune.
2. We _____ ball every Saturday afternoon.
3. He _____ the strongest swimmer in the school.
4. They _____ very good friends of mine.
5. It _____ a great deal of money to build a railroad.
6. John and Tom always _____ to school together.
7. Birds _____; fishes _____; snakes _____; dogs _____ on four legs; mankind alone _____ upright.
8. You _____ so badly that I can hardly read your letter. Your brother _____ much better.
9. The farmer _____ the seed; but the sun and the rain _____ it grow.
10. My uncle _____ me a dollar whenever he _____ to visit us.
11. Kangaroos _____ very long hind legs.
12. A spider _____ eight legs; a beetle _____ six.
13. My pony _____ apples out of my hand.
14. The grocer _____ tea, sugar, salt, and molasses.
15. The company of soldiers _____ up the hill in the face of the enemy.
16. The grapes _____ in clusters on the vine.

II.

In the chapter 79 exercise, point out all the subjects and all the objects.
Mention the number of each substantive and of each verb.

III.

Do the same with chapter 85, Exercise II.

CHAPTER 97[62]
Special Rules for the Number of Verbs

401. A compound subject usually takes a verb in the plural number.

> The king and his son *fear* treachery.
> Thomas and I *are* friends.
> The dog and the cat *have* no liking for each other.

402. A compound subject expressing but a single idea sometimes takes a verb in the singular number.

> The sole *end and aim* of his life *was* to get money.

This construction is comparatively rare in modern English, and should be used with great caution. It is for the most part confined to such idiomatic phrases as *end and aim* (equivalent to the single noun *purpose*), *the long and short of it*, etc.

403. Nouns that are plural in form but singular in sense commonly take a verb in the singular number.

> The *news is* good.
> Bad *news travels* fast.
> *Mathematics is* my favorite study.
> *Measles is* a troublesome disease.

In the older language most of these words were felt as plurals and accordingly took a plural verb. Thus, about 1600, we find both "This news is good," and "These news are good," for at this time the word *news* was still felt to mean "new things," and hence was sometimes plural in sense as well as in form.

404. With regard to some words of this class usage varies. Thus, *pains*, in the sense of *care* or *effort*, is sometimes regarded as a singular and sometimes as a plural. For example,

> Great pains has (*or* have) been taken to accomplish this.

405. Collective nouns take sometimes a singular and sometimes a plural verb.

When the persons or things denoted are thought of as individuals, the plural should be used. When the collection is conceived as a unit, the singular should be used.

> Some nouns are **plural in form but singular in sense** and commonly take a verb in the singular.
>
> ❧
>
> **Collective nouns** sometimes take a singular and sometimes a plural verb, depending on the context.

---

[62] This chapter may be omitted until review.

406. The distinction made in the foregoing rule (Section 405) is observed by careful writers and is consequently a matter of some importance. In many instances, however, the choice between the singular and the plural depends upon the feeling of the moment.

The following examples illustrate this distinction:

1. The people of the United States *are* discussing this question with great interest.

   [Here *the people of the United States* are thought of not as a whole (or, as we say, **collectively**), but as a number of **individuals** holding different opinions and engaged in a lively debate. Hence the verb is in the **plural**.]

2. The sovereign people *is* the final authority in a republic.

   [Here the people is thought of as a single, all-powerful source of political authority. Hence the verb is in the **singular**.]

3. The committee *is* of opinion that this measure ought not to pass.

   [Here the committee, being unanimous, or at any rate having come to some agreement amongst its members, expresses itself with a single voice as if one man were speaking for all. Hence the **singular** verb is proper.]

4. The committee *are* both individually and collectively much opposed to this measure.

   [Here the use of the word *individually* calls attention at once to the fact that the committee consists of a number of persons who think and feel as individuals; hence the **plural** *are* is natural.]

CHAPTER 98
Person of Verbs

407. Compare the following sentences:

> I walk.
> Thou walkest.
> He walks.

(1) The three pronouns *I, thou,* and *he* refer to different **persons**: *I* denotes the **speaker**; *thou* denotes the person **spoken to**; *he* denotes neither the speaker nor the person spoken to, but some third person whom we may call the **person spoken of.** (See chapter 68.)

(2) The **form** of the verb *walk* changes according as this verb is used with *I, thou,* or *he* as its subject.

(3) If we change any one of the **verb forms** without at the same time changing the **pronoun**, the sentence becomes bad English. We cannot say *I walkest,* or *I walks,* or *he walk.*

(4) If we change the subject of the sentence to a **noun in the singular number**, the verb will take the same form that it has when the subject is *he.* Thus,

> He walks.
> John walks.

408. Substantives and verbs are distinguished as to person.

409. There are three persons: first, second, and third.

> The **first person** denotes the speaker;
> the **second person** denotes the person spoken to;
> the **third person** denotes the person or thing spoken of.

410. A verb must agree with its subject in person.

411. We may now include in one rule the principle of agreement between a verb and its subject as explained in Sections 399 and 407:

A verb must agree with its subject in number and person.

Chapter 98 Exercises

I.

Write an account of some accident or adventure that you have had or that you have heard of. If you have written in the first person, change your story so that it shall be told of some other person. If you have told your story in the third person, imagine that the adventure happened to you, and write the story again in the first person.

What changes have you made in the form of each verb?

II.

Find some story in your history or reading book. Imagine that the incidents related happened to you, and tell the story in the first person.

What changes have you made in the form of each verb?

III.

Tell the person and number of each of the verbs and verb phrases below. If the form may belong to more than one person or number, mention all. Test your accuracy by using personal pronouns (*I, you, they,* etc.) with each form.

> Found, didst know, finds, acts, act, mentions, sells, sold, broughtest, brings, bringest, speak, spoke, broke, endeavors, dives, replied, puzzled, utters, knowest, hath, has, canst, can, is, are, leapest, fight, fought, has spoken, have, am, art, were.

IV.

In some page of your reading book find all the presents and preterites you can. Tell the person and number of each. A selection is provided for you in *Mother Tongue Student Workbook 2.*

CHAPTER 99
Personal Endings — Conjugating Verbs

Verb endings in English are mostly unchanged, even when the *person* of the subject changes.

❧

The second person singular pronoun *thou* is no longer used. Instead, the second person plural pronoun *you* is used for singular and plural situations.

❧

Today, only the present tense **third person singular** has a different ending **(-s):** *He walks.*

412. We may now gather up what we have learned in the preceding exercises and state it in an orderly manner.

413. Verbs change their form to indicate person and number.

414. The endings by means of which a verb indicates person and number are called personal endings.

In the **present tense** a verb has **two personal endings**:

-*est* for the second person singular[63] and
-*s* for the third person singular (old form, -*eth*).

The first person singular and all three persons in the plural are alike. The simplest form of the verb is used and no personal ending is added.

SINGULAR	PLURAL
1. I walk. (no ending)	We walk. (no ending)
2. Thou walk-est.	You walk. (no ending)
3. He walk-s (old form, walk-eth)	They walk. (no ending)

415. In the absence of a personal ending, the person and number of a verb are indicated by its subject.

416. Let us now examine the **preterite tense** with reference to the **personal endings**.

I walked.
Thou walkedst.
He (we, you, they) walked.

We see at once that there is but **one personal ending in the preterite**: -*(e)st* in the second person singular. The ending -*ed* indicates past time, and is not a personal ending.

417. The first and third persons of the preterite singular and all three persons of the preterite plural have no personal ending.

---

[63] Editor's Note: This book teaches "thou" as the second person **singular** pronoun. Today "you" is used in the place of "thou" and it follows the second person plural form (no ending added). Modern students will commonly see verbs conjugated with "you" in the second person singular, although technically it is the plural form.

418. We may draw up the following table of the **endings** which verbs take to distinguish **person** and **number**. Such endings are called the **personal endings**.

PRESENT TENSE		PRETERITE (PAST) TENSE	
SINGULAR	PLURAL	SINGULAR	PLURAL
1. (no ending)	1. (no ending)	1. (no ending)	1. (no ending)
2. -est, -st	2. (no ending)	2. -est	2. (no ending)
3. -s (old, -eth)	3. (no ending)	3. (no ending)	3. (no ending)

419. **Inflection**, as we learned in Section 4, is a change in the form of a word to indicate a change in its meaning.

Hence these changes in verb forms that we have just studied are a part of the inflection of the English verb.

420. The **inflection** of a verb is called its **conjugation**; to **inflect** a verb is to **conjugate** it.

In Section 414, then, we have conjugated the verb *walk* in the **present tense**.

421. We are now prepared to conjugate verbs in the **preterite tense**. Thus,

PRETERITE TENSE

SINGULAR	PLURAL
1. I walked.	1. We walked.
2. Thou walked-st.	2. You (*or* ye) walked.
3. He walked.	3. They walked.
1. I found.	1. We found.
2. Thou found-est.	2. You (*or* ye) found.
3. He found.	3. They found.

Walked is a weak verb; *found* is a strong verb.

Inflection is the change in the form of a word to change its meaning.

To **inflect** a verb is to **conjugate** it.

Chapter 99 Exercises

I.

In accordance with the model above, conjugate the following verbs in the present and the preterite tense[64]:

> Love, call, answer, shout, examine, stand, find, bind, bear, lose, sit, set, lie, lay, burn, fight, bring, catch, reach, spend, beat, declare, read, march, charge, enlarge, despise, praise, honor, foretell, prophesy, enter, depart.

II.

Mention the number and person of each verb in chapter 69, Exercise I.

III.

Conjugate the following verbs in the present tense, giving all three persons and both numbers. Use a pronoun as the subject of each verb.

> Stand, answer, compel, go, ask, fill, try, succeed, spend, earn, study, run, rescue, play, climb, flee, retreat, charge, descend, ride, act, smile, laugh, speed, descry, find, bring, discover, desire, retreat, succeed, drink, lead, bend.

IV.

Make fifteen sentences, each containing one of the verbs in III, above:

> (1) in the present tense, third person, singular number;
> (2) in the third person plural;
> (3) in the second person plural;
> (4) in the first person plural;
> (5) in the preterite tense, first person, singular number;
> (6) in the third person plural;
> (7) in the second person plural;
> (8) in the third person singular.

---

[64] This exercise may be indefinitely extended according to the needs of the pupils.

CHAPTER 100
Infinitive

> **Verbs** change their form as they change *tense*. Most verb forms have subjects.
>
> ❧
>
> The **infinitive** is a verb form **with no subject.**
>
> ❧
>
> Usually **infinitives** are formed with the *preposition* **to.**
>
> ❧
>
> **Infinitives** don't need to agree in person and number with the subject. They are "unlimited" and so take the name *infinitive.*

422. The **verb forms** hitherto discussed have all been such as, in connected speech, **have subjects**. That is, they have been forms that not only **express an action** or state, but are also capable of **asserting** it with reference to some person or thing. Thus, in

> The whale *smashed* the boat with his tail,

the verb *smashed* not merely expresses the action of breaking to pieces, but it asserts that the subject, *the whale*, actually performed that action in a given instance.

423. There are, however, two important classes of words which, though counted among verb forms, can never have subjects,[65] and are incapable of **asserting** an action or a state. They are called **infinitives** and **participles**. We must first give our attention to infinitives.

424. Let us examine the following sentence:

> The boy runs *to see* the fire.

We at once recognize *see* as a verb form. It expresses action and takes a direct object, *fire*. But we also observe two peculiarities which distinguish it, at a glance, from *runs*, the other verb in the sentence:

(1) The verb *runs* has a subject, *boy*; whereas *see* has no subject.

(2) *Runs* is in the third person and singular number, agreeing with its subject *boy*; whereas *see*, having no subject, has neither person nor number.

If we change the subject *boy* to the plural *boys*, the verb *runs* must be changed also, but nothing will happen to the form of *see*. Thus,

> The boys run to *see* the fire.

Similarly:

> I run *to see* the fire.
> We run *to see* the fire.

See, then, in all these sentences expresses the idea of action in the very simplest way. It is free from those limitations of **person** and **number** to which a verb that has a subject must conform. For this reason it is called an **infinitive**, that is, an "unlimited" verb form.

---

[65] Except in the so-called "infinitive clause" (see chapter 142).

We observe, also, that *see* is introduced by the preposition *to*, which in this use is called the **sign of the infinitive**.

425. The following sentence will make clear another peculiarity of the infinitive:

> *To obey* is a child's duty.

Here the subject of the sentence is *to obey*, which we recognize as an infinitive with its sign *to*. The infinitive, then, has at least one of the properties of a **noun**: it may be used as the **subject** of a sentence. Indeed, without changing the meaning, we could substitute the pure noun *obedience* for the infinitive in this sentence.

> *Obedience* is a child's duty.

Further study will show us that the infinitive has other properties of the noun, but this single specimen is enough for our present purpose. Having learned that the infinitive has **noun** properties, as well as **verb** properties, we are ready for the definition.

426. The infinitive is a verb form which partakes of the nature of a noun. It expresses action or state in the simplest possible way, without the limitations of person or number.

It is commonly preceded by the preposition *to*, which in this use is called the sign of the infinitive.

Strictly speaking, *to love, to speak,* and the like are infinitive phrases, consisting of the infinitive (*love, speak*) and the preposition. For convenience, however, we often speak of the whole phrase as the infinitive, as if the preposition were actually a part of the infinitive itself.

NOTE: Historically considered, the infinitive is not a verb at all, but a noun expressing action or state. Its real nature comes out if we compare "*To err* is human" with "*Error* is human"; "I have a horse *to sell*" with "I have a horse for *sale*"; "I desire *to see* it" with "I desire a *sight* of it." Yet the infinitive is so closely associated in our minds with the genuine verb that it would be unwise to refuse to admit it to a place among verb forms. Such a classification is in a manner justified by three important considerations:

(1) the infinitive is modified, as verbs are, by adverbs and not, like nouns, by adjectives;
(2) it behaves like a verb in taking one or more objects when its meaning allows;
(3) finally, the infinitive is systematically used to make certain verb phrases (like the so-called future tense) which supply the lack of genuine inflections in the English verb, and this would in itself be a strong reason for classifying it as a verb form.

The preposition *to* which comes before an infinitive is called the **sign of the infinitive.**

❧

Infinitives have some properties of nouns. Sometimes an infinitive is the subject of a sentence.

The **infinitive** is a **verb** form.

❧

Infinitives are modified by **adverbs** (not adjectives).

❧

Infinitives sometimes have a **direct object.**

Chapter 100 Exercises

I.
Make sentences of your own containing the following infinitives:

> To boast, to help, to leap, to fly, to flee, to lie, to lay, to ask, to advise, to assist, to order, to revenge, to describe, to injure, to disappear, to lose, to advance, to recognize, to travel, to transform, to spare, to suggest, to pursue, to remember, to remind, to define, to desert, to settle, to build, to plant, to exterminate, to destroy, to cultivate, to sow, to reap, to mow, to pacify, to burn, to descend, to modify, to persevere, to forgive, to puzzle, to explain.

II.
Insert an infinitive with *to* in each blank.

> EXAMPLE:
> Tom is too tired _____ his lesson.
> Tom is too tired *to study* his lesson.

1. Old Carlo was too well trained _____ cats.
2. Charles was in such a hurry that he could hardly spare time _____ his breakfast.
3. We are taught _____ our enemies.
4. Gerald rose very early and went down to the brook _____ for trout.
5. Little Bo-Peep has lost her sheep,
   And doesn't know where _____ them.
6. The fireman was obliged _____ from the locomotive to save his life.
7. The careless fellow has forgotten _____ the door.
8. Our orders were _____ against the enemy at daybreak.
9. Commodore Dewey did not hesitate _____ into Manila Bay.
10. The performing bear stood up on his hind legs and began _____ clumsily.

III.
Find the infinitives.

1. Lord Craven did me the honor to inquire for me by name.
2. Distress at last forced him to leave the country.
3. I know not what to think of it.
4. Our next care was to bring this booty home without meeting with the enemy.
5. To see judiciously requires no small skill in the seer.
6. The business of his own life is to dine.

7. The ladies are to fling nosegays; the court poets to scatter verses; the spectators are to be all in full dress.

8. Vathek invited the old man to dine, and even to remain some days in the palace.

9. Earth seemed to sink beneath, and heaven above to fall.

CHAPTER 101
Participles

427. Let us examine the following sentence:

> The boy sees in the courtyard a dog, *stretched* out and *gnawing* a bone.

We at once recognize *stretched* and *gnawing* as **verb forms**. They express **action**, and one of them, *gnawing*, takes a direct **object**, *bone*. But we observe, as in the infinitive already studied, two peculiarities which distinguish them, at a glance, from *sees*, the other verb in the sentence:

> (1) The verb *sees* has a **subject**, *boy*; whereas *stretched* and *gnawing* have no subjects. (*Dog* is the direct object of *sees*.)
>
> (2) *Sees* is in the third person and singular number, agreeing with its subject *boy*; whereas *stretched* and *gnawing*, having no subject, have neither **person** nor **number**.

If we change the subject *boy* to the plural *boys*, the verb *sees* must be changed also, but nothing will happen to the form of *stretched* or to that of *gnawing*. Thus,

> The boys see in the courtyard a dog, *stretched* out and *gnawing* a bone.

Similarly we may make *I* (first person) or *you* (second person) the subject of the sentence without changing *stretched* and *gnawing* at all.

Stretched and *gnawing*, then, in this sentence express the idea of action in a very simple way. Like the infinitive, they are free from those **limitations** of **person** and **number** to which a verb that has a subject must conform.

They differ, however, from infinitives in two important respects:

> (1) Their **forms** are not like that of the infinitive. They have endings *-ing* and *-ed*, which the infinitives *to stretch* and *to gnaw* do not possess; and they have not and cannot have the infinitive sign *to*.
>
> (2) They **describe** the noun *dog*, much as **adjectives** would do.

Indeed, without changing the structure of the sentence we could substitute genuine descriptive adjectives for *stretched* and *gnawing*. Thus,

---

The **participle** is a **verb** form **with no subject**.

❧

Participles do not change form to agree with the sentence's subject in person or number.

❧

Participles end in *-ed* or *-ing*.

❧

Participles describe nouns.

> **Participles** resemble adjectives. They describe or modify a noun or pronoun.
>
> ❧
>
> **Participles** *participate* (or share) the nature of adjectives.

The boy sees in the courtyard a dog, *stretched* out and
    gnawing a bone.
The boy sees in the courtyard a dog, *lean* and *fierce*.

From this resemblance to adjectives, *stretched* and *gnawing* are called **participles** because they *participate* (that is, share) in the nature of adjectives.

We have now learned that the **participle** has **adjective** properties as well as **verb** properties, and are ready for the definition.

428. The participle is a verb form which has no subject, but which, partaking of the nature of an adjective, expresses action or state in such a way as to describe or limit a substantive.[66]

Chapter 101 Exercise

Examples of participles may be seen in the following sentences:

Walking up to the front door, *I* rang the bell.
The policeman saw a *man sitting* on the steps.
He observed a fine *dog stretched* out on the hearth rug.
He tripped over a *rope extended* across his path.

In the following sentences pick out the **participles**. What noun or pronoun does each modify?

1. I see trees laden with ripening fruit.
2. In the green churchyard there were cattle tranquilly reposing upon the verdant graves.
3. The mob came roaring out, and thronged the place.
4. The girls sat weeping in silence.
5. Asked for a groat, he gives a thousand pounds.
6. Edward marched through Scotland at the head of a powerful army, compelling all ranks of people to submit to him.
7. The blackest desperation now gathers over him, broken only by red lightnings of remorse.
8. Arrived at Athens, soon he came to court.
9. Still the vessel went bounding onward.

---

[66] Historically considered the participle is not a verb at all, but a verbal adjective expressing action or state. Its real nature comes out if we compare "The scholar, *desiring* praise, studied hard" with "The scholar, *eager* for praise, studied hard"; "*Fatigued* with his journey, the traveler went to his room" with "*Weary* from his journey, the traveler went to his room." Yet the participle is commonly and conveniently classified among verb forms for reasons similar to those already given with regard to the infinitive (chapter 100). Like the infinitive, the participle is very important in making verb phrases which supply the place of inflections.

10. Enchanted with the whole scene, I lingered on my voyage.
11. So saying, from the pavement he half rose
    Slowly, with pain, reclining on his arm,
    And looking wistfully with wide blue eyes
    As in a picture.
12. I went home that evening greatly oppressed in my mind, irresolute, and not knowing what to do.
13. Methinks I see thee straying on the beach.
14. A mountain stood
    Threatening from high,
    and overlooked the wood.
15. The wondering stranger round him gazed.
16. The castaways haunted the shore of the little island, always straining their eyes in the vain hope that a ship might show itself on the horizon.
17. Jack said nothing, but stood looking quizzically at his cousin.
18. Hearing of the disaster, they had come to my assistance.
19. At the first fire, twenty or thirty of the assailants fell dead or wounded.
20. Egbert stood motionless, horrified at the sight.
21. Almost exhausted, and swimming with the greatest difficulty, Philip reached the pier at last.
22. I found him hiding behind a tree.

CHAPTER 102
Present Participle

429. English verbs have two simple participles: the present participle and the past participle.

430. The present participle ends in *-ing*.

Thus, the present participle of the verb *give* is *giv-ing;*

> that of *walk* is *walk-ing;*
> that of *kill, kill-ing;*
> that of *drink, drink-ing*, and so on.

431. The present participle usually describes an action as taking place at the same time with some other action. Thus,

> The dandy walked up the street, *flourishing* his cane.
> The enemy disputed their ground inch by inch, *fighting* with the fury of despair.
> Do you hear that nightingale *singing* in the wood?

432. The present participle may describe an action as having taken place before some other action. Thus,

> *Raising* his rifle and *taking* careful aim, Tom fired at the bear.
> *Mounting* his horse, the bandit rode off.
> *Walking* up to the stranger, John asked him his name.
> *Landing* at Calais, we proceeded to Paris.

433. The present participle is much used with the copula *is* (*was*, etc.), to make verb phrases expressing continued or repeated action.

> He *is chopping* wood.
> They *were traveling* in Italy last year.
> You *have been climbing* trees all day.

A verb phrase of this kind is called the **progressive form** of the verb.

CHAPTER 103
Past Participle of Weak Verbs

434. The past participle is always associated with the idea of past time or completed action.

The past participle is also called the *perfect participle*.

435. In form, past participles differ according as they come from

    (1) **weak verbs** or
    (2) **strong verbs**.

436. The past participle of any weak verb is identical in form with the preterite of that verb.[67]

Weak past participles, then, end in *-ed, -d, -t*, according as the preterite shows one or another of these terminations.

Thus, the **preterite** tense of the verb *stretch* is *stretched*; the **past participle** is also *stretched*.

> The rascal *stretched* a cord across the road.
> [Here *stretched* is the preterite, and has *rascal* for its subject.]

> I saw a cord *stretched* across the road.
> [Here *stretched* has no subject. It is a past participle and belongs to the noun *cord*, the object of *saw*.]

PRESENT	PRETERITE	PAST PARTICIPLE
He *kills* the dog.	He *killed* the dog.	The dog was *killed*.
He *spends* money.	He *spent* money.	Much money was *spent*.
He *meets* a friend.	He *met* a friend.	He was *met* by a friend.
He *buys* iron.	He *bought* iron.	Iron was *bought*.
The terrier *catches* rats.	The terrier *caught* rats.	The rat was *caught*.
He *shuts* the door.	He *shut* the door.	The door was *shut*.

The past participle, it will be seen, follows the weak preterite through all its irregularities.

The student may, at first, be troubled to distinguish between the preterite tense and the past participle in those verbs which have these two forms

---

The **past participle** has the idea of **past time** or **completed action**.

Past participle is also called **perfect participle**.

Look for verbs ending in *-ed, -d, or -t*.

Remember, past participles **do not** have a subject. Preterite (past) tense verbs do have a subject.

---

[67] The only exceptions to this rule are trivial variations in spelling.

alike, but he can make no mistake if he remembers that the past participle can never have a subject, and the preterite tense must always have a subject.

Chapter 103 Exercises

I.

Write in three columns, as in Section 436:
(1) the sentences that follow;
(2) the same sentences with the verbs changed to the preterite;
(3) sentences containing the past participle of each verb preceded by *was* or *has*. Thus,

PRESENT	PRETERITE	PAST PARTICIPLE
John *ties* his horse.	John *tied* his horse.	John's horse was *tied*. OR John has *tied* his horse.

1. The farmer sows his seed.
2. The maid sets the table.
3. The dog obeys his master.
4. The pupil answers the question.
5. The girl reads her book.
6. He spends his money freely.
7. He feels sorry for his faults.

II.

Give the present, the preterite, and the past participle of:

Quarrel, accept, tell, offer, hit, drown, flee, start, arrive, hear, convey, sleep, obey, cut, delay, sweep, sell, stay, feel, make, deal, beseech, creep, bring, shut, cast, keep, lose, catch, cost, leave.

CHAPTER 104
Past Participle of Strong Verbs

437. The past participle of strong verbs, like the preterite, shows a change from the vowel of the present tense.

> **Past participles** of strong verbs change their vowel.
>
> ❧
>
> **Past participles** of some verbs are the same as the preterite past tense. Check the list in the appendix to learn the forms.

All strong verbs had originally the ending *-en (-n)* in the past participle, but this ending has been lost in many verbs.

PRESENT INDICATIVE	PRETERITE INDICATIVE	PAST PARTICIPLE
He *rides*.	He *rode*.	He has *ridden*.
He *forgets*.	He *forgot*.	It is *forgotten*.
He *breaks* the stick.	He *broke* the stick.	The stick is *broken*.
He *sinks*.	He *sank*.	They *have sunk*.
He *begins*.	He *began* the game.	The game is *begun*.
He *digs* a pit.	He *dug* a pit.	The pit is *dug*.
He *finds* gold.	He *found* gold.	The gold was *found*.

The past participle without ending is sometimes identical in form with the preterite. The forms show great variety and must be learned by practice.

438. The strong past participles have suffered many changes of form, even in comparatively modern English. New forms have come up and been in fashion for a while, only to disappear from accepted usage, and old forms have sometimes been revived and have made good their position in the language.

Thus, the only past participle of *write* now in good use is *written*, which is really a very old form. A hundred years ago, however, *wrote* was an accepted form, and two hundred years ago *writ* was perfectly good. Hence, whereas we can say only "I have *written* a letter," our ancestors could say "I have *written* a letter," "I have *writ* a letter," or "I have *wrote* a letter."

Chapter 104 Exercises

Errors in the forms of the preterite and the past participle are very common among careless speakers. Most of the erroneous forms now heard were once in good use, but this does not make them correct now.[68]

I.

Write in three columns, as in Section 437,

(1) the sentences that follow;

(2) the same sentences with the verbs changed to the preterite;

(3) sentences containing the past participle of each verb preceded by *was* or *has*. Thus,

PRESENT	PRETERITE	PAST PARTICIPLE
Jack *wears* no hat.	Jack *wore* no hat.	No hat was *worn* by Jack.
		OR
		Jack has *worn* no hat.

1. Nobody knows the truth of the matter.
2. Henry writes to his mother every day.
3. The arrow strikes the target near the center.
4. The explosion throws down the wall.
5. January 1, 1901, begins a new century.
6. The boy stands on the burning deck.
7. A great banquet takes place tonight.
8. The old man sits in the sun.
9. The Mexican swings the lasso round his head.
10. Johnson swims in the lake every day.

II.

Make sentences containing

    (1) the preterite and

    (2) the past participle (preceded by *have* or *has*) of:

(a) Begin, drink, ring, run, shrink, sing, sink, spring, swim.

(b) Bear, bite, break, choose, drive, eat, fall, forget, freeze, hide, ride, shake, speak, steal, swear, take, tear, wear.

---

[68] See the appendix for the correct modern forms.

CHAPTER 105
Modifiers and Object of Infinitive or Participle

439. Infinitives and participles, like other verb forms, may be modified by adverbs or adverbial phrases.

> *To walk briskly* is good exercise.
> He ordered the company *to march forward at once.*
> The constable, *running with all his speed*, was scarcely able to overtake the thief.
> The carriage, *driven rapidly*, was soon out of sight.

440. An infinitive or a participle, like any other verb form, may take an object if its meaning allows.

> I wish *to find* gold.
> *To rouse* a *lion* is a dangerous game.
> Sudden a thought came like a full-blown rose,
>   *Flushing* his *brow.*
> We could see a woman *pulling* a small *boat.*

441. No word of any kind should be inserted between *to* and the infinitive.[69]

RIGHT		WRONG
I will try *to inform him thoroughly* in regard to this matter.		I will try *to thoroughly inform him* in regard to this matter.
Creditably to perform one's task is not always easy. Or, *To perform* one's task *creditably* is not always easy.	NOT	*To creditably perform* one's task is not always easy.

> **Adverbs or adverbial phrases** may modify infinitives and participles.
>
> ❧
>
> Infinitives and participles may have an **object**.
>
> ❧
>
> Do not insert any words between the preposition *to* and the infinitive.

---

[69] This rule of order is in strict accordance with the best usage, although it is habitually neglected by careless writers and sometimes deliberately violated by good writers and speakers who choose to defy it.

Chapter 105 Exercises

I.

In each of the following sentences insert an adverb or adverbial phrase to modify the infinitive.

1. I resolved to return to England.
2. His orders to me were to keep him in sight.
3. My first thought was to flee.
4. To rush towards her was my impulse.
5. What right have you, then, to upbraid me for having told you the truth?
6. The young man began to spend his money.

II.

Pick out the participles, and tell what noun or pronoun each modifies.
Mention all the modifiers and objects of the participles.

1. He occupied a farm of seventy acres, situated on the skirts of that pretty little village.
2. Mine was a small chamber, near the top of the house, fronting on the sea.
3. The listening crowd admire the lofty sound!
4. This life, which seems so fair,
   Is like a bubble blown up in the air.
5. Still is the toiling hand of Care;
   The panting herds repose.
6. His bridge was only loose planks laid upon large trestles.
7. She had a little room in the garret, where the maids heard her walking and sobbing at night.
8. The kind creature retreated into the garden, overcome with emotions.
9. The colonel, strengthened with some troops of horse from Yorkshire, comes up to the bridge.
10. Exhausted, I lay down at the base of the pyramid.

CHAPTER 106
Principal Parts of Verbs

442. Three forms of the verb are of so much consequence that they are called the principal parts.[70] These are:

(1) the first person singular of the present;
(2) the first person singular of the preterite;
(3) the past participle.

PRESENT	PRETERITE	PAST PARTICIPLE
I act	I acted	acted
I kill	I killed	killed
I bring	I brought	brought
I find	I found	found
I ride	I rode	ridden

In giving the principal parts of a verb the pupil may be sure of getting the past participle right if he remembers that it is always the form which we use after *I have.*

Thus, [*I have*] *found, ridden, brought.*

Chapter 106 Exercise

From the sentences in chapter 105, Exercise II, complete the following:

(1) Pick out all the presents and preterites and mention the subject of each.
(2) Select all the present and past participles and mention the substantive which each modifies.
(3) Tell whether the verb is weak or strong in each case.
(4) Give the principal parts of every verb.

---

[70] The importance of the present and the preterite is at once clear. Their difference in form serves to distinguish the time of actions. The importance of the past participle will appear in the chapters on the passive voice and the compound tenses.

CHAPTER 107
Verbal Nouns Ending in *-ing* (Gerunds)

443. Not all words that end in *-ing* are participles. There is a large class of **verbal nouns** that have this ending. Indeed, from any ordinary verb in the language a noun ending in *-ing* may be formed just as readily as a present participle.

> **Not all *-ing*** words are **participles.** Some are **verbal nouns.**
>
> ❧
>
> Present participles are **not** used as nouns.
>
> ❧
>
> If an *-ing* word is functioning as a noun in a sentence, it is a **verbal noun.**
>
> ❧
>
> **Verbal nouns** are also known as **gerunds.**

The distinction between **verbal nouns** ending in *-ing* and **present participles** is easy to make; for the present participle is never used as a noun. Consequently, if a word ending in *-ing* is the **subject** of a sentence, or the **object** of a verb or preposition, or stands in any other **noun** construction, it cannot be a participle.

444. The distinction just indicated may be seen in the following sentences:

> **Participle**
> *Walking* up the street, I met an old friend.

> **Verbal Noun**
> *Walking* is good exercise.
> I like *walking* on account of its good effect upon my health.
> He gave much attention to *walking*, because he thought it made him feel better.

In the first of these examples we see at once that *walking* is a **participle**, not a **noun**. It expresses action but has no subject, and it modifies the subject of the sentence, *I*, thus having the use of an adjective.

In the other examples, however, *walking* is not a participle, but a **noun**. In the second sentence it is the **subject**; in the third it is the **direct object** of the verb *like*; in the fourth it is the **object** of the preposition **to**.

445. **From nearly every English verb there may be formed a verbal noun ending in *-ing*. Such nouns are identical in form with present participles, but they have the construction, not of participles, but of nouns.**

NOTE: In the oldest form of English the present participle ended, not in *-ing* but in *-ende*, and the number of nouns in *-ing* was limited. At a later period a confusion of endings came about, so that there was no longer any distinction in form between verbal nouns in *-ing* and present participles. As a result of this confusion, nouns in *-ing* multiplied greatly in number, so that in modern English we can form one from almost any verb at pleasure.

446. Verbal nouns ending in *-ing* partake of the nature of the verbs from which they are formed. Hence:

1. Verbal nouns ending in *-ing* may take a direct or an indirect object if their meaning allows. Thus,

> *Giving them money* does not satisfy them.

Here the verbal noun *giving*, which is the subject of the sentence, takes both a direct object (*money*) and an indirect object (*them*), as the verb *give* might do.

2. A verbal noun ending in *-ing* may take an adverbial modifier.

> Eating *hastily* injures the health.

Here the verbal noun *eating* is the subject of the verb *injures*. It is, however, modified by the adverb *hastily*, precisely as if it were a verb.

But verbal nouns ending in *-ing*, like other nouns, may be modified by **adjectives**.

Thus, in the last example we may substitute the adjective *hasty* for the adverb *hastily* without changing the construction of the verbal noun *eating*.

ADVERBIAL MODIFIER	ADJECTIVE MODIFIER
Eating *hastily* injures the health.	*Hasty* eating injures the health.

447. That nouns ending in *-ing* are real nouns may be proved by substituting ordinary nouns in their places.

On thinking this matter over.	On consideration of this matter.
After resting.	After a rest.
By experimenting.	By an experiment.

448. Verbal nouns ending in *-ing* are similar in some of their constructions to infinitives used as nouns (Section 425). Thus,

---

Sidebar:

Verbal nouns may take a direct or indirect object.

Verbal nouns may be modified by **adverbs** *or* **adjectives**.

Verbal nouns are similar to infinitives used as nouns.

	INFINITIVE AS NOUN	VERBAL NOUN IN -ING
Subject	*To breathe* is natural to animals.	*Breathing* is natural to animals.
Subject and predicate nominative	*To see* is *to believe.*	*Seeing* is *believing.*

NOTE: Verbal nouns ending in *-ing* are sometimes called *infinitives* and sometimes *gerunds*.

Chapter 107 Exercise

In the following sentences pick out all the words ending in *-ing* and tell whether they are present participles or verbal nouns. Give your reasons.

1. Books, painting, fiddling, and shooting were my amusements.
2. We are terribly afraid of Prince Eugene's coming.
3. Upon hearing my name, the old gentleman stepped up.
4. After I had resided at college seven years, my father died and left me — his blessing.
5. The neighing of the generous horse was heard.
6. Joseph still continued a huge clattering with the poker.
7. Then came the question of paying.
8. The day had been spent by the king in sport and feasting, and by the conspirators in preparing for their enterprise.
9. He first learned to write by imitating printed books.
10. Here we had the pleasure of breaking our fast on the leg of an old hare, and some broiled crows.

CHAPTER 108
Future Tense

449. English verbs, as we have seen in chapter 90, have special forms of **inflection** to express **present** time and **past** time. Thus, *I find* and *I act* are in the present tense; *I found* and *I acted* are in the preterite tense.

> English forms the **future tense** with a **verb phrase**, not an inflectional change.
>
> ❧
>
> **Auxiliary verbs** are also known as **helping verbs.**
>
> ❧
>
> **Future tense** is formed with the **helping verb** *shall* or *will* combined with the **infinitive form** of the verb, **without** the *to* preposition.

Many languages have also an inflectional form for the **future tense**. In English, however, there is no such future inflection, and we are obliged, therefore, to use a **verb phrase** to express future time. Thus,

> I *shall visit* Chicago next month.
> You *will find* your horse in the stable.
> The ship *will sail* on Monday.
> We *shall march* up Main Street.

In these sentences the verb phrases *shall visit, will find, will sail,* and *shall march,* manifestly refer to **future time**. Each of them consists of an **auxiliary** verb (*shall* or *will*) followed by an **infinitive** (*visit, find, sail, march*) without the infinitive sign *to*.

450. The English future tense is a verb phrase consisting of the auxiliary[71] verb *shall* or *will*, followed by the infinitive without *to*.

451. A correct use of *shall* and *will* in the future tense is a matter of some difficulty.

The following table shows the proper form of the **future tense** for each of the three persons (1) in **assertions** and (2) in **questions**:

FUTURE TENSE

ASSERTIONS (DECLARATIVE)

SINGULAR NUMBER	PLURAL NUMBER
1. I shall fall.	We shall fall.
2. Thou wilt fall.	You will fall.
3. He will fall.	They will fall.

---

[71] Editor's note: Remember that today auxiliary verbs are commonly called helping verbs.

FUTURE TENSE

QUESTIONS (INTERROGATIVE)

SINGULAR NUMBER	PLURAL NUMBER
1. Shall I fall?	Shall we fall?
2. Shalt thou fall?	Shall you fall?
3. Will he fall?	Will they fall?

452. Very common errors are the use of *will* for *shall*,

> (1) in the **first person** in **assertions** and **questions** and
> (2) in the **second person** in **questions**.

In the following sentences the first person of the future tense is correctly formed:

I *shall fall.*	*Shall* I *fall?*
I *shall break* my arm.	*Shall* I *break* my arm?
We *shall die.*	*Shall* we *die?*

The italicized phrases express merely the action of the verb in **future** time. They do not indicate any **willingness** or **desire** on the part of the subject.

Contrast the following sentences, in which a verb phrase consisting of *I will* and the infinitive is used:

> I *will lend* you five dollars.
> I *will speak*, in spite of you.
> I *will* not *permit* such disorder.
> I *will do* my very best.
> I *will conquer* or die.

In these sentences the italicized phrases do not (as in the previous examples of *I shall*) express the action of the verb in future time. They express the **present willingness** or **desire** or **determination** of the subject to do something in the future.

Hence such verb phrases with *will* in the first person are not forms of the future tense. They are special verb phrases expressing willingness or desire.

453. In the first person *shall*, not *will*, is the auxiliary of the future tense in both assertions and questions. It denotes simple futurity, without expressing willingness, desire, or determination.

Be careful! It is easy to confuse *shall* and *will*.

ello

First person singular future tense should be formed with *shall* unless the speaker wants to express **desire** or **determination**, in which case *will* is used.

ello

Shall=action in future time

ello

Will=desire or determination for an action

Will in the first person is used in promising, threatening, consenting, and expressing resolution. It never denotes simple futurity.

> _I will give_ you a thousand dollars to do this. [Promise]
> _I will shoot_ the first man that runs. [Threat]
> _I will accompany_ you, since you wish it. [Consent]
> _I will fight_ it out on this line if it takes all summer. [Resolution]

454. _I'll_ and _we'll_ stand for _I will_ and _we will_, and are proper only when _I will_ and _we will_ would be correct. They can never stand for _I shall_ and _we shall_.

455. **The use of _will_ for _shall_ in the first person of the future is a common but gross error. Thus,**

> We _will_ all die some day.
> [Wrong, unless what one means is "We are determined to die." Say: "We _shall_."]

> I _will_ be glad to help you.
> [Say: "I _shall_ be glad."]

Such expressions as _I shall be glad, I shall he willing, I shall be charmed to do this_, express willingness not by means of _shall_ but in the adjectives _glad, willing, charmed_. To say "I will be glad to do this," then, would be wrong, for it would be to express volition twice. Such a sentence could only mean "_I am determined_ to be glad to do this."

456. **In the second person _shall you?_ not _will you?_ is the proper form of the future tense in questions.**

Will you? always denotes willingness, consent, or determination, and never simple futurity.

> FUTURE TENSE (simple futurity).

> _Shall_ you _vote_ for Jackson? [THAT IS, Are you going to vote for him as a matter of fact?]
> _Shall_ you _try_ to win the prize?
> _Shall_ you _go_ to Paris in June or in July?

> VERB PHRASE DENOTING WILLINGNESS, ETC.

> _Will_ you _lend_ me ten dollars as a favor?
> _Will_ you _try_ to write better?
> _Will_ you _insist_ on this demand?

Be careful! It is easy to confuse _shall_ and _will_.

❧

Shall you? is the proper form of **future tense in second person** questions.

❧

Shall=action in future time

❧

Will=desire or determination for an action

273

457. *Shall* in the **second** and **third persons** is not the sign of the **future** tense in declarative sentences.

It is used in **commanding, promising, threatening,** and **expressing resolution,** the volition being that of the speaker. Thus,

> Thou *shalt* not steal. [Command]
> You *shall* have a dollar if you run this errand. [Promise]
> You *shall* be punished if you defy me. [Threat]
> He *shall* be punished if he defies me. [Threat]
> You *shall* never see him again. [Determination]
> He *shall* leave the house instantly. [Determination]

Be careful! It is easy to confuse *shall* and *will.*

&.

In **second** and **third** persons, *will* is used for **future action.** *Shall* is used for **commands.**

Chapter 108 Exercises

I.

Express the thought in each of the following sentences by means of a verb phrase with *will* or *shall*.

1. I am determined to learn my lesson. (*I will?* or *I shall?*)
2. I am willing to accompany you. (*Will* or *shall?*)
3. You are sure to fall if you climb that tree. (*You will* or *you shall?*)
4. I am sure to fall if I climb that tree. (*I will* or *I shall?*)
5. He is not to go home till he has learned his lesson. (*He will not* or *he shall not?*)
6. We agree to lend you fifty dollars. (*We will lend* or *we shall lend?*)
7. We are going to lend you fifty dollars, as a matter of fact. (*We will* or *we shall?*)
8. We are determined to find the rascal who stole our dog.
9. We are certain to succeed in the search.
10. Columbus cannot fail to discover land if he sails on.
11. You are resolved to win this game, I see.
12. Are you willing to help me? *(Will you?* or *Shall you?)*
13. Are you to be punished? *(Will you?* or *Shall you?)*
14. Are we to be punished? *(Will we?* or *Shall we?)*

II.

Fill the blanks with *shall* or *will* as the sense requires. Give your reason for selecting one or the other word. In some cases either may be used.

1. I _____ lose my train if I stay any longer.
2. I _____ be tired to death by night.
3. We _____ break through the ice if we are not careful.
4. We _____ try to do our duty.
5. We _____ not be guilty of such a crime.
6. We _____ give you what you need.
7. I _____ send a letter to him at once, since you wish it.
8. "I _____ drown!" cried the poor fellow, who was struggling in the water.
    "Nobody _____ help me!"
9. He _____ misspell his words, in spite of all I can say.
10. They _____ not be captured if I can help it.
11. They _____ catch nothing if they fish in that stream.
12. I _____ catch one fish if I have to stay here all day.
13. I _____ catch cold in this carriage.
14. I _____ ride as fast as I can.

CHAPTER 109
Passive Voice[72]

458. We have already studied the difference between the **active** and the **passive** voice of verbs (chapter 41).

459. A verb is said to be in the active voice when it represents its subject as the doer of an act.

> Thomas *struck* John.
> The sleeping fox *catches* no poultry.
> The wave *washed* him overboard.

460. A verb is said to be in the passive voice when it represents its subject not as the doer of an action, but as receiving an action.

> John *was struck* by Thomas.
> The goose *was caught* by the fox.
> He *was washed* overboard by the wave.

461. In English there is no single verb form for the passive voice. Hence the **passive voice** must be expressed by a **verb phrase**, as in the examples above.

462. The passive voice of a verb is expressed by a verb phrase made by prefixing some form of the copula (*is, was,* etc.) to the past participle of the verb.

Thus in the second example in Section 460, the passive is expressed by *was caught,* a phrase consisting of

> (1) the **copula** *was* and
> (2) *caught,* the **past participle** of the verb *catch.*

463. In this way a verb may have passive forms for all tenses of the **indicative mood.**

To form the **passive voice**, a verb phrase is formed with a form of the **copula *to be*** with the **past participle** form of the verb.

❧

All **indicative mood verb tenses** may be put into the **passive form.**

---

[72] Here chapter 41 should be reviewed.

ACTIVE VOICE	PASSIVE VOICE

PRESENT TENSE

SINGULAR NUMBER

1. I strike.	I am struck.
2. Thou strikest.	Thou art struck.
3. He strikes.	He is struck.

PLURAL NUMBER

1. We strike.	We are struck.
2. You strike.	You are struck.
3. They strike.	They are struck.

PRETERITE [PAST] TENSE

SINGULAR NUMBER

1. I struck.	I was struck.
2. Thou struckest (*or* didst strike).	Thou wast (*or* wert) struck.
3. He struck.	He was struck.

PLURAL NUMBER

1. We struck.	We were struck.
2. You struck.	You were struck.
3. They struck.	They were struck.

FUTURE TENSE

SINGULAR NUMBER

1. I shall strike.	I shall be struck.
2. Thou wilt strike.	Thou wilt be struck.
3. He will strike.	He will be struck.

PLURAL NUMBER

1. We shall strike.	We shall be struck.
2. You will strike.	You will be struck.
3. They will strike.	They will be struck.

In modern usage, the second person singular pronoun *thou* is no longer used.

In its place, the second person **plural** pronoun *you* is used.

While *you* is applied in a singular use, the plural **form** of *you* is always used.

❧

For instance, one would never say, "You strikest," "You struckest," or "You wilt strike."

Instead, one always uses the plural form, "You strike," "You struck," and "You will strike."

Chapter 109 Exercises

I.

Find the passives. Give tense, person, and number. Mention the subject of each.

1. The spears are uplifted; the matches are lit.
2. Burton was staggered by this news.
3. Thus was Corinth lost and won.
4. Five hundred carpenters had been set at work.
5. Old Simon is carried to his cottage door.
6. You will be surprised at her good spirits.
7. George Brand was ushered into the little drawing room.
8. We shall be hit by the sharpshooters.
9. The house had been struck by lightning.
10. The art of writing had just been introduced into Arabia.
11. They are bred up in the principles of honor and justice.
12. He was carried away captive by the Indians.
13. The alarm bell will be rung when the foe appears.
14. For my own part, I swam as Fortune directed me, and was pushed forward by wind and tide.
15. Thus the emperor's great palace was built.
16. The stranger was surrounded, pinioned with strong fetters, and hurried away to the prison of the great tower.
17. Some of the cargo had been damaged by the sea water.
18. Our blows were dealt at random.
19. Nothing will be gained by hurry.
20. I shall be surprised if he succeeds.
21. The orchards were hewn down.
22. Panama was captured by Morgan, the buccaneer.
23. The bridge will be swept away by the flood.
24. My efforts had been rewarded with success.
25. The bank was robbed last night.

II.

Use in sentences some passive form of each of the following verbs:

> Delay, devour, pierce, set, send, bring, betray, fulfill, declare, conduct, guide, spend, read, feel, catch, sink, cut, find, steal, drink, ring.

CHAPTER 110
Active and Passive

Sentences with **transitive verbs** may be changed from **active to passive voice.**

❧

The **object** becomes the **subject.**

❧

Sentences with **intransitive verbs** may **not** be changed from active to passive voice.

464. Any sentence in which the verb of the predicate is **transitive** may be changed from the **active** to the **passive** form. Thus,

> ACTIVE   The dog *chased* the boy.
> PASSIVE   The boy *was chased* by the dog.

(1) The verb *(chased)* is changed from the **active voice** to the **passive** (becoming *was chased*).

(2) *Boy,* the **object** of the **active** verb *chased,* becomes the **subject** of the **passive** verb *was chased.*

(3) *Dog,* the subject of the active verb, becomes, in the passive sentence, a part of the complete predicate, and is the object of the preposition *by.*

465. In turning a sentence from the active voice to the passive, the object of the active verb becomes the subject of the passive.

466. An intransitive verb can have no passive voice.

Since it is the very nature of the passive voice that the object of the action should appear as the subject of the sentence, an intransitive verb, which takes no object, cannot be used in the passive.

Chapter 110 Exercises

I.

Change the active verbs to the passive voice. Note that the object of the active verb becomes the subject of the passive.

1. Theseus killed the Minotaur.
2. Fulton invented steamboats.
3. The President will veto the bill.
4. Dampier explored the coast of Australia.
5. The Normans conquered the Saxons.
6. A band of Indians attacked Deerfield.
7. A storm has disabled the fleet.
8. The miner had found gold in the bed of the stream.
9. John Greenleaf Whittier wrote "Snow-Bound."
10. The sun will soon melt the snow.

11. Edison invented the incandescent electric light.
12. The Romans conquered Spain.
13. The French settled Louisiana.
14. The Dutch colonized New York.
15. Bruce defeated the English at Bannockburn.
16. An English court declared Sir William Wallace guilty of treason.
17. Henry V defeated the French at Agincourt.
18. The Indians outwitted General Braddock.
19. Braddock had scorned Washington's advice.
20. The Angles and Saxons invaded and subdued Britain.

II.

Analyze the sentences from chapter 109, Exercise I, reproduced below.

1. The spears are uplifted; the matches are lit.
2. Burton was staggered by this news.
3. Thus was Corinth lost and won.
4. Five hundred carpenters had been set at work.
5. Old Simon is carried to his cottage door.
6. You will be surprised at her good spirits.
7. George Brand was ushered into the little drawing room.
8. We shall be hit by the sharpshooters.
9. The house had been struck by lightning.
10. The art of writing had just been introduced into Arabia.
11. They are bred up in the principles of honor and justice.
12. He was carried away captive by the Indians.
13. The alarm bell will be rung when the foe appears.
14. For my own part, I swam as Fortune directed me, and was pushed forward by wind and tide.
15. Thus the emperor's great palace was built.
16. The stranger was surrounded, pinioned with strong fetters, and hurried away to the prison of the great tower.
17. Some of the cargo had been damaged by the sea water.
18. Our blows were dealt at random.
19. Nothing will be gained by hurry.
20. I shall be surprised if he succeeds.
21. The orchards were hewn down.
22. Panama was captured by Morgan, the buccaneer.
23. The bridge will be swept away by the flood.
24. My efforts had been rewarded with success.
25. The bank was robbed last night.

CHAPTER 111
Complete or Compound Tenses

These **compound verb tenses** are formed by a **helping verb** plus the **past participle**.

❧

Perfect tense:
have (hast, has)

Pluperfect (Past Perfect):
had (hadst)

Future Perfect Tense:
shall have

Perfect Participle:
having

Perfect Infinitive:
to have

Passive Voice: The helping verb *been* is combined with the tenses above.

467. **Completed action** is denoted by special **verb phrases** made by prefixing to the **past participle** some form of the auxiliary *have.*

These are called the **complete** or **compound tenses.**

468. **The perfect tense denotes that the action of the verb is complete at the time of speaking. It is formed by prefixing *have (hast, has)* to the past participle.**

> I *have eaten* my breakfast.
> He *has filled* his pockets with apples.

469. **The pluperfect (or past perfect) tense denotes that the action was completed at some point in past time. It is formed by prefixing *had (hadst)* to the past participle.**

> When I reached the pier, the ship *had sailed.*
> After the bell *had rung* three times, the session began.

470. **The future perfect tense denotes that the action will be completed at some point of future time. It is formed by prefixing the future tense of *have (shall have,* etc.) to the past participle.**

> The ship will sail before I *shall have reached* the pier.

The future perfect tense is rare except in very formal writing.

471. A verb phrase made by prefixing *having* to the past participle is called the **perfect participle.**

> *Having knocked,* he waited for admittance.

472. A verb phrase made by prefixing *to have* to the past participle is called the **perfect infinitive.**

> He ought *to have studied* harder.

473. **In the passive voice of the complete tenses the past participle *been* follows the auxiliary.**

The flames *have been extinguished.*	Perfect Passive
The horse *had been driven* too hard.	Pluperfect Passive
When this happens, I *shall have been attacked* once too often.	Future Perfect Passive
He could not move, *having been crippled* by a fall.	Perfect Passive Participle
You ought *to have been* punished.	Perfect Passive Infinitive

Chapter 111 Exercise

I.

In the following sentences select all the verbs, give the tense, voice, person, and number of each, and point out the subject with which it agrees.

1. My eldest daughter had finished her Latin lessons, and my son had finished his Greek.
2. There has been a heavy thunderstorm this afternoon.
3. A multitude of humming birds had been attracted thither.
4. Our men had besieged some fortified house near Oxford.
5. I really have had enough of fighting.
6. All shyness and embarrassment had vanished.
7. The great tree has been undermined by winter floods.
8. He had lost his way in the pine woods.
9. Thousands had sunk on the ground overpowered.
10. A storm of mingled rain and snow had come on.
11. We had left our two servants behind us at Calais.
12. The patience of Scotland had found an end at last.
13. His passion has cast a mist before his sense.
14. The surgeon has set my arm very skillfully and well.
15. A strange golden moonlight had crept up the skies.
16. You will have finished your task by Saturday.
17. The wind has howled all day.
18. He had gasped out a few incoherent words.

II.

Pick out the infinitives and the participles. Give the tense of each infinitive (present or perfect) and of each participle (present, past, or perfect).

1. Columbus's crew had begun to despair.
2. I should like to have seen his face when he heard this news.
3. I ought to have known that the lizard was harmless.
4. 'T is better to have loved and lost
   Than never to have loved at all.
5. Having done my best, I am ready to endure whatever comes.
6. Having once suffered from the bite of a tarantula, Johnson was very much afraid even of harmless spiders.

CHAPTER 112
Progressive Verb Phrases, Part 1

Progressive Verb Phrases:

The action was on-going or progressing in the past.

&

Progressive verb phrases are formed by combining the **present participle** with the present tense form of "to be."

For example:

He *is* striking.

First person singular, present tense form of "to be" *(is)* combined with the present participle *striking.*

474. Examine the following sentences:

> I *struck* John. I *was striking* John.

In these two short sentences the predicates (*struck, was striking*) both refer to **past time,** but there is an obvious difference in their sense.

(1) The first predicate, *struck,* merely **states a fact** in past time. The form is that of the simple **preterite** tense.

(2) The second predicate, *was striking,* describes an act as **going on** or **progressing** in past time. Hence it is called the **progressive form** of the preterite tense. It is, we observe, a verb phrase made by prefixing the preterite of *be* (namely, *was*) to the present participle, *striking.*

475. **The progressive form of a tense represents the action of the verb as going on or continuing at the time referred to.**

476. **The progressive form is a verb phrase made by prefixing to the present participle some form of the verb *to be.***

He is striking.	They will be striking.
They were striking.	They have been striking.

477. The **progressive forms** of the present indicative active may be seen in the following table:

PRESENT TENSE, PROGRESSIVE FORM

SINGULAR	PLURAL
1. I am reading.	We are reading.
2. Thou art reading.	You are reading.
3. He is reading.	They are reading.

CHAPTER 113
Progressive Verb Phrases, Part 2

478. In the **passive**, the **progressive verb phrases** are made by prefixing *am being, is being, was being*, etc., to the past participle. Thus,

> I *am* always *being tormented* by this fellow.
> John *is being educated* in Germany.
> While the guard *was being changed*, the prisoner escaped.

479. Instead of the progressive form of the passive, English sometimes prefers a peculiar phrase consisting of the **verbal noun** in *-ing* preceded by some form of *be*.

Thus,

> The house *is building.*
> [Instead of: The house *is being built.*]

> Arrangements *were making* for a grand celebration.
> [Instead of: Arrangements *were being made.*]

> The book *is* now *printing.*
> [Instead of: *is* now *being printed.*]

NOTE: The word ending in *-ing* in these examples is not the present participle; it is the verbal noun in *-ing*. The construction is in fact the same as that in "I went a-fishing," "They were going a-Maying." "The old year lies a-dying," etc., in which *a* is a contraction of the preposition *on* ("I went *on* fishing"). The omission of *a-* disguises the real construction.

The use of the *-ing* phrase as a substitute for the passive is becoming less and less common, but the construction is often useful as well as elegant. Thus, if one wished to say that the building of a certain house had taken ten years, the progressive form of the passive would be intolerable:

> The house *had been being built* ten years.

But the *-ing* construction would be both neat and concise:

> The house *had been* ten years *building.*

Care should be taken, however, to avoid ambiguity. It would never do to say "The boy *was whipping,*" if one meant "The boy was *being whipped.*"

Passive **Progressive Verb Phrases:** The action was on-going or progressing in the past, in the passive voice.

❧

Passive **Progressive Verb Phrases** are formed by combining the **past participle** with *am being, is being, was being,* etc. For example:

John *is being* educated.

Is being is combined with the past participle *educated.*

Chapter 113 Exercise

Parse the verbs and verb phrases. If a form is progressive, mention the fact. Thus, in the first sentence, *were calling* is in the past tense, progressive form. (See chapter 72, additional review exercises, for instructions on how to parse a word.)

1. The church bells, with various tones, but all in harmony, were calling out and responding to one another.
2. A huge load of oak wood was passing through the gateway.
3. Many a chapel bell the hour is telling.
4. Edmund was standing thoughtfully by the fire.
5. A thick mist was gradually spreading over every object.
6. I have been walking by the river.
7. Merry it is in the good greenwood
   When the mavis and merle are singing.
   When the deer sweeps by, and the hounds are in cry,
   And the hunter's horn is ringing.
8. The morn is laughing in the sky.
9. Curly-headed urchins are gambolling before the door.

CHAPTER 114
Emphatic Verb Phrases

480. Compare the following sentences:

> I study.
> I do study.

In these two short sentences the predicates *(study, do study)* both refer to **present** time, but there is an obvious difference in their sense.

Emphatic Verb Phrases: The action is emphasized by adding the **helping verb "do"** to the **infinitive form** of the verb (without the prefix to).

&

For example:
I *do* study.
I *did* study.

Note that the helping verb *do* changes form to indicate past tense, but the infinitive form *study* remains.

> (1) The first predicate, *study*, merely **states a fact.** We recognize the form as that of the simple **present** tense.
> (2) The second predicate, *do study*, states the same fact, but with **emphasis**: "I *do* study." Hence it is called the **emphatic form** of the present tense. It is a verb phrase made by prefixing the present tense of *do* to the infinitive *study* (without the infinitive sign *to*).

Similarly we may use an emphatic preterite, "I *did* study," instead of the simple preterite "I studied."

481. The present or the preterite of a verb in the active voice may be expressed with emphasis by means of a verb phrase consisting of *do* or *did* and the infinitive without *to*.

Such a phrase is called the emphatic form of the present or the preterite tense.

482. The emphatic form is confined to the present and preterite tenses of the active voice.

NOTE: In questions and in negative sentences, the emphatic forms are used without the effect of emphasis. See Sections 64, 489, 490.

In older English the verb phrase with *do* or *did* in declarative sentences often carried no emphasis whatever, but was merely a substitute for the simple present or preterite.

Chapter 114 Exercise

Change the progressive and the emphatic forms to the ordinary tense forms. Tell which of the "emphatic" forms are *really* emphatic.

1. The wind did blow, the cloak did fly.
2. Glossy bees at noon do fieldward pass.
3. A second time did Matthew stop.
4. He did come rather earlier than had been expected.
5. She did look a little hot and disconcerted for a few minutes.
6. The dogs did bark, the children screamed,
   Up flew the windows all.
7. Our true friends do not always praise us.
8. But Knowledge to their eyes her ample page,
   Rich with the spoils of time, did ne'er unroll.
9. Beasts did leap and birds did sing,
   Trees did grow and plants did spring.
10. The noise of the wind and of the thunder did not awaken the king, for he was old and weary with his journey.
11. Why did you not tell me the news?
12. I did tell you everything that I had heard.
13. Where does Mr. Jackson live? I do not know.
14. You did give me some anxiety by your long absence.
15. Does this train go to Chicago?
16. The conductor says that it does.
17. I did not believe that Jones was guilty of intentional falsehood; but I did think that he was rather careless in his account of what took place.
18. What did he tell you about Thomas?

CHAPTER 115[73]
Imperative Mood

The form of the verb in an **imperative sentences** is called the **imperative mood.**

❧

The **imperative** of "to be" is simply **"be."** For example: *Be a man.*

❧

Imperative in **passive voice** is formed by combining *be* with a **past participle.** For example: *Be honored by your friends.*

❧

The **emphatic imperative** is formed by combining *do* with the *infinitive* (without *to*). For example: *Do go to market with me.*

483. An imperative sentence expresses a command or an entreaty in the second person.

Come here.	Go to your mother.
Love your enemies.	Forgive us our sins.

The form of the verb used in an imperative sentence is called the imperative mood.

484. The imperative mood has both voices, **active** and **passive**, but only one tense, — the **present**. It has both numbers, the **singular** and the **plural,** but only one person, the **second**. It has the same form for both the **singular** and the **plural** number.

485. In the active voice the imperative has the same form as the second person plural of the present indicative.

INDICATIVE MOOD	IMPERATIVE MOOD
(Declarative Sentences)	*(Imperative Sentences)*
You *learn* your lessons well.	*Learn* your lessons.
You *run* very fast.	*Run* home with this message.
You *waste* your time.	*Waste* nothing.

Exception. The imperative of the verb *to be* is *be.* Thus,

Be a man.	*Be* diligent in business.
Be good, and you'll be happy.	*Be* attentive.

486. In the passive voice the imperative is expressed by a verb phrase consisting of *be* and a past participle.

Be killed at your post rather than run away.
Be honored by your friends rather than by strangers.

487. The **emphatic form** of the imperative consists of the imperative *do,* followed by the infinitive without *to.*

Do go to market with me.
Do come to my house this afternoon.
Do try to be more careful.

---

[73] Here chapters 13-15 should be reviewed.

488. The subject of an imperative is seldom expressed unless it is emphatic.

The subject, when expressed, may precede the imperative: as, *you go, you read.*

In this use the subject is almost always emphasized in speaking. The construction is seldom heard except in familiar language.

In older English the subject often followed the imperative: as, *go thou, go you, hear ye.*

This use is now confined to the solemn style and to poetry.

489. In modern English the so-called emphatic form with *do* is often used when the subject of the imperative is expressed: as, — *do you go.*

In this use the emphatic force of *do* has disappeared.

490. Negative commands or entreaties are commonly expressed by means of the so-called emphatic form with *do*, which in this use has lost its emphatic force.

> *Do* not *skate* on thin ice.
> *Do* not *keep* bad company.
> *Do* not *interrupt* a conversation.
> *Do* not *talk* so idly.

The subject is very rarely expressed except in familiar language: as,

> Don't *you* believe him.
> Don't *you* do it.

491. In older English, **negative** commands and entreaties are often expressed by the simple imperative, followed by *not*. The subject, when expressed, precedes the *not.* Thus,

> *Look not* upon the wine when it is red.
> *Speak not*, but go.
> *Judge not*, that ye be not judged.
> If sinners entice thee, *consent* thou *not.*

This construction is common in the solemn style and in poetry.

> **Imperative mood** verbs rarely have a subject expressed unless it is **emphatic.**
>
> ❧
>
> In questions, *do* is used with the subject *you* expressed, but it no longer carries **emphasis.**

Chapter 115 Exercise

In each of the following imperative sentences pick out the verb. Mention the subject, when it is expressed; when not, supply it.

1. Let us have a walk through Kensington Gardens.
2. Do not forget the poor.
3. Hope not, base man, unquestioned hence to go!
4. Would ye be blest? Despise low joys, low gains.
5. Summon Colonel Atherton without a moment's delay.
6. Look up and be not afraid, but hold forth thy hand.
7. Mount ye! spur ye! skirr the plain!
8. O, listen, listen, ladies gay!
9. Toll ye the churchbell sad and slow.
10. You, Herbert and Luffness, alight,
    And bind the wounds of yonder knight.
11. Stay with us. Go not to Wittenberg.
12. Listen to the rolling thunder.
13. Call off your dogs!
14. Keep thine elbow from my side, friend.
15. Do not leave me to perish in this wilderness.
16. Saddle my horses! Call my train together.

Chapter 115 Additional Review Exercise[74]

You have now studied the inflections of the verb in the **indicative mood** (that is, in the set of forms used in most sentences) and the **imperative mood.** You are acquainted with the **present, preterite,** and **future tenses;** with the **complete tenses;** with the **infinitive** and **participle;** with the **progressive** and **emphatic verb phrases.** You have learned to distinguish **person** and **number.**

In the following passages tell all you can about the form and construction of each verb and verb phrase.

1. The more I give to thee, the more I have.
2. Comes the king back from Wales?
3. Dost thou not hear them call?

---

[74] Here chapters 90-115 should be reviewed.

4. The more we stay, the stronger grows our foe.
5. I know not, gentlemen, what you intend.
6. How long hast thou to serve, Francis?
7. A great portion of my time was passed in a deep and mournful silence.
8. The day, which had been tempestuous, was succeeded by a heavy and settled rain.
9. His courage was not staggered, even for an instant.
10. I was startled by the sound of trumpets.
11. The company was surprised to see the old man so merry, when suffering such great losses; and the mandarin himself, coming out, asked him, how he, who had grieved so much, and given way to calamity the day before, could now be so cheerful?

    "You ask me one question," cries the old man; "Let me answer by asking another: Which is the more durable, a hard thing or a soft thing; that which resists or that which makes no resistance?"

    "A hard thing, to be sure," replied the Mandarin.

    "There you are wrong," returned Shingfu. "I am now four-score years old; and, if you look in my mouth, you will find that I have lost all my teeth, but not a bit of my tongue."

CHAPTER 116
Nominative Absolute

492. Examine the following sentence:

> The general falling, the troops became discouraged.

In this sentence the noun *general* is not the **subject** or the **object** of any verb, nor is it in any other noun construction which we have so far studied.

The participle *falling* obviously belongs to *general*. **The phrase *the general falling* modifies the predicate *became discouraged*,** by giving the **time** or perhaps the **cause** of the discouragement. We might, indeed, substitute an adverbial phrase of time for this participial phrase without any material change in the sense:

> On the fall of the general the soldiers became discouraged.
> [Here *became discouraged* is modified by the phrase *on the fall of the general.*]

Other sentences illustrating this use of **nouns** and **participles** are the following:

> His friends requesting it, he surrendered his office.
> [Here the phrase *his friends requesting it* is equivalent to *because his friends requested it*: that is, it expresses **cause.**]

> The time having come, he mounted the scaffold.
> [Here the phrase *the time having come* is equivalent to *when the time had come*: that is, it expresses **time.**]

> He began to speak, the audience listening intently.
> [Here the phrase *the audience listening intently* expresses neither **time** nor **cause**, but merely one of the **circumstances** that attended the oration.]

We may, then, formulate the following rule:

493. A noun or pronoun, with a participle in agreement, may express the cause, time, or circumstances of an action.

This is called the absolute construction.

A **noun** or **pronoun,** with **a participle** in agreement, may express the **cause, time,** or **circumstances** of an action.

☙

The phrase modifies the predicate, as an adverbial phrase would.

☙

This is called the **absolute construction.**

☙

The **noun or pronoun** in an absolute construction is in the **nominative case.** It is called a **nominative absolute.**

The noun or pronoun is in the nominative case and is called a nominative absolute.

494. The **absolute** construction of the **nominative** is perfectly correct in English; but care should be taken not to use it with great frequency, since it is a loose and inexact way of designating the relations of thought, and an excessive employment of it tends to clumsiness and obscurity.[75]

495. It is not always necessary that a participle should be expressed in the nominative absolute construction. Sometimes **two substantives**, or a **substantive** and an **adjective** may be used together in this manner. In such cases, however, it is always easy to supply the participle *being* to separate the two.

Expressions of this kind are not numerous, but some of them are highly idiomatic. Thus,

> *Stephen* once *king,* anarchy reigned.
> [That is: Stephen once *being* king, or, in other words, As soon as Stephen became king.]

> The *rain over,* we ventured out.

> The *gate* once *open,* the cattle came trooping out of the yard.

> We stood silent, our *eyes full* of tears.

Chapter 116 Exercise

I.

In the following sentences point out all instances of the nominative absolute, and tell whether each expresses the time, place, or circumstance of the action.

1. Navigation was at a stop, our ships neither coming in nor going out as before.
2. Night coming on, we sought refuge from the gathering storm.
3. The song ended, she hastily relinquished her seat to another lady.
4. The house consisted of seven rooms, the dairy and cellar included.

---

[75] Students of Latin will see that the construction is of the same kind as the ablative absolute, so characteristic of Latin style. The absolute case in English was originally the dative. All dative case endings, however, disappeared, so that the dative of nouns became indistinguishable from the nominative; and hence the absolute case came to be felt as a nominative, and even pronouns (which kept a dative distinct in form from the nominative) have followed the analogy of nouns. Thus, we say "He being present, the game went on," and not "Him being present, the game went on," although *him* is the old dative of the personal pronoun *he*.

5. The resolution being thus taken, they set out the next day.
6. They had some difficulty in passing the ferry at the riverside, the ferryman being afraid of them.
7. She sat beneath the birchen tree,
   Her elbow resting on her knee.
8. The signal of battle being given with two cannon shot, we marched in order of battalia down the hill.
9. The dark lead-colored ocean lay stretched before them, its dreary expanse concealed by lowering clouds.
10. Next Anger rushed, his eyes on fire.
11. The last of these voyages not proving very fortunate, I grew weary of the sea.
12. The two Scottish generals, Macbeth and Banquo, returning victorious from this great battle, their way lay over a blasted heath.
13. The cottage was situated in a valley, the hills being for the most part crowned with rich and verdant foliage, their sides covered with vineyards and corn, and a clear, transparent rivulet murmuring along from east to west.
14. This done, the conspirators separated.
15. This being understood, the next step is easily taken.
16. This said, he picked up his pack and trudged on.

II.
Analyze the sentences in Exercise I.

CHAPTER 117
Cognate Object and Adverbial Objective

496. Some verbs that are regularly **intransitive** may be followed by a noun which resembles a direct object.

> The horse ran a *race.*
> The general smiled a sickly *smile.*
> He wept bitter *tears.*

In all these examples, the noun that follows the verb simply expresses once more, **in the form of a noun**, the action already expressed by the verb. Thus, the *race* is, to all intents and purposes, the *running* of the horse; the *tears* are the *weeping;* the *sickly smile* repeats the same idea already expressed in the verb *smiled.*

Nouns thus used are called **cognate objects.**

497. A verb that is regularly intransitive sometimes takes as a kind of object a noun whose meaning closely resembles its own.

A noun in this construction is called the cognate object of the verb and is in the objective case.[76]

The neuter pronoun *it* is used as a cognate object in such expressions as *go it, he went it,* and the like. These are colloquial or vulgar, but extremely idiomatic. The idiom was formerly much commoner than at present.

498. A **cognate object** merely repeats in some way the meaning of a verb whose **sense** is already **complete.**

A **direct object completes the meaning** of a verb by denoting that which receives or is produced by the action (see Section 156).

NOTE: A noun, or a phrase consisting of a **noun** and its modifiers, may be used as an **adverbial modifier.**

> (1) I have slept *hours.*
> (2) The man walked *miles* before he came to a house.
> (3) The messenger had been waiting *a long time.*
> (4) Robinson Crusoe remained *several years* in the island.
> (5) We rode on horseback *the whole way.*
> (6) Turn your head *this way.*

Intransitive verbs sometimes are followed by a **noun** which seems to be an object. **This is a cognate object.**

ᴁ

Cognate objects express the verb's action in the form of a noun.

ᴁ

Nouns used as the **cognate object** are in the **objective case.**

For example: The horse ran a *race.*

---

[76] *Cognate* means "related." The name is given to an object of this kind because of the close *relation* between its meaning and that of the verb.

(7) The sailor climbed the rope *hand over hand*.
(8) The plank is *two feet* wide.
(9) This rope is *several fathoms* too short.
(10) Thomas is *sixteen years* old.

In 1-7 the verbs are modified by the italicized words; in 8-10 these words modify adjectives (*wide, short, old*). A noun in this use is called an **adverbial objective.**

A noun used as an adverbial modifier is called an adverbial objective.

Chapter 117 Exercise

Pick out the cognate objects and the adverbial objectives, and parse each of them.

EXAMPLES:
Jane laughed a merry *laugh*.
Laugh: common noun, neuter gender, singular number, objective case; cognate object of the verb *laughed*.

The messenger ran three *miles*.
Miles: common noun, neuter gender, plural number, objective case; adverbial objective modifying *ran*.

1. But the skipper blew a whiff from his pipe,
   and a scornful laugh laughed he.
2. The wind blew a gale.
3. Everybody looked daggers at the intruder.
4. Speak the speech, I pray you, as I pronounce it to you
5. The hail was terrific. The sky seemed to rain stones.
6. The colonists endured oppression a long time.
7. The poet Gray worked upon his "Elegy" several years.
8. That mountain is distant five miles from this spot.
9. The soldiers marched Indian file.
10. The table is six feet long, four feet wide, and three feet high.
11. I cannot swim a yard farther.
12. The cannon carried four miles.
13. You will never accomplish anything that way.
14. The road ran a very long distance without a curve.

CHAPTER 118
Predicate Objective

499. Examine the following sentence:

> The people elected Adams president.

We observe that the transitive verb *elected* has **two objects,**

> (1) the **direct object,** *Adams,* and
> (2) a **second noun,** *president,* referring to the same person as the direct object and completing the sense of the predicate. This second noun we may call a **predicate objective.**

500. **Verbs of choosing, calling, naming, making, and thinking, may take two objects referring to the same person or thing.**

The first of these is the direct object, and the second, which completes the sense of the predicate, is called a predicate objective.

The **predicate objective** is often called the **complementary object,** because it completes the sense of the verb. It is sometimes called the **objective attribute.**

Examples may be seen in the following sentences:

> Washington called the man friend.
> The nobles made the prince their king.
> I call this headache a nuisance.
> Caesar appointed Brutus governor of a province.
> I thought him a rascal.
> The judge deemed him a criminal.
> The club chose Thomas secretary.

501. With some verbs an **adjective** may serve as a **predicate objective.** Thus,

> His rashness makes his friends *uneasy.*
> His companions thought him *gentlemanly.*
> I call such conduct *unwise.*

The fact that in these sentences the adjective stands in the same construction as the predicate objective may be seen by comparing the following examples:

Sometimes a transitive verb has two objects.

❧

The second object, which refers to the first object and completes the sense of the predicate, is a **predicate objective.**

PREDICATE OBJECTIVE	ADJECTIVE AS PREDICATE OBJECTIVE
His companions thought him a *gentleman*.	His companions thought him *gentlemanly*.
I call such conduct *folly*.	I call such conduct *unwise*.

502. **Predicate objectives** must be carefully distinguished from **nouns in apposition** with the direct object.

APPOSITIVE	PREDICATE OBJECTIVE
The pirates charged Kidd, their *captain*, with treachery.	The pirates elected Kidd *captain*.

> The **predicate objective** should not be confused with an **appositive.**
>
> ❧
>
> **A predicate objective** is needed to complete the meaning and cannot be omitted. **Appositives** may be omitted and the meaning of the sentence remains complete.

(1) In the first sentence the **appositive** *captain* is simply added to *Kidd* to **describe** Kidd. It might be omitted, without making the sense incomplete:

The pirates charged Kidd with treachery.

(2) In the second sentence the **predicate objective**, *captain*, is not a mere descriptive word, to be omitted at our pleasure. If we cut it out, the sense is incomplete.

"The pirates elected Kidd " would at once suggest the question: "Elected him *what?* Captain? or cook? or commodore?"

The **predicate objective** completes the meaning of the **verb**, forming a vital part of the statement.

NOTE: In this construction the **direct object** is, strictly speaking, the object of the **whole idea expressed by the verb and the predicate adjective or objective.** Compare "He *made* the child *quiet*" with "He *quieted* the child"; "He *made* the wall *white* " with "He *whitened* the wall." *Made quiet = quieted; made white =whitened;* and, since *child* is the object of *quieted* and *wall* the object of *whitened*, these same nouns are clearly the objects of the phrases *made quiet* and *made white*.

Chapter 118 Exercises

I.

Fill each blank with a predicate objective.

1. The boys elected Will Sampson _____ of the boat club.
2. I always thought your brother an excellent _____.
3. Do you call the man your _____?
4. The governor appointed Smith _____.
5. Everybody voted the talkative fellow a _____.
6. The pirates chose Judson _____.
7. The hunter called the animal a _____.
8. My parents named my brother _____.
9. I cannot think him such a _____.
10. The merchant's losses made him a poor _____.
11. You called my brother a _____.

II.

Fill each blank with a predicate adjective.

1. A good son makes his mother _____.
2. The jury declares the prisoner _____.
3. This noise will surely drive me _____.
4. I cannot pronounce you _____ of this accusation.
5. The sedate burghers thought the gay youngster very _____.
6. The travelers thought the river _____.
7. Our elders often think our conduct _____.
8. I call the boy _____ for his age.
9. Exercise makes us _____.
10. Nothing makes one so _____ as a good dinner.
11. Do you pronounce the prisoner _____?
12. Do you think us _____?

III.

Analyze the sentences in I and II. Your teacher may wish to have you diagram these sentences. Identify:

    (1) Whether the sentence is declarative, interrogative, imperative, or exclamatory.
    (2) The complete subject.
    (3) The complete predicate.
    (4) The simple subject.

(5) The simple predicate.

(6) The adjective modifiers.

(7) The adverb modifiers.

(8) The direct object and the transitive verb, or the predicate objective, or adjective used as predicate objective.

IV.

Pick out:

(1) transitive verbs,

(2) direct objects, and

(3) predicate objectives.

1. Pope had now declared himself a poet.
2. The people call it a backward year.
3. He called them untaught knaves.
4. He could make a small town a great city.
5. She called him the best child in the world.
6. A man must be born a poet, but he may make himself an orator.
7. Fear of death makes many a man a coward.
8. Ye call me chief.
9. The Poles always elected some nobleman their king.
10. He cared not, indeed, that the world should call him a miser; he cared not that the world should call him a churl; he cared not that the world should call him odd.

V.

The **predicate objective** becomes a **predicate nominative** when the verb is changed from the **active** voice to the **passive**.

Active Voice	Passive Voice
(Predicate Objective)	*(Predicate Nominative)*
The people elected Grant *president*.	Grant was elected *president* by the people.
I named my dog *Jack*.	My dog was named *Jack*.
They think such conduct *unwise*.	Such conduct is thought *unwise*.
The noise drove me *mad*.	I was driven *mad* by the noise.

Change the verbs in Exercises II and IV, above, to the passive voice.
What happens to the predicate objective or adjective?

CHAPTER 119[77]
Relative Pronouns

503. A **relative pronoun** introduces a subordinate clause, which it attaches to the main clause by referring directly back to a substantive in the main clause.

This substantive is called the **antecedent** of the **relative**.

504. A relative pronoun must agree with its antecedent in gender, number, and person; but its case is determined by the construction of its own clause and has nothing to do with the case of the antecedent.

505. The simple **relative pronouns** are *who, which, that, as,* and *what.*

Who and *which* are inflected as follows:

WHO	WHICH
(Singular and Plural)	*(Singular and Plural)*
Nominative: *who*	Nominative: *which*
Genitive: *whose*	Genitive: *whose*
Objective: *whom*	Objective: *which*

That, as, and *what* have no inflection. They have the same form for both nominative and objective and are not used in the genitive case.

As may be used as a relative pronoun when *such* stands in the main clause.

506. Examples of *who, which, that,* and *as,* in various constructions may be seen in the following sentences:

> He bowed to every *man whom* he met.
> Elizabeth was a *queen who* could endure no opposition.
> The *stone which* you have picked up is not gold ore.
> The *king that* succeeded Henry V was a mere child.
> The *house that* I bought last week has burned down.
> Such *money as* I have is at your service.

> **Relative pronouns:**
> *who*
> *which*
> *that*
> *as*
> *what*
>
> ❧
>
> **Relative pronouns** *who* **and** *which* change their form depending on its construction in the sentence. They are **inflected.**

---

[77] Here chapter 51 should be reviewed.

507. *Who* is either masculine or feminine, *which* is neuter, *that* and *as* are of all three genders.

The sentences in Section 506 illustrate the agreement of the relative with its antecedent in **gender**.

508. The plural of the relative pronouns does not differ in form from the singular. If the relative is the subject of a verb, however, the verb form must be singular or plural according as the relative pronoun refers to a singular or a plural antecedent.

Hence the rule that a relative pronoun must agree with its antecedent in **number** is of importance.

> The boy *who comes* to school late will be punished. [Singular]
> All the boys *who come* to school late will be punished. [Plural]

509. Relative pronouns have no distinction of form for the three persons; but they are regarded as agreeing in person with their antecedents.

Hence a verb which has for its subject a relative pronoun is in the same person as the antecedent of the relative. Thus,

> Why do you attack *me, who am* your friend? [First Person]
> It is *you who are* to blame. [Second Person]
> *He who speaks* to them shall die. [Third Person]

510. The case of a relative pronoun has nothing to do with its antecedent, but depends on the construction of its own clause.

> The general *who* was appointed immediately resigned.
> [*Who* is in the nominative, being the subject of *was appointed*.]

> He appointed the general, *who* immediately resigned.
> [*Who* is in the nominative, being the subject of *resigned*, although
>   its antecedent *general* is in the objective case.]

> These men *whom* you see standing about are waiting for work.
> [*Whom* is in the objective case, being the direct object of *see*. The
>   antecedent, *men*, is, on the contrary, in the nominative.]

511. A relative pronoun in the objective case is often omitted.

RELATIVE PRONOUN EXPRESSED	RELATIVE PRONOUN OMITTED
The stranger bowed to everyman *whom* he met.	The stranger bowed to every man he met.
The dog *that* you bought of Tom has run away.	The dog you bought of Tom has run away.
The listener heard every word *that* he said.	The listener heard every word he said.

This omission of the relative is common in conversation and in an easy and informal style of writing. In case of doubt, express the pronoun.

In analyzing a sentence in which the relative is omitted, it should be supplied.

Chapter 119 Exercises

I.

From chapter 51, Exercise III, (reproduced below) pick out all the relative pronouns:

> (1) tell their number, person, and gender;
> (2) designate their antecedents;
> (3) explain their case.

1. A sharp rattle was heard on the window, which made the children jump.
2. The small torch that he held sent forth a radiance by which suddenly the whole surface of the desert was illuminated.
3. He that has most time has none to lose.
4. Gray rocks peeped from amidst the lichens and creeping plants which covered them as with a garment of many colors.
5. The enclosed fields, which were generally forty feet square, resembled so many beds of flowers.
6. They that reverence too much old times are but a scorn to the new.
7. The morning came which was to launch me into the world, and from which my whole succeeding life has, in many important points, taken its coloring.
8. Ten guineas, added to about two which I had remaining from my pocket money, seemed to me sufficient for an indefinite length of time.
9. He is the freeman whom the truth makes free.
10. There was one philosopher who chose to live in a tub.

11. Conquerors are a class of men with whom, for the most part, the world could well dispense.
12. The light came from a lamp that burned brightly on the table.
13. The sluggish stream through which we moved yielded sullenly to the oar.
14. The place from which the light proceeded was a small chapel.
15. The warriors went into battle clad in complete armor, which covered them from top to toe.
16. She seemed as happy as a wave
    That dances on the sea.
17. He sang out a long, loud, and canorous peal of laughter, that might have wakened the Seven Sleepers.
18. Thou hadst a voice whose sound was like the sea.
19. Many of Douglas's followers were slain in the battle in which he himself fell.

II.

Review your work in chapter 51, Exercise II. Give your reason for using one relative rather than another. (The sentences are reproduced below.)

1. The house _____ stands yonder belongs to Colonel Carton.
2. Are you the man _____ saved my daughter from drowning?
3. The sailor's wife gazed at the stately ship _____ was taking her husband away from her.
4. A young farmer, _____ name was Judkins, was the first to enlist.
5. Nothing _____ you can do will help me.
6. The horses _____ belong to the squire are famous trotters.
7. James Adams is the strongest man _____ I have ever seen.
8. My friend, _____ we had overtaken on his way down town, greeted us cheerfully.
9. Behold the man _____ the king delighteth to honor!
10. That is the captain _____ ship was wrecked last December.

III.

Make twelve sentences containing the pronouns:

> who, whom, which, whose, of which, that, as

IV.

Fill each blank with the proper form of the copula (*am, is, are*). Note the person and number of the antecedent in each sentence, and observe that the relative must agree with it.

1. You find fault with *me,* who _____ not to blame.
2. *You* who _____ present are all members of the society.
3. *We* who _____ in good health should have sympathy for the sick.
4. *He* who _____ fond of good books will never feel lonely.
5. *Those* of you who _____ ready may start at once.

6. *I, who* _____ a poor swimmer, shall never win the prize.
7. *Nobody* who _____ young ever really expects old age.
8. *Such* of us as _____ aware of the facts have little doubt of the man's innocence.

CHAPTER 120
Gender of Relatives

> The **relative pronoun** *which* is used to refer to living creatures but not people, regardless of gender.
>
> ❧
>
> The **genitive relative pronoun** *whose* is used to refer to all living creatures and people, regardless of gender.
>
> ❧
>
> The **relative pronoun** *which* is usually preferred to refer to non-animal objects.

512. The relative *which* is commonly used in referring to the lower animals unless these are regarded as persons. This is true even when *he* or *she* is used of the same animals (see chapter 43). Thus,

> The horse *which* I bought yesterday is a good trotter. *He* can go a mile in less than three minutes.

The genitive form *whose* is freely used of all living creatures, whether they would be designated by the pronoun *he*, by *she*, or by *it*. Thus,

> The *lady whose* purse was lost offered a large reward.
>
> The *general whose* men were engaged in this battle was complimented by the commander-in-chief.
>
> The *butterfly, whose* wing was broken, fell to the ground. It was picked up immediately by one of the birds.

In the case of things without animal life, however, the tendency is to use *of which* instead of *whose*, unless euphony forbids.[78] Thus, of the sentences that follow, though both are grammatical, the second is more in accordance with modern usage:

> The *tree, whose* top had been struck by lightning, was cut down.
> The *tree*, the top *of which* had been struck by lightning, was cut down.

The choice between *whose* and *of which* is rather a question of style than of grammar. A cultivated ear is the best guide.

---

[78] *Whose* is particularly common when the relative is restrictive (Section 514).

CHAPTER 121
Descriptive and Restrictive Relatives

Descriptive relatives introduce a descriptive fact. Descriptive relatives are not preceded by a comma.

❧

Restrictive relatives limit the antecedent. Restrictive relative pronouns **are preceded by a comma.**

❧

Who, which, and *that* are common **restrictive relatives.**

513. **Relative pronouns** have two uses, which may be distinguished in the sentences that follow:

> The hat, which is black, belongs to me.
> The hat which is black belongs to me.

In the first sentence, the relative clause (*which is black*) merely **describes** the hat by adding a fact about it. In speaking, a pause is made between the antecedent (*hat)* and the relative (*which*).

In the second sentence, the relative clause is very closely connected with the antecedent (*hat*), and there is no pause between them. The relative clause serves to designate the particular hat which is meant; that is, the relative confines or **restricts** the meaning of the noun.

In the first of these uses, the relative is called a **descriptive relative**; in the second, a **restrictive relative**.

514. **A relative pronoun that serves merely to introduce a descriptive fact is called a descriptive relative.**

A relative pronoun that introduces a clause confining or limiting the application of the antecedent is called a restrictive relative.

515. A descriptive relative is preceded by a **comma;** a restrictive relative is not.

516. *Who, which,* and *that* are all common as restrictive relatives; but some writers prefer *that,* especially in the nominative case.

Chapter 121 Exercises

In Exercises II and III from chapter 51 (reproduced below), explain why each relative as descriptive or restrictive.

Exercise II sentences:
(Look back to your work from chapter 51 to see which relative pronouns you chose, or repeat the exercise and fill in the blanks with relative pronouns.)

1. The house _____ stands yonder belongs to Colonel Carton.

2. Are you the man _____ saved my daughter from drowning?
3. The sailor's wife gazed at the stately ship _____ was taking her husband away from her.
4. A young farmer, _____ name was Judkins, was the first to enlist.
5. Nothing _____ you can do will help me.
6. The horses _____ belong to the squire are famous trotters.
7. James Adams is the strongest man _____ I have ever seen.
8. My friend, _____ we had overtaken on his way down town, greeted us cheerfully.
9. Behold the man _____ the king delighteth to honor!
10. That is the captain _____ ship was wrecked last December.

Exercise III sentences:
1. A sharp rattle was heard on the window, which made the children jump.
2. The small torch that he held sent forth a radiance by which suddenly the whole surface of the desert was illuminated.
3. He that has most time has none to lose.
4. Gray rocks peeped from amidst the lichens and creeping plants which covered them as with a garment of many colors.
5. The enclosed fields, which were generally forty feet square, resembled so many beds of flowers.
6. They that reverence too much old times are but a scorn to the new.
7. The morning came which was to launch me into the world, and from which my whole succeeding life has, in many important points, taken its coloring.
8. Ten guineas, added to about two which I had remaining from my pocket money, seemed to me sufficient for an indefinite length of time.
9. He is the freeman whom the truth makes free.
10. There was one philosopher who chose to live in a tub.
11. Conquerors are a class of men with whom, for the most part, the world could well dispense.
12. The light came from a lamp that burned brightly on the table.
13. The sluggish stream through which we moved yielded sullenly to the oar.
14. The place from which the light proceeded was a small chapel.
15. The warriors went into battle clad in complete armor, which covered them from top to toe.
16. She seemed as happy as a wave
    That dances on the sea.
17. He sang out a long, loud, and canorous peal of laughter, that might have wakened the Seven Sleepers.
18. Thou hadst a voice whose sound was like the sea.
19. Many of Douglas's followers were slain in the battle in which he himself fell.

CHAPTER 122
The Relative Pronoun "What"

517. The relative pronoun *what* is often equivalent to *that which*.

Thus, in the second of the sentences below, *what* has exactly the sense of *that which* in the first:

> *What* is a **relative pronoun** and often carries the sense of *that which*.

(1) The fire destroyed *that which* was in the building.

[*That*, the antecedent of *which*, is a demonstrative pronoun and is the direct object of *destroyed*. The relative pronoun *which* is the subject of *was*.]

(2) The fire destroyed *what* was in the building.

[*What*, being equivalent to *that which*, has two constructions. It serves both as the direct object of *destroyed* and as the subject of *was*.]

518. In this use, *what* has a **double construction:**

(1) the construction of the **omitted** or **implied antecedent** *that*;
(2) the construction of the **relative** *which*.

In parsing *what*, mention both of its constructions.

Chapter 122 Exercise

Change each *what* to *that which*. Explain the constructions of *that* and *which*.

1. We seldom imitate what we do not love.
2. He gives us what our wants require.
3. What's mine is yours, and what is yours is mine.
4. What you have said may be true.
5. What I have is at your service.
6. The spendthrift has wasted what his father laid up.
7. What I earn supports the family.
8. What supports the family is Tom's wages.

CHAPTER 123
Compound Relative Pronouns

519. The compound relative pronouns are formed by adding -*ever* or -*soever* to *who, which,* and *what*.

The forms in -*soever* are used in the solemn style or for special emphasis.

520. The compound relative pronouns are thus inflected:

SINGULAR AND PLURAL

Nominative:	whoever (whosoever)	whichever (whichsoever)
Genitive:	whosever (whosesoever)	— —
Objective:	whomever (whomsoever)	whichever (whichsoever)

Whatever (whatsoever) has no inflection. The nominative and the objective are alike, and the genitive is supplied by the phrase *of whatever (of whatsoever).*

The phrase *of whichever (of whichsoever)* is used instead of *whosever* exactly as *of which* is used instead *of whose* (chapter 120).

521. The compound relative pronouns may include or imply their own antecedents and hence may have a double construction.

> *Whoever* sins, *he* shall die.
> [Here *he*, the antecedent of *whoever*, is the subject of *shall die*, and *whoever* is the subject of *sins*.]

> *Whoever* sins shall die.
> [Here the antecedent *he* is omitted, being implied in *whoever*. *Whoever* has therefore a double construction, being the subject both of *sins* and of *shall die*.]

> *Whoever* runs away is a coward.
> *Whatever* he does is right.
> *Whichever* he chooses will be right.

Compound relative pronouns:

whoever
whosever
whomever
whichever

❧

The suffix -*soever* is added in solemn style or special emphasis.

CHAPTER 124
Relative Adjectives and Adverbs

522. *Which, what, whichever,* and *whatever* are often used as adjectives. Thus,

> He gave me *what money* was on hand.
> I will take *whichever seat* is vacant.
> He has lost *whatever friends* he had.

523. A noun limited by the adjectives *what, whatever, whichever,* may have the same double construction that these relatives have when they are used as pronouns (Sections 518 and 521).

Thus, in the first sentence above, *what money* is both the **direct object** of *gave* and the **subject** of *was.*

524. A number of **adverbs** are closely related in meaning to the **relative pronouns.** Thus, in

> The town *where* this took place is a frontier settlement,

the word *where* is an **adverb of place**, but it is connected with *town* in much the same way in which a **relative pronoun** is connected with its antecedent. Indeed we might substitute for *where* the phrase *in which.*

Similarly,

> The time *when [= at which]* this took place was five o'clock.

525. The most important **relative adverbs** are:

> Where, whence, whither, wherever, when, whenever,
> while, as, how, why, before, after, till, until, since.

Such words **connect** subordinate clauses with main clauses as **relative pronouns** do. Hence they are called **relative** or **conjunctive adverbs.** They will be further studied in chapter 134.

> **The words** *which, what, whichever, and whatever* can be used as **adjectives.**
>
> ❧
>
> **Relative adverbs:**
> *where, whence, whither, wherever, when, whenever, while, as, how, why, before, after, till, until, since.*
>
> ❧
>
> **Relative** or **conjunctive adverbs** connect subordinate clauses with main clauses.

Chapter 124 Exercises

I.

In each of the following sentences explain the construction of *that* and of *which*. Then change *that which* to *what* and explain the double construction of *what.*

1.   That which man has done, man can do.

2. I will describe only that which I have seen.
3. That which was left was sold for old iron.
4. That which inspired the inventor was the hope of final success.
5. Captivity is that which I fear most.
6. That which we have, we prize not. That which we lack, we value.
7. I thought of that which the old sailor had told of storms and shipwrecks.
8. Give careful heed to that which I say.
9. That which offended Bertram most was his cousin's sneer.
10. That which is done cannot be undone.

Substitute *whatever* for *that which* whenever you can.

II.

Explain the construction of the relatives.

1. Whoever he is, I will loose his bonds.
2. Give this message to whomever you see.
3. Give this letter to anyone whom you see.
4. Whatsoever he doeth shall prosper.
5. Everything that he does shall prosper.
6. I owe to you whatever success I have had.
7. I owe to you any success that I have had.
8. Whoever deserts you, I will remain faithful.
9. He gave a full account of whatever he had seen.
10. Whichever road you take, you will find it rough and lonely.

CHAPTER 125[79]
Interrogative Pronouns, Etc.

526. The pronouns *who, which,* and *what* are often used in **asking questions**.

527. In this use they are called **interrogative pronouns**.

> *Who* is your best friend?
> *Whose* coat is this?
> *Whom* do you see in the street?
> *What* is the name of your sled?
> *Which* of the three is the best scholar?

528. The forms of the interrogative pronouns are the same as those of the corresponding relatives (see chapter 119).

529. The **objective** *whom* often begins a question (as in the third example above). In such cases, care should be taken not to write *who*.

So also in such sentences as "*Whom* did you give it to?" where *whom* is the object of the preposition.

530. *Which* and *what* are often used as **interrogative adjectives.** Thus,

> *Which* seat do you prefer?
> In *what* state were you born ?

531. The interrogative adjective *what* is common in **exclamatory sentences** (chapter 14). Thus,

> *What* a rascal he is!
> *What* weather we are having!
> *What* heroes they are!

In this use *what* in the singular is often followed by the indefinite article *a* or *an,*

532. *Where, when, whence, whither, how, why,* may be used as **interrogative adverbs.** Thus,

> *When* did you visit Naples?
> *How* do you spell this word?

Interrogative pronouns:
who
which
what
whom
whose

Interrogative pronouns are used in **asking questions.**

Interrogative adjectives:
which
what

Interrogative adverbs:
where
when
whence
whither
how
why

---

[79] Here chapter 12 should be reviewed.

Chapter 125 Exercises

I.

Write fifteen interrogative sentences, using all the forms of the interrogative pronouns and adjectives.

II.

Give the gender, number, and case of the interrogative pronouns, and tell what nouns the interrogative adjectives limit. Mention the interrogative adverbs.

1. Who told you that I was going to London?
2. What is the meaning of this terrible summons?
3. Who are these strange-looking men?
4. What dost thou want? Whence didst thou come?
5. What is the creature doing here?
6. Which of you is William Tell?
7. Where did we go on that memorable night? What did we see? What did we do? Or rather, what did we not see, and what did we not do?
8. Of what crime am I accused? Where are the witnesses?
9. Whom shall you invite to the wedding?
10. Whose are the gilded tents that crowd the way
    Where all was waste and silent yesterday?
11. Whom did you see at my uncle's?
12. What strange uncertainty is in thy looks?
13. Which of you trembles not that looks on me?
14. To whom are you speaking?
15. From whom did you hear this news?

III.

Write ten exclamatory sentences beginning with *what*.

CHAPTER 126
The Infinitive as a Noun

533. The infinitive is often used as a pure **noun**.

534. The infinitive, with or without an object or modifiers, may be used as the subject of a sentence.

The **infinitive** is often used as a **noun**.

ﻋ

The **infinitive** may be the **subject of a sentence.**

ﻋ

The **infinitive** may be the **predicate nominative.**

ﻋ

The **infinitive** may be standing in the predicate when *it* is used as the subject.

> *To steal* is disgraceful.
> *To kill* a man is a crime.
> *To read* carefully improves the mind.

The infinitive as subject is especially common with *is* and other forms of the verb *be*.

535. The infinitive may be used as a predicate nominative.

> His fault is *to talk* too much.
> His custom is *to ride* daily.

In this construction it is possible to have **two infinitives**, one as the subject and the other as a predicate nominative. Thus,

> *To act* thus is *to forfeit* our respect.

536. An infinitive often stands in the predicate when the neuter pronoun *it* is used as the subject of a sentence. Thus,

> It is good *to be* here.
> [Instead of: *To be* here is good.]

> It is a crime *to kill* a man.
> It is human *to err*; it is divine to forgive.

In this construction the infinitive is still in sense the subject, for *it* has little meaning and serves merely to introduce the sentence.

In this use *it* is often called an **expletive** (or "filler").

Chapter 126 Exercises

I.

Replace each infinitive by a verbal noun ending in *-ing* and each noun ending in *-ing* by an infinitive. Thus,

To laugh is peculiar to man.   *Laughing* is peculiar to man.
To fish is great sport.   *Fishing* is great sport.

1. To toil is the lot of mankind.
2. To hunt was Roderick's chief delight.
3. To aim and to hit the mark are not the same thing.
4. To swim is easy enough if one has confidence.
5. Wrestling is a favorite rural sport in the South of England.
6. To cross the river was Washington's next task.
7. To be poor is no disgrace.
8. Begging was the poor creature's last resource.
9. Waiting for a train is tedious business.
10. To desert one's flag is disgraceful.
11. Feeling fear is not being a coward.

II.

Analyze the sentences in I, above.

III.

Explain the construction of the infinitives.

1. To save money is sometimes the hardest thing in the world.
2. It is delightful to hear the sound of the sea.
3. It was my wish to join the expedition.
4. Pity it was to hear the elfin's wail.
5. To be faint-hearted is indeed to be unfit for our trade.
6. Her pleasure was to ride the young colts and to scour the plains like Camilla.
7. 'T is thine, O king, the afflicted to redress.
8. The queen's whole design is to act the part of mediator.

CHAPTER 127[80]
The Infinitive as a Modifier

The **infinitive** with *to* is common as an **adverbial modifier** and an **adjective modifier**.

ক

Complementary infinitives complete or define the meaning of the verb.

ক

Infinitives of purpose add something new to a complete statement.

537. The **infinitive** with *to* is common as an **adverbial modifier** of verbs and adjectives and as an **adjective modifier** of nouns.

538. In each of the following sentences the verb of the predicate is followed by an infinitive:

1. The cat hastened *to climb* a tree.
2. The ogre ceased *to laugh*.
3. The whole company began *to shout*.
4. The midshipman tried *to do* his duty.
5. Everybody wishes *to enjoy* life.
6. Antony prompted the Romans *to avenge* Caesar.
7. I permitted him *to call* me friend.
8. We go to school *to learn*.
9. Brutus addressed the people *to calm* their agitation.
10. The lawyer rose *to address* the court.
11. He bent his bow *to shoot* a crow.
12. You must not sell the horse *to buy* the saddle.

The force of the infinitive varies considerably in the different sentences.

In numbers 1-7 the infinitive **completes** or **defines** the **meaning** of the verb.

In this use infinitives are called **complementary infinitives.**

The verbs of numbers 1-7 do not make complete and definite sense without the added infinitive; whereas in numbers 8-12 the part of the sentence that precedes the infinitive makes complete sense by itself.

The infinitive in these cases does not serve to **complete** or **define** the sense of the verb, but to add something new—namely, the **purpose** of the action, — to a statement already complete.

---

[80] For the so-called infinitive clause, see chapter 142.

> **Complementary infinitives** and **infinitives of purpose** are both considered **adverbial phrases**.
>
> ❧
>
> **Infinitives** that modify the meaning of a noun are **adjective modifiers**.
>
> ❧
>
> **Infinitives** that modify the meaning of an adjective are **adverbial modifiers**.

Both the **complementary infinitive**[81] and the **infinitive of purpose** may be regarded as **adverbial phrases** modifying the verb.

539. An infinitive may modify a verb by completing its meaning, or by expressing the purpose of the action.

540. An infinitive may be used to modify the meaning of a noun or an adjective.

In this use the infinitive is said to **depend on** the noun or the adjective which it limits. It may be regarded as an adjective modifier of the noun and an adverbial modifier of the adjective.

NOUNS	ADJECTIVES
Desire *to rule* is natural to men.	All men are eager *to rule*.
Quickness *to learn* was his strong point.	He was quick *to see* the point.
There is no need *to summon* assistance.	It was necessary *to call* for help.
The ability *to laugh* is peculiar to mankind.	Only human beings are able *to laugh*.
His will *to do* right was strong.	He was willing *to try* anything.

---

[81] After some verbs, the infinitive approaches the construction of a pure noun. In such case it is often regarded as the object of the verb. Thus, "I desire *to see* you" (compare "I desire a *sight* of you"). It is simpler, however, to regard all such infinitives as complementary phrases and to treat them as adverbial modifiers. For it is impossible to distinguish the construction of the infinitive after certain adjectives (for example, in "I am eager *to see* you") from its construction after such verbs as *wish* and *desire*.

Chapter 127 Exercises

I.
Explain the construction of each infinitive:
- (1) as noun,
- (2) as complementary infinitive,
- (3) as infinitive of purpose,
- (4) as adjective modifier of a noun.

1. All men strive to excel.
2. I have several times taken up my pen to write to you.
3. The moderate of the other party seem content to have a peace.
4. There was not a moment to be lost.
5. He chanced to enter my office one day.
6. The lawyer had no time to spare.
7. They tried hard to destroy the rats and mice.
8. This was very terrible to see.
9. He continued to advance in spite of every obstacle.
10. Even the birds refused to sing on that sullen day.
11. The bullets began to whistle past them.
12. The fox was quick to see this chance to escape.
13. That gaunt and dusty chamber in Granby Street seemed to smell of seaweed.
14. Resolved to win, he meditates the way.
15. The explorer climbs a peak to survey the country before him.

II.
Make sentences containing each of these words followed by an infinitive:

VERBS: begins, try, hoped, omits, endeavored, neglects, resolved, strove, undertook, determined, dares, venture, desires, wishes, longs, feared.

ADJECTIVES AND PARTICIPLES: able, ready, unwilling, glad, loth, reluctant, eager, sorry, disposed, determined, pleased, shocked, gratified, content, disturbed.

CHAPTER 128
Potential Verb Phrases

541. Several auxiliary verbs are used to form verb phrases indicating ability, possibility, obligation, or necessity.

Such verb phrases are called **potential phrases**, that is, "phrases of possibility."

542. The auxiliary verbs used in **potential phrases** are: *may, can, must, might, could, would,* and *should.* They are followed by the infinitive without *to.*[82]

> I *may give* him a small present.
> He *can overcome* all his difficulties.
> We *might help* them if we tried.
> They *could catch* fish in the river.
> If he *should fall,* he *would be killed.*

543. The **potential phrases** may show a great variety of forms: present, preterite, and perfect, active and passive. Thus,

I may send.	I may be sent.
I might send.	I might be sent.
I may have sent.	I may have been sent.
I might have sent.	I might have been sent.

Such phrases may be easily arranged in paradigms, like that in the chart shown in chapter 109.

They are often called, collectively, the **potential mood.**

544. *Can* is regularly used to indicate that the subject **is able** to do something. *May* is frequently used to indicate that the subject is **permitted** to do something.

Thus, "You *can* cut down that tree" means "You are able to cut it down," that is, you have strength or skill enough to do so; whereas "You *may* cut

---

> Helping verbs used in **potential phrases:**
> *may*
> *can*
> *must*
> *might*
> *could*
> *would*
> *should*
>
> ❦
>
> *Can* indicates the subject is **able** to do something.
>
> *May* indicates the subject is **permitted** to do something.

---

[82] The fact that *give,* etc., in such phrases as *can give,* are infinitives is not apparent from modern English. We use the verb phrase as a whole without thinking of its parts or their grammatical relation to each other. A study of older English, however, makes the origin and history of the phrases clear. We may also see the nature of these constructions by comparing also "I can *strike*" with "I am able *to strike,*" "I may *strike*" with "I am permitted *to strike,*" "I must *strike*" with "I am obliged *to strike,*" and so on.

down that tree" means simply "You are allowed or permitted to cut it down," and implies nothing as to your ability to carry out the permission.

Hence, in **asking permission** to do anything, the proper form is, "*May I?*" not "*Can I?*" For example, "*May I* go to the party this evening?" is the correct form, and not "*Can I* go to the party this evening?"

NOTE: The use of *can* for *may* to express permission is a very common form of error, but should be carefully avoided. With negatives, however, *can* is the common form rather than *may* except in questions. Thus,

> QUESTION: "*May* I not (*or* Mayn't I) go to the party this evening?"
> ANSWER: "No, you *cannot* go this evening; but if there is a party next week you *may* go to that."

545. *May* often indicates **possibility** or **doubtful intention.**

> I *may* go to town this afternoon.
> [That is, It is possible that I shall go.]

546. *Must* expresses **necessity** or **obligation.** Thus,

> Brave men *must* meet death fearlessly.
> You *must* not disobey the law.

Must, though originally a preterite tense, is in modern English almost always used as a present.

547. **Necessity** in past time may be expressed by *had to* with the infinitive.

> He *had to pay* dear for his sport.

548. The irregular verb *ought* expresses **moral obligation**, as distinguished from mere **necessity.**

Ought with the **present** infinitive expresses a moral obligation in present time.

Ought with the **perfect** infinitive expresses a moral obligation in past time.

> Children *ought to obey* their parents. [Present]
> They *ought* not *to act* so selfishly. [Present]
> He *ought* not *to have made* such a mistake. [Past]
> The general *ought to have consulted* the commander-in-chief.

549. *Ought* (like *must*) was originally a preterite, but in modern English is always used in a present sense.

May often indicates **possibility** or **doubtful intention.**

ᘔ

Must expresses **necessity** or **obligation.**

ᘔ

Ought expresses **moral obligation.**

550. *Had* should never be prefixed to *ought*.

CORRECT	INCORRECT
I *ought* to go to school.	I *had ought* to go to school.
John *ought not* to have hit me.	John *hadn't ought* to have hit me.
He ought to go, *oughtn't* he?	He ought to go, *hadn't* he?

551. The preterite *should* is often used in the sense of *ought*. Thus,

> One *should* always *do* one's best.
> You *should have given* me the letter.

552. In subordinate clauses after *if, though, when, until*, etc., *shall* and *should* are used in **all three persons** unless the subject is thought of as **wishing** or **consenting**, when *will* and *would* are correct.

> If *he shall* offend, he will be punished.   [Futurity]
> If *he should* offend, he would be punished.   [Futurity]
> If *you should* try, you could do this.   [Futurity]
> If *I would* consent, all would be well.   [Willingness]
> If *you would* agree, I should be glad.   [Willingness]

When duty or obligation is expressed, *should* is of course the auxiliary for all three persons (see Section 551), in both principal and subordinate clauses.

Chapter 128 Exercises

I.

Pick out the potential verb phrases. Explain the meaning of each phrase.

1. She might have held back a little longer.
2. The French officer might as well have said it all aloud.
3. Is it possible that you can have talked so wildly?
4. An honest man may take a knave's advice.
5. If he cannot conquer he may properly retreat.
6. I arrived at Oxford with a stock of erudition that might have puzzled a doctor, and a degree of ignorance of which a schoolboy would have been ashamed.
7. From the hall door she could look down the park.
8. Early activity may prevent late and fruitless violence.
9. Lear at first could not believe his eyes or ears.
10. May I come back to tell you how I succeed?

11. We might have had quieter neighbors.
12. It must then have been nearly midnight.
13. We must have walked at least a mile in this wood.
14. When bad men combine, the good must associate.
15. I ought to be allowed a reasonable freedom.
16. He must and shall come back.
17. Something must have happened to Erne.
18. He would not believe this story, even if you should prove it by trustworthy witnesses.
19. Would you help me if I should ask it?
20. Should you care if I were to fail?
21. You should obey me if you were my son.
22. If he should visit Chicago, would he call on me?
23. I would go if the others would.

II.
Analyze the sentences in I, above.

CHAPTER 129
Subjunctive Mood

553. Besides the inflections of the **indicative** and the **imperative,** the English verb has a set of forms which belong to the **subjunctive mood**.

> **Subjunctive mood** verb forms follow the prefix *if.*

554. In older English the special **subjunctive** forms were common in a variety of uses, and this is still true of poetry and the solemn style. In ordinary modern prose, however, such forms are rare, and in conversation they are hardly ever heard, except in the case of the **copula** *be.*

555. The main forms of the subjunctive mood may be seen in the following paradigm.

SUBJUNCTIVE MOOD

PRESENT TENSE

SINGULAR NUMBER	PLURAL NUMBER
1. If I be.	If we be.
2. If thou be.	If you (*or* ye) be.
3. If he be.	If they be.

PRETERITE TENSE

SINGULAR NUMBER	PLURAL NUMBER
1. If I were.	If we were.
2. If thou wert.	If you (*or* ye) were.
3. If he were.	If they were.

If is prefixed to each of these forms because it is in clauses beginning with *if* that the subjunctive is commonest in modern English. *If,* however, is of course no part of the subjunctive inflection.

556. In other verbs, the **subjunctive active** has the same forms as the **indicative**, except in the **second** and **third persons singular** of the **present** tense, which are like the **first** person:

INDICATIVE	SUBJUNCTIVE
1. I find.	If I find.
2. Thou findest.	If thou *find*.
3. He finds.	If he *find*.

557. In the **passive subjunctive**, the subjunctive forms of the copula (Section 555) are used as auxiliaries:

> Present, *if I be struck;*
> Preterite, *if I were struck.*

558. **Progressive verb phrases** in the subjunctive may be formed by means of the copula:

> Present, *if I be striking;*
> Preterite, *if I were striking.*

The present is rare; the preterite is in common use.

559. In the **future** and **future perfect** verb phrases the auxiliary is *shall* for all three persons. Thus,

> If I (he) shall strike, if thou shalt strike.
> If I (he) shall have struck, if thou shalt have struck.

Volition, however, may be expressed by *will.*

> If I *will* consent, he will begin at once.
> Nothing can be done if you *will* not help.
> If Jack *will* study, he can learn his lesson.

In an advanced study of English grammar it is worth while to attempt to distinguish the subjunctive from the indicative by historical and logical tests, even when its forms are identical with those of the indicative. But the beginner should not be expected to split hairs. It is enough if he learns to recognize those forms in which the subjunctive really differs from the indicative. When he comes to study the constructions of the subjunctive in later chapters, he will be able in some cases to distinguish between the subjunctive and the indicative character of certain identical forms, but till then the matter should be left largely in abeyance.

CHAPTER 130
Subjunctives in Wishes and Exhortations

560. The English subjunctive was once very common in both dependent and independent clauses; but it is now confined to a few special constructions.

561. The subjunctive is often used in wishes or prayers.

Heaven *forgive* him!	God *forbid!*
The Lord *help* the poor creatures!	God *grant* us peace!
The Lord *be* with you!	The saints *protect* you!
God *help* our country!	Oh! That my father *were* here!
	Oh! That money *grew* on trees!

In the first seven examples, the wish is expressed in an independent sentence. In the last two, the construction is subordinate—the *that*-clause being the object of an unexpressed "I wish" (or the like).

The verbs *may* and *would* in such expressions of wish as *"May* all go well with you!" *"Would that* I were with him!"* were originally subjunctives. *Would* stands for *I would,* that is, *I should wish.*

562. **Exhortations** in the first person plural sometimes take the subjunctive in elevated or poetical style. Thus,

> *Strike we* a blow for freedom!
> [That is, in plain prose, Let us strike a blow for
> freedom!]

In ordinary language such exhortations are regularly expressed by *let us* followed by the infinitive. Thus,

> *Let us* tell our friends.
> *Let us* seek for gold.
> *Let us* try this road.
> *Let us* not be cowardly.

In this construction *let* is a verb in the imperative, *us* is its object, and the infinitive (*tell, seek,* without *to*) depends on *let.*

Subjunctive is often used in wishes or prayers.

☙

Sometimes *I wish* is unexpressed but implied.

☙

Ordinarily, speakers use **let us** (or *let's*) combined with the **infinitive** in making appeals or exhortations.

CHAPTER 131
Subjunctive in Concessions, Conditions, Etc.

563. The **subjunctive** is used after *though, although,* to express a **concession** not as a fact but as a **supposition.** Thus,

> Though this *be* true, we need not be anxious.
> Though he *were* my brother, I should condemn him.

The **indicative** is regularly used after *though* and *although* when the concession is stated as a **fact.** Thus,

> Though he *is* my brother, he does not resemble me.
> Though John *was* present, he took no part in the proceedings.

564. After *if* and *unless,* expressing **condition,** the **subjunctive** may be used in a variety of ways.

> 1. If this *be* true, I am sorry for it.
>   [It MAY or MAY NOT be true.]
>
> 2. If he *find* this out, he will be angry.
>   [He MAY or MAY NOT find it out.]
>
> 3. If this *were* true, I should be sorry for it.
>   [It is NOT true; hence I am NOT sorry.]
>
> 4. If this *had been* true, I should have been sorry for it.
>   [It was NOT true; hence I was NOT sorry.]

565. In conditional clauses, the **present subjunctive** denotes either **present** or **future** time. It suggests a doubt as to the truth of the supposed case, but not decisively. (See examples 1 and 2, above.)

The **preterite subjunctive** refers to **present** time. It implies that the supposed case **is not a fact.** (Example 3)

The **pluperfect subjunctive** refers to **past** time. It implies that the supposed case **was not a fact.** (Example 4)

566. **Condition** is sometimes expressed by the **subjunctive** without *if.* In this construction the verb precedes the subject. Thus,

> *Were* my brother here, he would protect me.
> [That is: If my brother were here...]

> *Had* you my troubles, you would despair.
> [That is: If you had my troubles...]

Subjunctive is used with *though* and *although* to express a **concession.**

ॐ

Condition is sometimes expressed by the **subjunctive.**

Had the boat *capsized*, every man of them would have been drowned.

In modern English, this construction is confined to *were* and *had*; but it was formerly common with other verbs.

567. After *as if (as though)*, the **preterite subjunctive** is used. Thus,

> He acts as if he *were* angry.
> [NOT: as if he *was* angry.]

> You speak as if I *were* your enemy.
> [NOT: as if I *was*.]

568. The **subjunctive** is occasionally used after *that, lest, before, until*, etc., in subordinate clauses referring to the future and commonly expressing **purpose**. Thus,

> Sustain him, that he *faint* not.
> I will help him, lest he *die*.
> We will abide until he *come*.

These constructions are confined to poetry and the solemn style.

569. In ordinary English we say,

> Hold him up, so that (*or* in order that) he *may* not *fall*.
> We will wait till he *comes*.

Thus old **subjunctive** constructions are in modern English often replaced by the **indicative** or by **potential verb phrases** with *may, might, should*.

CHAPTER 132
Various Uses of the Subjunctive

570. The **subjunctive** is sometimes used to express not what **is** or **was** but what **would be** or **would have been** the case. Thus,

> It *were better* to eat husks than to starve.
> It *had been better* for him if he had never been born.

This construction is old-fashioned. Modern English commonly uses *would be* or *would have been* instead: as,

> It *would be better* to eat husks than to starve.

571. The **preterite subjunctive** *had* is common in *had rather* and similar phrases. Thus,

> I *had rather* die than be a slave.
> You *had better* be careful.
> I *had as lief* do it as not.

Had in this construction is sometimes regarded as erroneous or inelegant; but the idiom is old and well established, and has first-rate modern usage in its favor.

Chapter 132 Exercises

I.

Make a table of all the indicative and subjunctive forms of the verbs *be, have, do, bind, declare,* in the present and preterite active. (See Section 555.)

Make a similar table for the present and preterite passive of *send, bind, declare.*

II.

Explain the form, use, and meaning of each subjunctive.

1. Mine be a cot beside the hill.
2. Ruin seize thee, ruthless king!
3. It were madness to delay longer.
4. Of great riches there is no real use, except it be in the distribution.
5. King though he be, he may be weak.
6. "God bless you, my dear boy!" Pendennis said to Arthur.
7. It is Jove's doing, and Jove make me thankful!

8. If this were played upon a stage now, I could condemn it as an improbable fiction.
9. Go we, as well as haste will suffer us,
    To this unlooked for, unprepared pomp.
10. If this be treason, make the most of it!
11. "Walk in." "I had rather walk here, I thank you."
12. He looks as if he were afraid.
13. I should have answered if I had been you.
14. God in thy good cause make thee prosperous!
15. These words hereafter thy tormentors be!
16. Had I a son, I would bequeath him a plough.
17. There's matter in't indeed if he be angry.
18. I wish I were at Naples this moment.
19. If he were honest, he would pay his debts.
20. If wishes were horses, beggars might ride.
21. No man cried, "God save him!"
22. By heaven, methinks it were an easy leap
    To pluck bright honor from the pale-faced moon.
23. Unless my study and my books be false,
    That argument you held was wrong in you.
24. Take heed lest thou fall.
25. Though he be angry, he can do no harm.

CHAPTER 133
The Thought in the Sentence

Complete thought is expressed by **combining words into sentences.**

❧

Laws govern the structure of sentences according to definite principles so that we can understand one another.

❧

Simple sentences need words that **modify** the subject and predicate to convey shades of meaning and complexity.

❧

Clauses may serve as **nouns, adjective modifiers,** or **adverbial modifiers.**

572. We have now studied the main facts and principles of English grammar, that is, we have observed how those **signs** that we call **words** perform their task of **signifying,** or **expressing, thought.**

Thought, as we have seen, may be rudely and imperfectly uttered by means of **single words.** For its complete expression, however, words must be **combined into sentences.** This combination, too, must be made in accordance with definite principles, or laws; otherwise language would be so confused that nobody could understand his neighbor.

In studying the laws that govern the structure of sentences, we have found that a very simple thought may be expressed in a very simple sentence, consisting of a single noun and a single verb.

Such sentences, however, do not carry us far. To make clear the various shades of meaning which our language has to convey, words and groups of words must be used to **modify** the subject and predicate; and this process of modification results in the building up of complicated sentences that sometimes consist of several **clauses.**

Such complicated sentences, however, may always be **analyzed** (or broken up) into their **elements,** — and in this process of **analysis** we are able to see clearly the relations which the different parts of the sentence bear to each other in their common task, — **the full and exact expression of thought.**

Among these elements of expression, we have found that **subordinate clauses** are of great importance; for by means of them the meaning of a sentence may be changed or **modified** at pleasure.[83]

Subordinate clauses, as we have learned, may serve as **nouns,** as **adjective modifiers,** or as **adverbial modifiers,** and they may be connected with the main clause by various words (such as relative pronouns, relative adverbs, and subordinate conjunctions), — each of which has its special office in the common work of language.

We must now carry our study of the **thought in the sentence** a step farther, and ask what are the main varieties of thought that are expressed

---

[83] In connection with this chapter the summary chapter on the Structure of Sentences (chapter 57) should be consulted if the matter is not fresh in the pupils mind.

> What **categories** of thought can we observe that are typically expressed by **subordinate clauses?**
>
> ❧
>
> Let's find out in the coming chapters.

by the different kinds of subordinate clauses. To this study the chapters that follow are devoted.[84]

We shall find that most subordinate clauses may be easily classified in accordance with their meaning. We shall also observe that the **subordinate conjunction** or other word which introduces such a clause not only serves as a connective but also suggests, in most cases, what the general sense of the clause is to be.

These chapters are not intended to be worked through mechanically. Still less are they meant to be committed to memory. Their purpose is to lead the student to recognize, in his own speech, oral or written, and in the speech of others, some of the important varieties of human thought, and to see **how language behaves in expressing these different ideas.**

----

[84] Chapters 134-142

CHAPTER 134[85]
Subordinate Clauses Classified

Subordinate clauses may be **classified** into **nine** categories of ideas. **See the list at the bottom of this page.**

❧

Study the: relative pronouns,

compound relatives,

chief relative adverbs,

interrogative pronouns,

interrogative adverbs,

and

subordinative conjunctions

listed in the text.
You should be able to identify these words.

573. **Subordinate** or **dependent clauses** express a great variety of ideas and are attached to main clauses by different kinds of words.

The word which attaches a subordinate clause to a main clause is said to **introduce** the subordinate clause.

574. A subordinate clause may be introduced by:

(1) a relative or an interrogative pronoun
(2) a relative or an interrogative adverb
(3) a subordinate conjunction

The **relative pronouns** are: *who, which, what, that* (=*who* or *which*), *as* (after *such*), and the **compound relatives** *whoever, whichever, whatever*. Their uses have already been studied (chapter 119).

The chief **relative adverbs** are: *when, whenever, since, until, before, after, where, whence, whither, wherever, why, as, how.*

The **interrogative pronouns** are: *who, which, what.*

The **interrogative adverbs** are: *when, where, whence, whither, how, why.*

The most important **subordinate conjunctions** are: *because, since* (= *because*), *though, although, if, unless, that* (in order that, so that), *as, as if, as though, than.* Their meaning will be explained in what follows.

575. Subordinate clauses may be used:

as **adjective modifiers**
as **adverbial modifiers**
as **substantives**

576. The ideas expressed by subordinate clauses may be classified under:

(1) time or place	(6) condition
(2) cause	(7) comparison
(3) concession	(8) indirect statement
(4) purpose	(9) indirect question
(5) result	

---

[85] The present chapter is for reference and review. It summarizes chapters 135-141.

CHAPTER 135
Clauses of Place and Time

577. An adjective or an adverbial clause may express place or time.

I. ADJECTIVE CLAUSES

> An **adjective** or **adverbial clause** may express **place** or **time**.
>
> ❧
>
> **Adjective clauses** of **place and time** may begin with **relative pronouns.**
>
> ❧
>
> **Adverbial clauses** of **place and time** may begin with **relative adverbs.**

The town *where John lives* is called Granby.
The lion returned to the cave *whence he had come.*
Show me the book *in which you found the poem.*
There was no water in the desert *through which he passed.*
The general fell at the moment *when the enemy began to flee.*
Her father died on the day *on which she was born.*

II. ADVERBIAL CLAUSES

The soldier died *where he fell.*
He found his knife *where he had left it.*
You make friends *wherever you are.*
Whither thou goest, I will go.
Washington lived *when George III was king.*
The poor fellow works *whenever he can.*
We cannot start *while the storm is raging.*
Jack rose from bed *as the clock struck six.*
We reached our inn *before the sun went down.*
Everybody waited *until the speaker had finished.*
When the iron is hot, then is the time to strike.

578. Adjective clauses of place and time may be introduced by relative pronouns (see examples above).

579. Adjective and adverbial clauses of place and time may be introduced by relative adverbs: as,

PLACE: *where, whence, whither, wherever, whithersoever, wherefrom, whereto,* etc.

TIME: *when, whenever, while, as, before, after, until, since.*

Chapter 135 Exercise

Identify the relative pronoun or adverb in each sentence from Section 577, above.

CHAPTER 136
Causal and Concessive Clauses

An **adverbial clause** may express **cause.**

&

Causal clauses begin with conjunctions *because, since, as,* or *inasmuch as.*

&

An **adverbial clause** may express **concession.**

&

Concessive clauses begin with *though, although,* or *even if.*

580. An adverbial clause may express cause.

> The shepherd fled *because he was afraid of the wolf.*
> The bell is ringing *because there is a fire.*
> *Since you will not work,* you shall not eat.

581. **Causal clauses** are introduced by *because, since, as, inasmuch as,* and other subordinate conjunctions of like meaning.

Since is an adverb when it expresses time (Section 579), a conjunction when it expresses cause.

582. An adverbial clause may denote concession.

583. A **concessive clause** is usually introduced by a subordinate conjunction, *though, although,* or *even if.* It **admits** (or concedes) some fact or supposition **in spite of which** the assertion in the main clause is made.

> *Although Smith is an Englishman,* he has never seen London.
> I admired the man, *though he was my enemy.*
> *Though this be madness,* yet there's method in't.
> Such an act would not be kind, *even if it were just.*

584. For the distinction between the **indicative** and the **subjunctive** in concessive clauses, see Section 563.

Chapter 136 Exercises

I.
Make:
(1) ten complex sentences containing clauses of time
(2) ten containing clauses of place
(3) ten containing causal clauses
(4) ten containing concessive clauses

II.
Use each of the following words to introduce a subordinate clause in a complex sentence:

> where, since, if, because, until, when, though

For each sentence, tell whether the clause that you have made expresses time, place, cause, or concession.

CHAPTER 137
Clauses of Purpose and of Result

585. A subordinate clause may express purpose or result.

A **subordinate clause** may express **purpose** or **result.**

≈

Purpose clauses begin with the subordinate conjunction *that* or a *that*-phrase.

≈

Result clauses begin with *so that*, or *that.*

≈

Clauses of purpose or result may be either an **adverbial modifier** or a **substantive clause.**

I. CLAUSES OF PURPOSE.

Brutus smote Caesar *that Rome might be free.*
I will do my best *that no lives may be lost.*
The sailors cast anchor *so that the ship might not drift on the rocks.*
The bandits fought desperately *in order that they might not be taken alive.*
Guide him faithfully *lest he lose his way.*

II. CLAUSES OF RESULT.

The castle was very old, *so that it fell after a short bombardment.*
The messenger was *so* tired *that he could scarcely stand.*
The duke received me *so* courteously *that I was quite enchanted.*

586. **Clauses of purpose** may be introduced by the subordinate conjunction *that* or by a phrase containing it (*so that, in order that, to the end that,* etc.).

Negative clauses of purpose may be introduced by *that . . . not* or by *lest.* *Lest* is often followed by the subjunctive (see Section 568).

587. **Clauses of result** may be introduced by the phrase *so that,* consisting of the adverb *so* and the subordinate conjunction *that;* or by *that* alone, especially when *so, such,* or some similar word stands in the main clause.

588. A clause of **purpose** or of **result** may be either an **adverbial modifier** (as in the examples in Section 585), or a **substantive clause:** as,

My purpose was *that the wall should be undermined.*
[Predicate Nominative]

The mayor ordered *that the city gates should be shut.*
[Object]

The result was *that nobody came.*
[Predicate Nominative]

His speech had this result, *that everybody went to sleep.*
[Appositive]

589. Purpose is often expressed by the infinitive with *to* or *in order to*, and result by the infinitive with *as to*.

> He worked hard *to earn* his living.
> They rowed so hard *as to be* quite *exhausted*.

CHAPTER 138
Conditional Sentences

590. Study the following sentence:

> Caesar deserved death if he was a tyrant.

The sentence consists of two clauses:

(1) "Caesar deserved death" (the main clause)
(2) "if he was a tyrant" (the subordinate clause)

The *if*-clause does not state anything **as a fact.** It simply expresses a supposition, or **condition**, on the truth of which the truth of the assertion made in the main clause depends.

Such a sentence is called a **conditional sentence**, because it states a fact not absolutely but conditionally.

Other examples of conditional sentences are:

> If money were plenty, nobody would care for it.
> If you call at ten o'clock, I shall be at home.
> Nobody will help you if you do not help yourself.

591. A clause that expresses a condition or supposition introduced by *if,* **or by some equivalent word or phrase, is called a conditional clause.**

A sentence that contains a conditional clause is called a conditional sentence.

592. A **conditional sentence** in its simplest form consists of two parts:

(1) A subordinate clause, commonly introduced by *if,* and expressing the **condition.**
(2) A main clause expressing the **conclusion,** that is, the statement asserted as true in case the condition expressed in the *if-c*lause is true.

The conditional clause is often called the **protasis,** and the conclusion is often called the **apodosis.**

593. The main clause of a conditional sentence is not necessarily declarative. It may be interrogative, imperative, or exclamatory.

> If this story were false, what should you do?
> Stand still if you value your life.
> What a pity it would be if he should fail!

A **conditional sentence** states a fact **conditionally**.

❧

A **conditional clause** is introduced by *if* or equivalent word or phrase.

❧

Conditional sentences contain **two parts:**
1. Subordinate *if*-clause,
2. Main conclusion clause.

❧

Protasis= *if*-clause
Apodosis= conclusion clause

594. A conditional clause is usually introduced by the conjunction *if*, but sometimes by other conjunctions or phrases: as, *provided* (or *provided that*), *granted that, supposing, on condition that*.

595. In a conditional sentence, either the condition or the conclusion may come first.

> The dog must be punished if he steals.
> If the dog steals, he must be punished.

596. A **negative condition** is commonly introduced by *if ... not,* or *unless.*

CHAPTER 139
Adverbial Clauses — Comparison

A adverbial clause may express **comparison.**

❧

Adverbial comparison clauses begin with *as if, as,* or *than.*

As if is followed by *were* not *was.*

597. An adverbial clause introduced by *as if* may express comparison.

The man acted *as if he were crazy.*
You look *as if you were very happy.*
The Arabs treated me as kindly *as if I had been a Moslem.*

598. The subjunctive *were*, not the indicative *was*, is used after *as if*.

599. *As* and *than*, as subordinate conjunctions, introduce **clauses of comparison**.

Albert is as tall as I [am].
Henry is taller than I [am].
I like you better than [I like] him.
You cannot run as fast as he [can].
You can play ball better than he [can].

When the verb is omitted, the substantive that follows *as* or *than* is in the same case in which it would stand if the verb were expressed. Thus,

Albert is taller than *I.* [Not: than *me.*]
I like you better than *him.* [Not: than *he.*]

Chapter 139 Exercises

I.
Fill the blanks below with *he* or *him* as the construction requires.

1. You are older than _____.
2. You can run faster than _____.
3. I am as strong as _____.
4. We are as careful as _____.
5. James is a better scholar than _____.

II.
Tell whether the subordinate clauses express time, place, cause, concession, condition, purpose, result, or comparison.

1. As flattery was his trade, he practiced it with the easiest address imaginable.
2. Whenever Macbeth threatened to do mischief to any one, he was sure to keep his word.

3. His armor was so good that he had no fear of arrows.
4. We admire his bravery, though it is shown in a bad cause.
5. He talks as if he were a Spaniard.
6. The marble bridge is the resort of everybody, where they hear music, eat iced fruits, and sup by moonlight.
7. It was a fortnight after this, before the two brothers met again.
8. It was impossible for me to climb this stile, because every step was six feet high.
9. The troops were hastily collected, that an assault might be made without delay.
10. Let us therefore stop while to stop is in our power.
11. King Robert was silent when he heard this story.
12. If others have blundered, it is your place to put them to right.
13. If Milton had any virtues, they are not to be found in the Doctor's picture of him.
14. Where foams and flows the glorious Rhine,
    Many a ruin wan and gray
O'erlooks the cornfield and the vine,
    Majestic in its dark decay.
15. It was impossible for me to advance a step; for the stalks were so interwoven that I could not creep through.
16. If he is not here by Saturday, I shall go after him.
17. He laid his ear to the ground that he might hear their steps.
18. My passage by sea from Rotterdam to England was more painful to me than all the journeys I had ever made by land.
19. Weeds were sure to grow quicker in his fields than anywhere else.

CHAPTER 140
Direct and Indirect Statements

600. In a **direct quotation** the words of another are repeated exactly as he spoke or wrote or thought them.

> He said: "There is gold in this old river bed."
> My friend writes: "I am going to Mexico this winter."
> "I have to work for a living," said the ant.
> "The goose is fat and tender," thought the fox.

601. In an **indirect quotation** the words or thoughts of another are repeated **in substance**, but not always in exactly their original form.

An indirect quotation takes the form of a subordinate clause dependent on some word of *saying* or *thinking*, and introduced by the conjunction *that*.

> He said *that there was gold in this old river bed.*
> My friend writes *that he is going to Mexico this winter.*
> The ant said *that he had to work for a living.*
> The fox thought *that the goose was fat and tender.*

602. **A substantive clause introduced by *that* may be used with verbs and other expressions of telling, thinking, knowing, and perceiving, to report the words or thought of a person in substance, but with some change of form.**

Such clauses are said to be in the indirect discourse.

603. **Direct quotations** begin with a **capital letter**, unless the quotation is a fragment of a sentence. They are enclosed in **quotation marks**.

Indirect quotations begin with a **small letter.** They usually have no quotation marks.

604. Statements in the **indirect discourse** are usually the objects of verbs of *telling, thinking,* etc.; but they may be in other substantive constructions.

> Some one reported *that the enemy was retreating.*
> [Object]
>
> *That the enemy was retreating* was rumored throughout the camp.
> [Subject]

A direct quotation repeats the words of another exactly and is placed in quotation marks.

❧

An indirect quotation takes the form of a **subordinate clause** introduced by *that*.

The rumor was *that the enemy was retreating*.
[Predicate Nominative]

The rumor *that the enemy was retreating* was false.
[Appositive]

Chapter 140 Exercises

I.

Change the following statements to the form of indirect discourse after "He said that."

> EXAMPLE: "I found this diamond in South Africa."
> He said that he found that diamond in South Africa.

1. "I shall sail for Yokohama next Tuesday."
2. "My grandfather has given me a gold watch."
3. "I am not fond of poetry."
4. "I honor the memory of Mr. Gladstone."
5. "Lieutenant Peary has just returned from the Arctic regions."
6. "You will certainly visit the pyramids."
7. "John is stronger than Thomas."
8. "This bird's wing has been broken."
9. "The trapper is struggling with a huge bear."
10. "My home is on the prairie."
11. "Louisiana formerly belonged to France."

II.

Copy the sentences in indirect discourse that you have made in Exercise I.

Turn each sentence back into the direct form and compare the results with the original sentences.

CHAPTER 141
Indirect Questions

605. We have learned to recognize sentences like the following as **interrogative sentences** and to write them with an interrogation point:

Who is president?	What shall you do?
Which man is he?	Is the dog mad?

Such interrogative sentences are called **direct questions.**

606. A question expressed in the form actually used in asking it is called a direct question.

If, now, we prefix "He asked" to the sentences given in Section 605, we have our choice between two forms of expression:

(1) We may keep the **direct form** of question. Thus,

He asked: "Who is president?"
He asked: "Is the dog mad?"

(2) We may change the form of the question while keeping its substance. Thus,

He asked who was president.
He asked whether (*or* if) the dog was mad.

Each of these new sentences contains a question, but this is no longer expressed in the direct form. It has become the **dependent clause** of a **complex sentence,** the main clause being *he asked.*

Such a clause is called an **indirect question.**

607. An indirect question expresses the substance of a direct interrogation in the form of a subordinate clause.

608. Indirect questions depend on verbs or other expressions of asking, doubting, thinking, perceiving, and the like.

He knew *what the man's name was.*
[Direct question: "What is the man's name?"]

John saw *who his companion pretended to be.*
[Here the question which presented itself to John's mind was: "Who does my companion pretend to be?"]

An interrogative sentence is a **direct question.**

⸙

A direct question may be written as a **quotation** and placed in quotation marks.

⸙

A question may be put into **indirect form** by putting the question into a **dependent clause**. Study the examples in Section 608.

The guide tried to discover *which way led out of the cave.* [Here the question which the guide proposed to himself was: "Which way leads out of the cave?"]

609. Both **direct** and **indirect questions** may be introduced:

(1) by the interrogative pronouns *who, which, what;*
(2) by the interrogative adverbs *when, where, whence, whither, how, why.*

Indirect questions may be introduced by the subordinate conjunctions *whether* and *if.*

The farmer asked Tom *whether* (or *if) he liked fruit.* [The farmer's question was: "Do you like fruit?"]

610. **Indirect questions** should be carefully distinguished from **relative clauses**.

Our guide found the road *which led home.* [Relative]
Our guide found *which road led home.* [Indirect question]

In the first sentence, *which* is a **relative pronoun** referring to its **antecedent** *road*, the object of *found*. We cannot express the clause as a question.

In the second sentence, the object of *found* is the **whole clause.** There was a **direct question** in the guide's mind: "Which road leads home?" *Which* is an **interrogative adjective**, and no antecedent is thought of.

> **Direct** and **indirect** questions may begin with: *who, which, what* and *when, where, whence, whither, how, why.*
>
> ❦
>
> **Indirect** questions may begin with: *whether, if.*

Chapter 141 Exercise

Pick out the substantive clauses. Give the construction of each (as subject, object, etc.), and tell whether it is an indirect statement or an indirect question.

1. That fine feathers do not make fine birds has always been taught by philosophers.
2. Here we halted in the open field, and sent out our people to see how things were in the country.
3. I do not imagine that you find me rash in declaring myself.
4. What became of my companions I cannot tell.
5. I should now tell what public measures were taken by the magistrates for the general safety.
6. You see, my lord, how things are altered.
7. Now the question was, what I should do next.
8. He said that he was going over to Greenwich. I asked if he would let me go with him.
9. That the tide is rising may be seen by anybody.

10. Ask me no reason why I love you.

11. That Arnold was a traitor was now clear enough.

12. I doubt whether this act is legal.

13. I am not prepared to say that Knox had a soft temper; nor do I know that he had an ill temper.

14. There are two questions, — whether the Essay will succeed, and who or what is the author.

15. The shouts of storm and successful violence announced that the castle was in the act of being taken.

16. The stranger inquired where the mayor lived.

17. That all is not gold that glitters was found out long ago.

18. I demanded why the gates were shut.

19. I doubt if I ever talked so much nonsense in my life.

20. I solemnly assure you that you are quite mistaken.

21. The prince soon concluded that he should never be happy in this course of life.

22. I know not what others may think.

23. Tell me not that life is a dream.

24. I think you are mistaken.

CHAPTER 142
Infinitive Clauses

> **Infinitive clauses** have a **substantive** in the **objective case** with an **infinitive**.
>
> ❧
>
> **Infinitive clauses** may be the **object of** certain **verbs**.
>
> ❧
>
> The **substantive** is the **subject of** the **infinitive**.

611. Compare the following sentences:

> John's friends wished that he should succeed.
> John's friends wished him to succeed.

These sentences say the same thing, but in different ways.

In the first sentence, the direct object of *wished* is the **noun clause** *that he should succeed*. In the second, the object must be *him to succeed*, since this group of words expresses *what* John's friends wished, precisely as the noun clause does in the first sentence.

What is the construction of the objective *him?* It is not the object of *wished;* for *I wish him* would make no sense. It appears to be a kind of **subject of the infinitive** *to succeed*, since it tells *who* is to succeed and replaces *he*, which stands as the subject of *should succeed* in the first sentence.[86]

612. **A kind of clause, consisting of a substantive in the objective case followed by an infinitive, may be used as the object of certain verbs.**

Such clauses are called infinitive clauses, and the substantive is said to be the subject of the infinitive.

613. An infinitive clause is usually equivalent in meaning to a noun clause with *that*.

614. **Infinitive clauses** are used:

> (1) after verbs of *wishing, commanding*, and the like, and
> (2) after some verbs of *believing, declaring*, and *perceiving*.[87] Thus,

> My father wishes *me to become a lawyer.*
> I believe *him to he an honorable man.*

615. A **predicate pronoun** after *to be* in an infinitive clause is in the **objective case,** agreeing with the subject of the infinitive. Thus,

> You know the culprit to be *him.*

---

[86] In Section 426 we learned that the infinitive has no subject. The construction which we are now studying may be regarded as a peculiar exception to that rule.

[87] After verbs of *wishing*, etc., they express purpose; after verbs of *thinking*, etc., they are in indirect discourse.

You believe my brother John to be *me*.
We know it to be *her*.

Contrast the **predicate nominative** in:

You know that the culprit is *he*.
You believe that my brother John is *I*.
The culprit was thought to be *he*.
My brother was believed to be *I*.
It was known to be *she*.

616. After *see, hear, feel,* and some other verbs, the infinitive without *to* is used. Thus,

I saw the sailor *climb* the rope.
The hunter heard the lion *roar* in the distance.
I felt his pulse *beat* feebly.
They watched the boat *drift* slowly down the stream.
They could not perceive him *move*.

Chapter 142 Exercise

Make ten sentences containing infinitive clauses after verbs of *wishing, commanding, believing, declaring,* etc.

CHAPTER 143
Elliptical Sentences

617. Compare the following sentences:

> *If it is possible,* we shall start for Chicago tomorrow.
> *If possible,* we shall start for Chicago tomorrow.

The meaning is the same, but in the second sentence the words *it is* are omitted. These words must be supplied (or understood) to make the sentence grammatically complete. Such an omission is called **ellipsis**, and the sentence is said to be **elliptical.**

618. **The omission of a word or words necessary to the grammatical completeness of a clause or sentence is called ellipsis.**

A clause or sentence that shows ellipsis is said to be elliptical. Ellipsis is a Greek word meaning "omission."

619. In analyzing an elliptical clause or sentence the omitted words should be supplied.

620. Various kinds of elliptical sentences are common in English. Examples follow, with the omitted words supplied in brackets.

> **The omission of a word or words** that are necessary to the grammatical completeness of a clause or sentence is called **ellipsis.**
>
> ❧
>
> To **analyze** an elliptical sentence, you must supply the missing words.

1. [I] thank you.
2. [I] pray come here.
3. When [he is] angry, he is dangerous.
4. Though [they were] weary and footsore, the wayfarers trudged along.
5. If [it is] necessary, I can lend you the money.
6. The man [whom] you met is a famous politician.
7. The ruins [which] you see were caused by an earthquake.
8. We must escape now if [we] ever [escape].
9. John is five years older than I [am old].
10. Gold is heavier than iron [is heavy].
11. You weigh more than I do [weigh].
12. He likes John better than [he likes] me.
13. The garrison held out as long as [it was] possible.
14. While [we were] climbing the mountain, we saw a bear.
15. Why [is] this disturbance?
16. His hair was light, his eyes [were] blue.

17. Some went east, others [went] west.[88]

Chapter 143 Exercise

Supply the ellipsis in each of the following elliptical sentences.

1. When in need of help, apply to me.
2. The leader they chose was called Pedro.
3. A good conscience is better than gold.
4. You are much taller than I.
5. Tom likes you better than me.
6. Though beaten, I am not discouraged.
7. I will send you the money tomorrow, if possible.
8. Why all this noise?
9. Some of us are studying arithmetic, others algebra.
10. The book you were reading has been returned to the library.
11. I don't believe you know your lesson.
12. What next?
13. When inclined to lose your temper, count twenty before you speak.
14. "Whither bound?" asked the captain.
15. Beetles have six legs, spiders eight.
16. Your boat is painted white, George's green.
17. I bought this hat at Sampson's.
18. These apples, though handsome enough, are rather hard.

---

[88] Some expressions, originally elliptical, have become so idiomatic in their shortened form that no ellipsis is felt and no words need be supplied in order to complete the construction. Thus in "He acts as if he were crazy," *as if* may be regarded as a compound conjunction connecting the clauses, and it is unnecessary to expand the sentence into "He acts as [he would act] if he were crazy" in order to analyze it.

Appendix A: The English Language

The English language has a history that extends back for some fifteen hundred years.

In the fifth century of the Christian era, England was inhabited by various tribes of the ancient Britons, who spoke a language altogether different from English. They had been for four centuries under the rule of the Roman Empire, and consequently Latin, the language of the Romans, was used to some extent in the larger cities. In the main, however, the Britons spoke a tongue resembling that of the modern inhabitants of Wales, who are their descendants.

In the fifth century the island was invaded by several wild, piratical tribes, whose home was in northern Germany, in the low countries on the eastern and southern shores of the North Sea. Of these tribes the most important were the Angles and the Saxons, whose language was similar to that tongue which has since become Dutch.

In a long war, or rather a series of wars, the Angles and Saxons made themselves masters of Britain. They became civilized and began to cultivate literature. Their language, which they usually called "English" (that is, "the tongue of the *Angles*"), gradually spread through most of the island. In Wales, however, the ancient Britons continued to use their own language, which is still spoken by their descendants, the Welsh; and in the northern part of Scotland, Gaelic, which is akin to Welsh, and identical to all intents and purposes with the native language of Ireland, has never died out.

The oldest period of our language is commonly called either Anglo-Saxon (from the Angles and Saxons) or Old English.

In the year 1066, England was invaded by the Normans, a Scandinavian tribe who had got possession of Normandy (in northern France) about a hundred and fifty years before. At the time of the Norman Conquest, the Normans had given up their native Scandinavian and spoke a dialect of French.

From the middle of the eleventh century to about the year 1400, two languages were common in England: (1) English, which was spoken by the majority of the people, and which was a descendant of the language of the Anglo-Saxons, and (2) French, which was the language of the court and of high society.

Gradually, however, the speaking of French died out amongst the inhabitants of England, except as an accomplishment, and the English tongue became the only natural language of Englishmen, whether they were of Anglo-Saxon or of Norman descent.

Meantime, however, the Old English or Anglo-Saxon language had become very much changed. By the year 1400 it had lost most of its inflections, and had adopted a large number of new words from French and Latin. Thus, in the following passage, most of the words printed in Roman type are of

Anglo-Saxon origin, whereas the italicized words come from Latin or French.

While he was *divided* betwixt these *reflections*, and *doubt*ful of what he should do, Bruce was looking upward to the roof of the *cabin* in which he lay; and his eye was *attracted* by a spider, which, hanging at the end of a long thread of its own spinning, was *endeavoring*, as is the *fashion* of that *creature*, to swing itself from one beam in the roof to another, for the *purpose* of *fixing* the line on which it meant to stretch its web. The *insect* made the *attempt* again and again without *success*; and at length Bruce *counted* that it had *tried* to *carry* its *point* six times, and been as often un*able* to do so.

The period of English from about 1200 to 1500 is usually called the Middle English period, to distinguish it from Old English or Anglo-Saxon on the one hand, and, on the other, from Modern English, the form of the language with which we are now familiar.

Even within that period which we call the Modern English period, our language has undergone many changes in pronunciation, in form, and in construction. Both Shakespeare and Tennyson, for example, are counted as Modern English writers, but we do not need to be told that Shakespeare's language is considerably different from that of Tennyson.

The explorations, discoveries, and conquests of the people of Great Britain have resulted in the spread of their language to all parts of the world, so that it is now not merely the language of England, but, to a considerable extent, that of Scotland, Ireland, North America, Australia, and India. Besides this, there is no quarter of the globe where English-speaking persons cannot be found.

Appendix B: Lists of Verbs

EDITOR'S NOTE: These verb lists are reproduced from the original *Mother Tongue Book II*. See Appendix G for a consolidated verb list that is a handy reference of all these verbs in one alphabetical list.

In lists I and II, only such verb forms are given as are indisputably correct in accordance with the best prose usage of the present day. The pupil may feel perfectly safe, therefore, in using the forms registered in these lists.[89]

I.

STRONG VERBS IN WHICH THE PRETERITE AND THE PAST PARTICIPLE DIFFER IN FORM.

[A few verbs (marked ❖) which are seldom or never used in ordinary language are included in this list. These have various irregularities. A few verbs are partly strong and partly weak.]

PRESENT TENSE	PRETERITE (PAST) TENSE	PAST PARTICIPLE
arise	arose	arisen
am (*subjunc.* be)	was	been
awake	awoke, awaked	awaked
bear	bore	borne, born[1]
beat	beat	beaten
beget	begot	begotten
begin	began	begun
bid, *command*[2]	bade	bidden
bite	bit	bitten
blow	blew	blown
break	broke	broken
chide	chid	chidden
choose	chose	chosen
❖cleave[3], *split*	cleft, clove (clave)	cleft, cleaved (cloven, *adj.*)
come	came	come
do	did	done
draw	drew	drawn
drink	drank	drunk (drunken, *adj*)
drive	drove	driven
eat	ate	eaten

---

[89] The omission of a form from the lists, then, does not necessarily indicate that it is "wrong" or even objectionable. There is considerable diversity of usage with regard to the strong verbs, and to state the facts at length would take much space. An attempt to include archaic, poetical, and rare forms in the same list with the usual modern forms is sure to mislead young students. Hence the lists here presented are confined to forms about whose correctness there can be no difference of opinion. Archaic and poetical tense forms are treated in the following pages.

PRESENT TENSE	PRETERITE (PAST) TENSE	PAST PARTICIPLE
fall	fell	fallen
fly	flew	flown
forbear	forbore	forborne
forget	forgot	forgotten
forsake	forsook	forsaken
freeze	froze	frozen
give	gave	given
go	went (*weak*)	gone
grow	grew	frown
hew	hewed (*weak*)	hewn
hide	hid	hidden
know	knew	known
lade[1]	laded (*weak*)	laded, laden
lie, *recline*[2]	lay	lain
ride	rode	ridden
ring	rang	rung
rise	rose	risen
♣ rive	rived (*weak*)	riven, rived
run	ran	run
see	saw	seen
♣ seethe, *transitive*	sod, seethed	seethed (sodden, *adj.*)[3]
shake	shook	shaken
shave	shaved (*weak*)	shaved (shaven, *adj.*)
show	showed (*weak*)	shown
shrink	shrank	shrunk (shrunken, *adj.*)
♣ shrive	shrove, shrived	shriven, shrived
sing	sang	sung
sink	sank	sunk
slay	slew	slain
slide	slid	slid, slidden
smite	smote	smitten
sow	sowed (*weak*)	sowed, sown
speak	spoke	spoken

[1]*Load* has *loaded* in both preterite and past participle. *Laden* is sometimes used as the past participle of *load*.

[2]*Lie*, "to tell a falsehood," has *lied* in both preterite and past participle.

[3]*Seethe*, intransitive, has usually *seethed* in both preterite and past participle. It is in rather common literary use.

PRESENT TENSE	PRETERITE (PAST) TENSE	PAST PARTICIPLE
spring	sprang	sprung
steal	stole	stolen
strew	strewed (*weak*)	strewn
stride	strode	stridden
strike	struck	struck (stricken, *adj.*)[1]
strive	strove	striven
swear	swore	sworn
swell	swelled (*weak*)	swelled, swollen
swim	swam	swum
take	took	taken
tear	tore	torn
thrive	throve, thrived	thriven, thrived
throw	threw	thrown
tread	trod	trodden
wear	wore	worn
weave	wove	woven
write	wrote	written

[1]Stricken is also used as a participle in a figurative sense. Thus we say: "The community *was stricken* with pestilence," but "The dog was *struck* with a stick."

Bear, break, drive, get (beget, forget), speak, stink, swear, tear, have archaic preterites in a: *bare, brake, drove, gat, spake,* etc.

Beat, beget (forget), bite, break, forsake, hide, ride, shake, speak, weave, write, and some other verbs, have archaic forms of the past participle like those of the preterite. The participles in *-en,* however, are now the accepted forms. *Chid* and *trod* are common participial forms.

Bid, "to command," has sometimes *bid* in both preterite and past participle; *bid,* "to offer money," has these forms regularly.

Begin, drink, ring, shrink, sing, sink, spring, swim, often have in poetry a *u*-form (*begun, sung,* etc.) in the preterite as well as in the past participle. This form (though good *old* English)[90] should be carefully avoided in modern speech.

Some verbs have rare or archaic weak forms alongside of the strong forms. Thus *shined,* preterite and past participle of *shine; showed,* past participle of *show.*

Ate and *eaten* are preferred to *eat* (pronounced ĕt).

Miscellaneous archaisms are *writ* for *wrote* and *written, rid* for *rode* and *ridden, strewed* and *strown* for *strewn.*

Quoth, "said," is an old strong preterite. The compound *bequeath* has *bequeathed* only.

---

[90] It is a remnant of the old preterite plural. In Anglo-Saxon, the principal parts of *begin* were: present, *beginne;* pret., *began* i pret. pl., *begunnon;* p.p., *begunnen.*

II.

STRONG VERBS AND IRREGULAR WEAK VERBS HAVING THE PRETERITE AND THE PAST PARTICIPLE ALIKE. [The strong verbs are italicized.]

PRESENT TENSE	PRETERITE AND PAST PARTICIPLE	PRESENT TENSE	PRETERITE AND PAST PARTICIPLE
abide	*abode*	*grind*	*ground*
behold	*beheld*	*hang*	*hung*, hanged[4]
bend	bent	have	had
bereave	bereft, bereaved[1]	hear	heard
beseech	besought	*heave*	*hove*, heaved[1]
bet	bet	hit	hit
bid (money)	bid	*hold*	*held*
bind	*bound*	hurt	hurt
bleed	bled	keep	kept
breed	bred	lay	laid
bring	brought	lead	led
build	built	leave	left
burst	*burst*	lend	lent
buy	bought	*let*	*let*
cast	cast	light	lighted *or* lit[2]
catch	caught	lose	lost
cling	*clung*	make	made
cost	cost	mean	meant
creep	crept	meet	met
cut	cut	pay	paid
deal	dealt	put	put
dig	*dug*	read	read
dwell	dwelt	reave (*archaic*)	reft, reaved
feed	fed	reeve	rove
feel	felt	rend	rent
fight	*fought*	rid	rid
find	*found*	say	said
flee	fled	seek	sought
fling	*flung*	sell	sold
get	*got*[3]	send	sent

[1]The adjective form is *bereaved:* as, "The bereaved father."

[2]So both *light*, "to kindle," and *light*, "to alight." The verb *alight* has usually *alighted* in both preterite and past participle.

[3] The archaic participle *gotten* is used in the compounds *begotten* and *forgotten*, and as an adjective ("*ill-gotten* gains"). Many good speakers also use it instead of the past participle *got*, but *got* is the accepted modern form.

[4] *Hanged* is used only of execution by hanging.

PRESENT TENSE	PRETERITE AND PAST PARTICIPLE	PRESENT TENSE	PRETERITE AND PAST PARTICIPLE
set	set	stave	stove, staved
shed	shed	*stick*	*stuck*
shine	*shone*	*sting*	*stung*
shoe	shod	*stink*	*stunk*
shoot	shot	*string*	*strung*
shut	shut	sweep	swept
sit	*sat*	*swing*	*swung*
sleep	slept	teach	taught
sling	*slung*	tell	told
slink	*slunk*	think	thought
slit	*slit*	thrust	thrust
spend	spent	*wake*	*woke*, waked
spin	*spun*	weep	wept
spit	*spit*	wet	wet
split	split	*win*	*won*
spread	spread	*wind*	*wound*
stand	*stood*	*wring*	*wrung*

[1] Usage varies with the context. We say, "The crew *hove* the cargo overboard," but NOT "She *hove* a sigh."

Observe that the following verbs have all three of the principal parts alike: *bet, burst, cast, cost, cut, hit, hurt, let, put, rid, set, shut, slit, spit, split, spread, thrust, wet.*

Bend, beseech, bet, build, burst, catch, dwell, rend, split, wet, have archaic or less usual forms in -ed: *bended, beseeched, betted,* etc. *Builded* is common in the proverbial "He *builded* better than he knew." *Bursted* is common as an adjective: "a *bursted* bubble."

Miscellaneous archaisms are the preterites *sate* for sat, *trode* for trod, *spat* for *spit.*

Dive has *dived*; but *dove* (an old form) is common in America.

Plead has preterite and past participle *pleaded.* Plead (pronounced *plĕd*) is avoided by careful writers and speakers.

Blend, leap, lean, have usually *blended, leaped, leaned*; but *blent, leapt, leant* are not uncommon.

Clothe has commonly *clothed*; but *clad* is common in literary use, and is regular in the adjectives *well-clad, ill-clad* (for which ordinary speech has substituted *well-dressed, badly* or *poorly dressed*).

Prove has preterite and past participle *proved.* The past participle *proven* should be avoided.

Work has preterite and past participle *worked. Wrought* in the preterite and past participle is archaic, but is modern as an adjective (as in *wrought iron*).

III.

The following verbs vary between -ed and -t (-d) in the preterite and the past participle. In some of them, this variation is a mere difference of spelling; in others it implies also a difference in pronunciation. In writing, the -ed forms are preferred in most cases; in speaking, the -t forms (when these indicate a different pronunciation) are very common.

PRESENT	PRETERITE (PAST) AND PAST PARTICIPLE
bless	blessed, blest[1]
burn	burned, burnt[2]
curse	cursed, curst[1]
dare	dared (*less common* durst)
dream	dreamed, dreamt
dress	dressed, drest
gird	girded, girt[2]
kneel	kneeled, knelt[2]
knit	knit, knitted[2]
learn	learned, learnt[3]
pen, *shut up*	penned, pent[2]
quit	quitted, quit[2]
shred	shredded, shred[2]
smell	smelled, smelt[2]
speed	sped, speeded[2]
spell	spelled, spelt
spill	spilled, spilt[2]
spoil	spoiled, spoilt
stay	stayed, staid
sweat	sweated, sweat[2]
wed	wedded (*p.p. also* wed)[2]

[1] The adjectives are usually pronounced *blessèd, cursèd*. Compare also the adjective *accursèd*.
[2] Both forms are in good use.
[3] Both forms are in good use. The adjective is pronounced *learnèd*.

IV.

The following verbs have regular *-ed* forms in modern prose, but in poetry and the high style sometimes show archaic forms. Only the modern forms should be used in ordinary speech and writing.

PRESENT TENSE	PRETERITE (PAST) TENSE	PAST PARTICIPLE
crow	crowed, *crew*	crowed, *crown*
freight	freighted	freighted, fraught (*figurative*)
grave	graved	graved, *graven*
engrave	engraved	engraved, *engraven*
mow	mowed	mowed, *mown*
sew	sewed	sewed, *sewn*
shape	shaped	shaped, *shapen*
shear	sheared, *shore*	sheared, *shorn*
wax	waxed	waxed, *waxen*

V.

DEFECTIVE VERBS.

The present tense of *may, can, shall,* is an old strong preterite. Hence the first and third persons singular are alike: *I may, he may.* The actual preterites of these verbs are weak forms: *might, could, should. Must* is the weak preterite of an obsolete *mot,* and is almost always used as a present tense (Section 546).

Dare and *owe* originally belonged to this class. *Owe* has become a regular weak verb, except for the peculiar preterite *ought,* which is used in a present sense (see Section 548); *dare* has in the third person *dare* or *dares,* and in the preterite *dared,* more rarely *durst.* The archaic *wot* "know," preterite *wist,* also belongs to this class. *Will* is inflected like *shall,* having *will* in the first and third singular and *would* in the preterite.

Appendix C: Conjugation of the Verb *To Be*

INDICATIVE MOOD	
SINGULAR	PLURAL
PRESENT TENSE	
1. I am.	We are.
2. Thou art.	You are.
3. He is.	They are.
PRETERITE (PAST) TENSE	
1. I was.	We were.
2. Thou wast (wert).	You were.
3. He was.	They were.
FUTURE TENSE	
1. I shall be.	We shall be.
2. Thou wilt be.	You will be.
3. He will be.	They will be.
PERFECT TENSE	
1. I have been.	We have been.
2. Thou hast been.	You have been.
3. He has been.	They have been.
PLUPERFECT TENSE	
1. I had been.	We had been.
2. Thou hadst been.	You had been.
3. He had been.	They had been.
FUTURE PERFECT TENSE	
1. I shall have been.	We shall have been.
2. Thou wilt have been.	You will have been.
3. He will have been.	They will have been.

SUBJUNCTIVE MOOD	
SINGULAR	PLURAL
PRESENT TENSE	
1. If I be. 2. If thou be. 3. If he be.	If we be. If you be. If they be.
PRETERITE (PAST) TENSE	
1. If I were. 2. If thou wert. 3. If he were.	If we were. If you were. If they were.
FUTURE TENSE	
1. If I shall be. 2. If thou shalt be. 3. If he shall be.	If we shall be. If you shall be. If they shall be.
PERFECT TENSE	
1. If I have been. 2. If thou have been. 3. If he have been.	If we have been. If you have been. If they have been.
PLUPERFECT TENSE	
1. If I had been. 2. If thou hadst been. 3. If he had been.	If we had been. If you had been. If they had been.
FUTURE PERFECT TENSE	
1. If I shall have been. 2. If thou shalt have been. 3. If he shall have been.	If we shall have been. If you shall have been. If they shall have been.

IMPERATIVE MOOD. *Present. Sing, and Pl.* Be [thou or you].
INFINITIVE. *Present,* to be; *perfect,* to have been.
PARTICIPLES. *Present,* being; *past,* been; *perfect,* having been.

Appendix D: Conjugation of the Verb *To Strike*

ACTIVE VOICE

INDICATIVE MOOD

SINGULAR	PLURAL
PRESENT TENSE	
1. I strike. 2. Thou strikest. 3. He strikes.	We strike. You strike. They strike.
PRETERITE (PAST) TENSE	
1. I struck. 2. Thou struckest. 3. He struck.	We struck. You struck. They struck.
FUTURE TENSE	
1. I shall strike. 2. Thou wilt strike. 3. He will strike.	We shall strike. You will strike. They will strike.
PERFECT TENSE	
1. I have struck. 2. Thou hast struck. 3. He has struck.	We have struck. You have struck. They have struck.
PLUPERFECT TENSE	
1. I had struck. 2. Thou hadst struck. 3. He had struck.	We had struck. You had struck. They had struck.
FUTURE PERFECT TENSE	
1. I shall have struck. 2. Thou wilt have struck. 3. He will have struck.	We shall have struck. You will have struck. They will have struck.

SUBJUNCTIVE MOOD	
SINGULAR	PLURAL
PRESENT TENSE	
1. If I strike. 2. If thou strike. 3. If he strike.	If we strike. If you strike. If they strike.
PRETERITE (PAST) TENSE	
1. If I struck. 2. If thou struck. 3. If he struck.	If we struck. If you struck. If they struck.
PERFECT TENSE	
1. If I have struck. 2. If thou have struck. 3. If he have struck.	If we have struck. If you have struck. If they have struck.
PLUPERFECT TENSE	
1. If I had struck. 2. If thou had struck. 3. If he had struck.	If we had struck. If you had struck. If they had struck.

IMPERATIVE MOOD. *Present. Sing, and Pl.* Strike [thou or you].

INFINITIVE. *Present,* to strike; *perfect,* to have struck.

PARTICIPLES. *Present,* striking; *past,* struck; *perfect,* having struck.

PASSIVE VOICE

INDICATIVE MOOD	
SINGULAR	PLURAL
PRESENT TENSE	
1. I am struck. 2. Thou art struck. 3. He is struck.	We are struck. You are struck. They are struck.
PRETERITE (PAST) TENSE	
1. I was struck. 2. Thou wast (*or* wert) struckest. 3. He was struck.	We were struck. You were struck. They were struck.
FUTURE TENSE	
1. I shall be struck. 2. Thou wilt be struck. 3. He will be struck.	We shall be struck. You will be struck. They will be struck..
PERFECT TENSE	
1. I have been struck. 2. Thou hast been struck. 3. He has been struck.	We have been struck. You have been struck. They have been struck.
PLUPERFECT TENSE	
1. I had been struck. 2. Thou hadst been struck. 3. He had been struck.	We had been struck. You had been struck. They had been struck.
FUTURE PERFECT TENSE	
1. I shall have been struck. 2. Thou wilt have been struck. 3. He will have been struck.	We shall have been struck. You will have been struck. They will have been struck.

SUBJUNCTIVE MOOD

SINGULAR	PLURAL
PRESENT TENSE	
1. If I be struck. 2. If thou be struck. 3. If he be struck.	If we be struck. If you be struck. If they be struck.
PRETERITE (PAST) TENSE	
1. If I were struck. 2. If thou wert struck. 3. If he were struck.	If we were struck. If you were struck. If they were struck.
PERFECT TENSE	
1. If I have been struck. 2. If thou have been struck. 3. If he have been struck.	If we have been struck. If you have been struck. If they have been struck.
PLUPERFECT TENSE	
1. If I had been struck. 2. If thou had been struck. 3. If he had been struck.	If we had been struck. If you had been struck. If they had been struck.

IMPERATIVE MOOD. *Present. Sing, and Pl.* Be [thou or you] struck.

INFINITIVE. *Present*, to be struck; *perfect*, to have been struck.

PARTICIPLES. *Present*, being struck; *past*, struck; *perfect*, having been struck.

Appendix E: Use of Capital Letters

1. Every sentence begins with a capital letter.

2. Every line of poetry begins with a capital letter.

3. The first word of every direct quotation begins with a capital letter.

   > NOTE: This rule does not apply to quoted fragments of sentences.

4. Every proper noun or abbreviation of a proper noun begins with a capital letter.

5. Most adjectives derived from proper nouns begin with capital letters: as, *America, Indian, Swedish, Spenserian.*

   > NOTE: Some adjectives derived from proper nouns have ceased to be closely associated in thought with the nouns from which they come, and therefore begin with small letters. Thus, *voltaic, galvanic, mesmeric, maudlin, stentorian.*

6. Every title attached to the name of a person begins with a capital letter.

Mr. Thomas Smith	C.J. Adams, *M.D.*
John Wilson, *Esq.*	*President* Grant
Miss Allerton	*Professor* Whitney
Dr. F.E. Wilson	*Sir* Walter Raleigh

7. In titles of books, etc., the first word, as well as every important word that follows, begins with a capital letter.

8. The interjection *O* and the pronoun *I* are always written in capital letters.

9. Personal pronouns referring to the deity are often capitalized.

   > NOTE: Usage varies: the personal pronouns are commonly capitalized, the relatives less frequently. The rule is often disregarded altogether when its observance would result in a multitude of capitals; so in the Bible and in many hymn books and works of theology.

10. Common nouns and adjectives often begin with capital letters when they designate the topics or main points of definitions or similar statements. Such capitals are called *emphatic* (or *topical*) *capitals*.[91]

> NOTE: Emphatic (or topical) capitals are analogous to capitals in the titles of books (see Rule 7), but their use is not obligatory. They are especially common in textbooks and other elementary manuals.

---

[91] Editor's note: In modern usage, capitals are rarely used for emphasis.

Appendix F: Rules of Punctuation[92]

The common marks of punctuation are:

the period
the interrogation point (question mark)
the exclamation point
the comma
the semicolon
the colon
the dash
marks of parenthesis and
quotation marks

The **hyphen** and the **apostrophe** may be conveniently treated along with marks of punctuation.

End Marks

1. The **period**, the **interrogation point (question mark)**, and the **exclamation point** are used at the end of sentences. Every complete sentence must be followed by one of these three marks.

The end of a declarative or an imperative sentence is marked by a period. But a declarative or an imperative sentence that is likewise exclamatory may be followed by an exclamation point instead of a period.

The end of a direct question is marked by an interrogation point.

An exclamatory sentence in the form of an indirect question is followed by an exclamation point: as,

"How absolute the knave is!"

2. A **period** is used after an abbreviation.

3. An **exclamation point** is used after an exclamatory word or phrase.

> NOTE: This rule is not absolute. Most interjections take the exclamation point. With other words and with phrases, usage differs; if strong feeling is expressed, the

[92] The main rules of punctuation are well fixed and depend on important distinctions in sentence structure and consequently in thought. In detail, however, there is much variety of usage, and care should be taken not to insist on such uniformity in the pupils' practice as is not found in the printed books which they use. If young writers can be induced to indicate the ends of their sentences properly, much has been accomplished.

exclamation point is commonly used, but too many such marks deface the page.

Commas

The comma is used,

1. After a noun (or a phrase) of direct address (a *vocative nominative*). Thus,

    > John, tell me the truth.
    > Little boy, what is your name?

    NOTE: If the noun is exclamatory, an exclamation point may be used instead of a comma.

2. Before a direct quotation in a sentence. Thus,

    > The cry ran through the ranks, "Are we never to move forward?"

    NOTE: When the quotation is long or formal, a colon, or a colon and a dash, may be used instead of a comma, especially with the words *as follows*.

3. After a direct quotation when this is the subject or the object of a following verb. Thus,

    > "They are coming; the attack will be made on the
    > center," said Lord Fitzroy Somerset.
    > "I see it," was the cool reply of the duke.

NOTE: If the quotation ends with an interrogation point or an exclamation point, no comma is used.

4. To separate words, or groups of words, arranged in a coordinate series, when these are not connected by *and, or,* or *nor.*

If the conjunction is used to connect the last two members of the series but omitted with the others, the comma may be used before the conjunction.

> I found two saws, an axe, and a hammer.
> They were so shy, so subtle, and so swift of foot, that it was
> difficult to come at them.
> It would make the reader pity me to tell what odd,
> misshapen, ugly things I made.
> They groaned, they stirred, they all uprose.

NOTE 1: Commas may be used even when conjunctions are expressed, if the members of the series consist of several words, or if the writer wishes to emphasize their distinctness.

NOTE 2: Clauses in a series are commonly separated by semicolons unless they are short and simple (see "Commas and Dependent Clauses" of this appendix).

5. To set off words and phrases out of their regular order. Thus,

> Seated on her accustomed chair, with her usual air of apathy and want of interest in what surrounded her, she seemed now and then mechanically to resume the motion of twirling her spindle. - SCOTT

6. To separate a long subject from the verb of the predicate. Thus,

> To have passed them over in an historical sketch of my literary life and opinions, would have seemed to me like the denial of a debt. - COLERIDGE

7. To set off an appositive noun or an appositive adjective, with its modifiers. Thus,

> I have had the most amusing letter from Hogg, the Ettrick minstrel.

> There was an impression upon the public mind, natural enough from the continually augmenting velocity of the mail, but quite erroneous, that an outside seat on this class of carriages was a post of danger. - DE QUINCY

NOTE 1: Many participial and other adjective phrases come under this head. Thus,

> The genius, seeing me indulge myself on this melancholy prospect, told me I had dwelt long enough upon it. - ADDISON

NOTE 2: If a noun and its appositive are so closely connected as to form one idea, no comma is used. Thus,

> My friend Jackson lives in San Francisco.

NOTE 3: An intensive pronoun (*myself*, etc.) is not separated by a common from the substantive which it emphasizes.

NOTE 4: A series of words or phrases in apposition with a single substantive is sometimes set off, as a whole, by a comma and a dash.

8. To set off a subordinate clause, especially one introduced by a descriptive relative. Thus,

> I am going to take a last dinner with a most agreeable family, who have been my only neighbors ever since I have lived at Weston. - COWPER

NOTE: No comma is used before a restrictive relative. Thus,

> I want to know many things which only you can tell me. Perhaps I am the only man in England who can boast of such good fortune.

9. To set off a phrase containing a nominative absolute. Thus,

> They had some difficulty in passing the ferry at the riverside, the ferryman being afraid of them. -DEFOE

10. To set off *however, nevertheless, moreover,* et., and introductory phrases like *in the first place, on the one hand,* etc.

11. To set off a parenthetical expression. For this purpose commas, dashes, or marks of parenthesis may be used.

When the parenthetical matter is brief or closely related to the rest of the sentence, it is generally set off by commas. Thus,

> I exercised a piece of hypocrisy for which, I hope, you will hold me excused. - THACKERY

When it is longer and more independent, it is generally marked off by dashes, or enclosed in marks of parenthesis. The latter are less frequently used at present than formerly.

> The connection of the mail with the state and the executive government - a connection obvious, but yet not strictly defined - gave to the whole mail establishment an official grandeur. - DE QUINCEY

NOTE: Brackets are used to indicate insertions that are not part of the text.

Colons, Semicolons, and Commas with Clauses

The clauses of a compound sentence may be separated by colons, semicolons, or commas.

1.   The colon is used:

   (a) To show that the second of two clauses repeats the substance of the first in another form, or defines the first as an appositive defines a noun. Thus,

   This was the practice of the Grecian stage. But Terence made an innovation in the Roman: all his plays have double actions. - DRYDEN

   (b) To separate two groups of clauses one or both of which contain a semicolon. Thus,

   At the time, news such as we had heard might have been long in penetrating so far into the recesses of the mountains; but now, as you know, the approach is easy, and the communication, in summer time, almost hourly: nor is this strange, for travelers after pleasure are become not less active, and more numerous, than those who formerly left their homes for purposes of gain.
   - WORDSWORTH

   NOTE: The colon is less used now than formerly. The tendency is to use a semicolon or to begin a new sentence.

2.   The semicolon is used when the clauses are of the same general nature and contribute to the same general effect, especially if one of more of them contain commas. Thus,

   The sky was cloudless; the sun shone out bright and warm; the songs of birds, and hum or myriads of summer insects filled the air; and the cottage garden, crowded with every rich and beautiful tint, sparkled in the heavy dew like beds of glittering jewels. - DICKENS

3.   The comma may be used when the clauses are short and simple (see "Commas," Section 4, note in this appendix.)

   NOTE: The choice between colon, semicolon, and comma is determined in many cases by the writer's feeling of the closer or the looser connection of the ideas expressed by the several clauses, and is to some extent a matter of taste.

Commas and Dependent Clauses

1.   In a complex sentence, the dependent clause is generally separated from the main clause by a comma. But when the dependent clause is short and the connection close, the comma may be omitted.

NOTE: A descriptive relative clause is preceded by a comma, a restrictive relative clause is not (see chapter 121, section 515).

2. The clauses of a series, when in the same dependent construction, are often separated by semicolons to give more emphasis to each Thus,

> [Mrs. Battles] was none of your lukewarm gamesters, your half-and-half players, who have no objection to take a hand if you want one to make up a rubber; who affirm that they have not pleasure in winning; that they like to win one game and lose another; that they can while away an hour very agreeably at a card table, but are indifferent whether they play or no; and will desire an adversary, who has slipped a wrong card, to take it up and play another. - LAMB

Quotation Marks _____

1. A direct quotation is enclosed in quotation marks.

    NOTE: If the quotation stands by itself and is printed in different type, the marks may be omitted.

2. A quotation within a quotation is usually enclosed in single quotation marks.

3. In a quotation consisting of several paragraphs, quotation marks are put at the beginning of each paragraph and at the end of the last.

    NOTE: For the punctuation before a quotation, see "Commas" sections 2 and 3.

4. When a book, poem, or the like, is referred to, the title may be enclosed in quotation marks or italicized.

Dashes _____

1. Sudden changes in thought and feeling or breaks in speech are indicated by dashes. Thus,

> Eh!—what—why—upon my life, and so it is—Charley, my boy, so it's you, is it? - LEVER

2. Parenthetical expressions may be set off by dashes (see "Commas" Section 11, p. 370).

A colon, or colon and dash, may precede an enumeration, a direct quotation, or a statement formally introduced, - especially with _as follows,_ *namely,* and the like. Before an enumeration a comma and a dash may be used.[93] Thus,

> There are eight parts of speech: — nouns, pronouns, adjectives, verbs, adverbs, prepositions, conjunctions, and interjections.
> OR —
> There are eight parts of speech, — nouns, pronouns, etc.

The dash is sometimes used to strengthen a comma (as in the last paragraph but one).

Apostrophe and Hyphen

1. The apostrophe is used:

    (a) To mark the omission of a letter or letters in contractions.
    (b) As a sign of the possessive or genitive.
    (c) To indicate the plural of letters, signs, etc.

4. The hyphen is used:

    (a) When the parts of a word are separated in writing.
    (b) Between the parts of some compound words. (See the dictionary in each case.)

---

[93] Editor's note: the colon and dash is rarely used together in modern usage, nor is a dash often used after a comma. Instead, a colon is used alone to introduce a list. Likewise, a dash is used alone to set off a break in thought.

The Mother Tongue Student Workbook 1 and *The Mother Tongue Student Workbook 2* each have practice exercises for punctuation and capitalization taken from the sentences below and from works of literature.

EXERCISE[94]

Explain the use of the capitals and the marks of punctuation in the following passages:

1. "It will be midnight," said the coachman, "before we arrive at our inn."
2. We give thee heart and hand,
   Our glorious native Land.
3. Yet, though destruction sweep those lovely plains,
   Rise, fellow men! Our country yet remains!
4. After a dreadful night of anxiety, perplexity, and peril, the darkness slowly disappeared.
5. As he that lives longest lives but a little while, every man may be certain that he has no time to waste.
6. At its western side is a deep ravine or valley, through which a small stream rushes.
7. "The Vision of Sir Launfal" was written by James Russell Lowell.
8. Will not your trip to Bath afford you an opportunity to visit us at Weston?
9. "That is my brother," said Jack.
10. Dr. Adams, the eminent surgeon, took charge of the case.
11. We ran on, the dogs pursuing us, until we reached the bridge.
12. A quotation - especially if it is a long quotation - should always be to the point.
13. She hastened downstairs, ordered the servants to arm themselves with the weapons first at hand, placed herself at their head, and returned immediately.
14. Is it your will, brethren, that this man be elected to the council?
15. Hark! how the pitiless tempest raves!
16. Tom, however, was not pleased with the prospect.
17. Nothing, I trust, will interfere with your plan.
18. The fisherman wades in the surges;
    The sailor sails over the sea;
    The soldier steps bravely to battle:
    The woodman lays axe to the tree.
19. Neither witch nor warlock crossed Mordaunt's path, however.
20. It was late one evening that a carriage, drawn by mules, toiled up one of the passes of the Apennines.

---

[94] These exercises appear in the revised edition (1908) of *The Mother Tongue*.

Appendix G: Rules of Syntax[95]

1. A **noun** is the **name** of a person, place, or thing. A **pronoun** is a word used instead of a noun. It designates a person, place or thing without naming it. Nouns and pronouns are called **substantives**.

2. The **subject** of a verb is in the **nominative case**.

3. A substantive standing in the predicate after an intransitive or passive verb, and referring to the same person or thing as the subject, is called a **predicate nominative**. A predicate nominative agrees with the subject and is therefore in the **nominative case**.

4. A substantive used for the purpose of **addressing** a person directly, and not connected with any verb, is called a **vocative**. A vocative is regarded as in the **nominative case**, and is often called a **nominative of direct address**.

5. A substantive used as an **exclamation** is called an **exclamatory nominative**.

6. A substantive, with a participle, may express the cause, time, or circumstances of an action. This is called the **absolute construction**. The substantive is in the **nominative case** and is called a **nominative absolute**.

7. The **possessive case** denotes ownership of possession.

8. The **object** of a verb or preposition is in the **objective case**.

9. A substantive that completes the meaning of a transitive verb is called its **direct object**.

10. Verbs of *choosing, calling, naming, making,* and *thinking* may take **two objects** referring to the same person or thing. The first of these is the **direct object**, and the second, which completes the sense of the predicate, is called a **predicate objective**.

11. Some transitive verbs may take **two objects,** a **direct object** and an **indirect object**. The indirect object denotes the person or thing toward who or toward which is directed the action expressed by the rest of the predicate.

12. A verb that is regularly intransitive sometimes takes as an object a noun whose meaning closely resembles its own. A noun in this

---

[95] For convenience, a few definitions are included in this summary.

construction is called the **cognate object** of the verb and is in the **objective case**.

13. A noun used as an adverbial modifier is called an **adverbial objective**.

14. An **appositive** is in the same case as the substantive which it limits or defines.

15. A pronoun must agree in **number** and **gender** with the substantive for which it stands or to which it refers.

16. **Relative pronouns** connect dependent clauses with main clauses by referring directly to a substantive in the main clause. The substantive to which a pronoun refers is called its **antecedent**. A relative pronoun must agree with its antecedent in **gender, number,** and **person**. The case of a relative pronoun has nothing to do with its antecedent, but depends on the construction of its own clause.

17. A relative pronoun in the objective case is often omitted.

18. The relative pronoun *what* is often equivalent to *that which*. In this use, *what* has a **double construction**:
    (1) the construction of the omitted or implied antecedent *that*;
    (2) the construction of the relatives *which*.

19. The **compound relative pronouns** may include or imply their own antecedents and hence may have a **double construction**.

20. An **adjective** is a word which describes or limits a substantive. An adjective is said to **belong** to the substantive which it describes or limits.

21. According to their position in the sentence, adjectives are often classified as **attributive, appositive**, and **predicate adjectives**.
    (1) An attributive adjective is closely attached to its noun and regularly precedes it.
    (2) An appositive adjective is added to its noun to explain it, like and appositive substantive.
    (3) A predicate adjective completes the predicate, but describes or limits the subject.
For the use of an adjective as **predicate objective**, see Section 134.

22. The **comparative degree**, not the superlative, is used in comparing two persons or things. The superlative is used in

comparing one person or thing with two or more persons or things.

23. An **adverb** is a word which modifies a verb, an adjective, or another adverb.

24. **Relative adverbs** introduce subordinate clauses and are similar in their use to relative pronouns.

25. A verb is a word which **asserts**.

26. A verb must agree with its subject in **person and number**.

27. A **compound subject** with *and* usually takes a verb in the plural number.

28. A **compound subject** with *or* or *nor* takes a verb in the singular number if the substantives are singular.

29. Nouns that are **plural in form but singular in sense** commonly take a verb in the singular number.

30. **Collective nouns** take sometimes a singular and sometimes a plural verb. When the persons or things denoted are though of as **individuals**, the plural should be used. When the collection is regarded as a **unit**, the singular should be used.

31. A verb is in the **active voice** when it represents its subject as the **doer** of an act.

32. A verb is in the **passive voice** when it represents its subject as the **receiver** or the **product** of an action. The object of the active verb becomes the subject of the passive.

33. The **indicative** is the mood of **simple assertion** or **interrogation**, but it is used in other constructions also.

34. The **imperative** is the mood of **command** or **request**.

35. The **subject** of an **imperative** is seldom expressed unless it is emphatic. The subject, when expressed, may precede the imperative: as, *You go, You read*.

36. The **subjunctive mood** is used in certain special constructions of **wish, condition**, and the like.

37. An **infinitive**, with or without a complement or modifiers, may be used as the **subject** of a sentence.

38. An **infinitive** may be used as a **predicate nominative**.

39. An **infinitive** may be used as the **object** of the prepositions *about, but, except.*

40. An **infinitive** may modify a verb by **completing** its meaning, or by expressing the **purpose** of the action.

41. An **infinitive** may modify a **noun** or an **adjective**.

42. A kind of **clause**, consisting of a substantive in the objective case followed by an **infinitive**, may be used as the object of certain verbs.

>   Such clauses are called **infinitive clauses,** and the substantive is said to be the subject of the infinitive.
>   The **subject of an infinitive** is in the objective case.
>   **Infinitive clauses** are used:
>   (1) after verbs of *wishing, commanding,* and the like, and
>   (2) after some verbs of *believing, declaring,* and *perceiving.*

43. The constructions of **participles** are similar to those of adjective.

44. A **participle** is said to **belong** to the substantive which it describes or limits.

45. An **infinitive** or a **participle**, like any other verb form, may take an **object** if its meaning allows.

46. **Infinitives** and **participles**, like other verb forms, may be **modified** by adverbs, adverbial phrases, or adverbial clauses.

47. **Verbal nouns** in *-ing* have the form of present participles, but the construction of nouns.

48. **Verbal nouns** in *-ing* have certain verb properties.

>   (1) Verbal nouns in *-ing* may take a **direct** or an **indirect** object if their meaning allows.
>   (2) A verbal noun in *-ing* may take an **adverbial modifier.**

But verbal nouns in *-ing*, like other nouns, may be **modified** by **adjectives**.

49. A **preposition** is a word placed before a substantive to show its relation to some other word in the sentence. The substantive which follows a preposition is called its **object** and is in the **objective case**.

50. A **conjunction** connects words or groups of words.

51. A **coordinate conjunction** connects words or groups of words that are independent of each other.

52. A **subordinate conjunction** connects a subordinate clause with the clause on which it depends.

53. An **interjection** is a cry or other exclamatory sound expressing surprise, anger, pleasure, or some other emotion or feeling.

54. Interjections usually have no grammatical connection with the phrases or sentences in which they stand. Sometimes, however, a substantive is connected with an interjection by means of a preposition.

Appendix H: Student Reference Lists

Some of the irregularities of English just need to be studied and memorized. This appendix includes study aids to help master those things. Prepositions and their use, tricky verb usage (lie/lay, raise/rise, hang/hang, bear/bear/bare/bore), and a consolidated list of strong and irregular weak verbs are all included here.

Common English Prepositions

Bolded prepositions are especially common.

aboard	**beside**	in place of	regarding
about	besides	in spite of	regardless of
above	between	including	round
across	**beyond**	inside	save
after	**but**	instead of	since
against	**by**	into	than
ahead of	by means of	like	**through**
along	circa	minus	**throughout**
amid	**concerning**	near,	**till**
amidst	despite	next to	**to**
among	**down**	**of**	toward
around	**during**	**off**	towards
as	**except**	**on**	**under**
as far as	except for	on account of	underneath
as of	excluding	on behalf of	unlike
aside from	far from	on top of	until
at	following	onto	**up**
athwart	**for**	opposite	**upon**
atop	**from**	**out**	versus
barring	**in**	out of	via
because of	in accordance with	outside	**with**
before	in addition to	**over**	with regard to
behind	in case of	past	**within**
below	in front of	plus	**without**
beneath	in lieu of	prior to	

Idiomatic Phrases with Particular Prepositions _____

Some idiomatic phrases are used with particular prepositions. It is important when writing to use the correct preposition with these words. Here is a list of some common expressions and their correct prepositions.

a critic of	complain about	grow up	participation in
abide by *a rule*	concern for	happy about	pay for
abide in *a place*	conform to	hatred of	planning to
according to	confusion about	hope for	popular with
adapt from *something*	consist of	identical with *or* to	prepare for
adapt to *a situation*	dependent on	impressed with	preoccupied with
afraid of	desire for	in a world where	protested against
agreed to	differ about *or* over *a*	inconsistent with	proud of
angry at	*question*	infer from	provide for
apologize for	differ from *in some*	inferior to	reason for
approval of	*quality*	interested in	regarded as
ask about	differ with *a person*	interest in	respect for
ask for	disappointed by *or* in	jealous of	similar to
attributed to	*a person*	look for	sorry for
awareness of	disappointed in *or*	look forward to	study for
aware of	with *a thing*	look up	success in
based on	disintegrates into	love of	sure of
belief in	evolved from	made of	talk about
belong to	familiar with	make up	think about
blame on	far from	married to	tired of
bring up	find out	necessary to	trust in
capable of	fondness for	need for	understanding of
care for	fond of	oblivious of	work for
careless about	give up	originating in	worried about
certain of	grasp of	opposed to	worry about

Idioms Following Prepositions _____

Some idiomatic phrases begin with particular prepositions. Once again, it is important when writing to use the correct preposition with these words. Here is a list of some common expressions that begin with a preposition, and their meaning.

above reproach: perfect
at any rate: whatever happens, no matter what happens
at one's disposal: available for one's use
at fault: causing a problem or accident

at first: in the beginning
at last: finally, after some delay
at a loss: unsure of what to do or say
at once: immediately
at present: now

at rest: not moving, still

at stake: to be won or lost

at the wheel: in control

behind the scenes: influencing events secretly; unseen

behind schedule: not on time

beside the point: irrelevant

beyond help: cannot be helped

beyond reproach: perfect

by accident: not on purpose

by all means: by any possible method

by courtesy of: with the help, permission, sponsorship of

by default: the unearned or unchosen outcome, *win by default*

by hand: without the use of machinery

by heart: from memory

by mistake: accidentally

by oneself: alone

by the way: incidentally (used to introduce a new, unrelated topic)

for good: permanently

for good measure: in addition to the required amount

for a living: as a profession

for instance: for example

for now/ for the time being: until some other arrangement/decision is made

for one thing: because of one reason (out of several)

for sale: intended to be sold

for sure: definitely

for a while: for a period of time

from cradle to grave: from the beginning to the end

from head to foot: completely

from scratch: from raw ingredients/materials; without anything pre-made

from time to time: occasionally

in addition to: also

in advance: before something begins; early

in any case: whatever happens

in brief: concisely

in charge: in command; responsible for

in common: shared by two or more people

in control: having the power

in danger: likely to be harmed (opposite: out of danger/out of harm's way)

in a daze: unable to think clearly; confused

in debt: owing money (opposite: out of debt)

in demand: wanted by many people

in earnest: seriously; determined; sincerely

in the end: after everything is finished (describes a final outcome)

in fact: in reality; really

in a hurry: doing something quickly

in itself: without anything else

in the long run: in the end; eventually

in mint condition: perfect; as though brand-new

in a minute/moment/second: soon; quickly (used to tell how much longer it will be until something happens)

in no time: very soon; very quickly (used to tell how quickly something happened)

in season: (fruit or vegetables) ripe and available for sale at that time of year (opposite: out of season)

in trouble: blamed or punished for doing something wrong; in a difficult situation (opposite: out of trouble)

in vain: without success

in vogue: stylish

in the wrong: responsible for an error; guilty

inside out: with the inner side out

of course: certainly; as one would expect; as everyone knows

off and on: (describes a situation that exists at some times, but not others, over a period of time)

on account of: because of

on the air: in the process of broadcasting (on radio or television)

on all fours: (people) on hands and knees; (animals) on all four feet

on demand: when requested or demanded

on fire: burning; in flames (not burning as in turning black from staying in the oven too long)

on hand: available; in stock

on the lookout: watchful

on the one hand: (used to introduce the first side of an argument)

on one's own: alone; without assistance

on the other hand: alternatively (used with "on the one hand" to introduce a contrasting side of an argument)

on purpose: deliberately

on sale: being sold at a reduced price

on second thought: after thinking further

on a shoestring: with very little money

on the spur of the moment: spontaneously; on a sudden impulse

on time: at the correct time

on the verge of: very close to (an achievement)

out of the blue: unexpectedly

out of breath: panting from a shortage of oxygen (usually due to physical exertion)

out of character: different from a person's known character

out of order: not functioning

out of the ordinary: unusual

out of practice: unable to do something as well as one once could because of lack of recent practice

out of the question: not to be considered; not an option

out of shape: not in top physical condition because of lack of exercise (opposite: in shape)

out of sight: not able to be seen; hidden (opposite: in sight)

out of town: not in the city/town where one normally resides (opposite: in town)

out of tune: (of music/musical instruments) not at the correct pitch (opposite: in tune)

out of work: unemployed

to a certain extent: partly

under one's breath: in a whisper; not intending to be heard

under the circumstances: because of the current situation/circumstance

under control: able to be controlled or influenced (opposites: out of control/out of hand)

under fire: being shot at; being criticized

under the impression that: having the idea/belief that

under the influence of: affected by (usually alcohol or drugs)

up in the air: uncertain (with regard to the outcome of a situation)

with the naked eye: without the use of a lens

with regard/respect to: concerning; about

with a vengeance: more than usual; angrily

within reason: that is reasonable

Confusing Verb Usage _____

	LAY	**L**IE	**L**IE
Definition	to put or place (something)	to rest or recline	to tell a falsehood
Strong or weak	strong	strong	strong
Verb class	transitive verb, takes a direct object	intransitive verb, does not take a direct object	intransitive verb, does not take a direct object
Principal parts	lay, laid, (have) laid	lie, lay (have) lain	lie, lied, (have) lied
Example	**Lay** your homework on the teacher's desk.	**Lie** down and take a nap.	Do not **lie** to your parents.

	RAISE	**R**ISE
Definition	to cause to go up, to grow up, to set up right, to lift	to get up, come up
Strong or weak	weak	strong
Verb class	transitive verb, takes a direct object	intransitive verb, does not take a direct object
Principal parts	raise, raised, (have) raised	rise, rose, (have) risen
Example	The students **raise** their hands when they have questions.	They **rise** when the judge enters the courtroom.

	HANG	**HANG**
Definition	to attach something without support from below	to put to death by tying a rope about the neck and suspending the body.
Strong or weak	strong	weak
Verb class	transitive verb, takes a direct object	transitive verb, takes a direct object
Principal parts	hang, hung, (have) hung	hang, hanged, (have) hanged
Example	She **hung** the picture on her wall.	The criminal was **hanged** for his crimes.

	SIT	**SET**
Definition	to rest or be seated	to put or place something
Strong or weak	strong	weak
Verb class	intransitive verb, does not take a direct object	transitive verb, takes a direct object
Principal parts	sit, sat, (have) sat	set, set, (have) set
Example	The boy **sat** under the tree and read a book.	The boy **set** the book on the table.

	BEAR	**BEAR**	**BARE**	**BORE**
Definition	bring forth	carry	to uncover, expose	to drill a hole
Strong or weak	strong	strong	weak	weak
Verb class	intransitive verb, does not take a direct object	transitive verb, takes a direct object	transitive verb, takes a direct object	transitive verb, takes a direct object
Principal parts	bear, bore, (have) born/borne	bear, bore, (have) born	bare, bared, (have) bared	bore, bored, (have) bored
Example	She **bore** a son.	His suffering was a lot to **bear**.	She **bared** her soul to her friend.	He **bored** a hole in the tree.

Consolidated List of Strong and Irregular Weak Verbs_____

Irregular weak verbs shown in bold print.

PRESENT TENSE	PRETERITE (PAST) TENSE	PAST PARTICIPLE (SHOWN WITH *HAVE*)
arise	arose	(have) arisen
am (*subjunc.* be)	was	(have) been
awake	awoke, awaked	(have) awaked
bear	bore	(have) borne, born[1]
beat	beat	(have) beaten
become	became	(have) become
beget	begot	(have) begotten
begin	began	(have) begun
bend	**bent**	**(have) bent**
bet	**bet**	**(have) bet**
bid, *command*	bade	(have) bidden
bid (money)	**bid**	**(have) bid**
bind	bound	(have) bound
bite	bit	(have) bitten
bleed	**bled**	**(have) bled**
blow	blew	(have) blown
break	broke	(have) broken
breed	**bred**	**(have) bred**
bring	**brought**	**(have) brought**
build	**built**	**(have) built**
burst	burst	(have) burst
cast	**cast**	**(have) cast**
catch	**caught**	**(have) caught**
chide	chid	(have) chidden
choose	chose	(have) chosen
cleave, *split*	cleft, clove (clave)	(have) cleft, cleaved (cloven, *adj.*)
cling	clung	(have) clung
come	came	(have) come
cost	cost	(have) cost
creep	**crept**	**(have) crept**
cut	**cut**	**(have) cut**
deal	**dealt**	**(have) dealt**
dig	dug	(have) dug
do	did	(have) done
draw	drew	(have) drawn
drink	drank	(have) drunk (drunken, *adj*)
drive	drove	(have) driven
dwell	**dwelt**	**(have) dwelt**
eat	ate	(have) eaten
fall	fell	(have) fallen

Irregular weak verbs shown in bold print.

PRESENT TENSE	PRETERITE (PAST) TENSE	PAST PARTICIPLE (SHOWN WITH *HAVE*)
feed	**fed**	**(have) fed**
feel	**felt**	**(have) felt**
fight	fought	(have) fought
find	found	(have) found
flee	**fled**	**(have) fled**
fling	flung	(have) flung
fly	flew	(have) flown
forbear	forbore	(have) forborne
forget	forgot	(have) forgotten
forsake	forsook	(have) forsaken
freeze	froze	(have) frozen
get	got	(have) got
give	gave	(have) given
go	**went**	**(have) gone**
grind	ground	(have) ground
grow	grew	(have) frown
hang	hung	(have) hung
hang, *execute*	hanged	(have) hanged
have	**had**	**(have) had**
hear	**heard**	**(have) heard**
heave	hove, **heaved**	(have) hove, **heaved**
hew	hewed (*weak*)	(have) hewn
hide	hid	(have) hidden
hit	**hit**	**(have) hit**
hold	held	(have) held
hurt	**hurt**	**(have) hurt**
keep	**kept**	**(have) kept**
know	knew	(have) known
lade	laded	**(have) laded, laden**
lay, *put or place, transitive*	laid	(have) laid
lead	**led**	**(have) led**
leave	**left**	**(have) left**
lend	**lent**	**(have)lent**
let	let	(have) let
lie, *recline, intransitive*	lay	(have) lain
lie, *tell a falsehood*	lied	(have) lied
light	**lighted, lit**	**(have) lighted, lit**
lose	**lost**	**(have) lost**
make	**made**	**(have) made**
mean	**meant**	**(have) meant**

Irregular weak verbs shown in bold print.

PRESENT TENSE	PRETERITE (PAST) TENSE	PAST PARTICIPLE (SHOWN WITH *HAVE*)
pay	**paid**	**(have) paid**
put	**put**	**(have) put**
read	**read**	**(have) read**
reeve	**rove**	**(have) rove**
rend	**rent**	**(have) rent**
rid	**rid**	**(have) rid**
ride	rode	(have) ridden
ring	rang	(have) rung
rise	rose	(have) risen
rive	**rived**	**(have) riven, rived**
run	ran	(have) run
say	**said**	**(have) said**
see	saw	(have) seen
seek	**sought**	**(have) sought**
seethe, *transitive*	sod, seethed	(have) seethed (sodden, *adj.*)
sell	sold	(have) sold
send	**sent**	**(have) sent**
set	**set**	**(have) set**
shake	shook	(have) shaken
shave	**shaved**	(have) shaved (shaven, *adj.*)
shed	**shed**	**(have) shed**
shine	shone	(have) shone
shoe	**shod**	**(have) shod**
shoot	**shot**	**(have) shot**
show	**showed**	(have) shown
shut	**shut**	**(have) shut**
shrink	shrank	(have) shrunk (shrunken, *adj.*)
sing	sang	(have) sung
sink	sank	(have) sunk
sit	sat	(have) sat
slay	slew	(have) slain
sleep	**slept**	**(have) slept**
slide	slid	(have) slid, slidden
sling	slung	(have) slung
slink	slunk	(have) slunk
slit	slit	(have) slit
smite	smote	(have) smitten
sow	sowed (*weak*)	(have) sowed, sown
speak	spoke	(have) spoken
spend	**spent**	**(have) spent**

Irregular weak verbs shown in bold print.

PRESENT TENSE	PRETERITE (PAST) TENSE	PAST PARTICIPLE (SHOWN WITH *HAVE*)
spin	spun	(have) spun
spit	spit	(have) spit
split	**split**	**(have) split**
spread	**spread**	**(have) spread**
spring	sprang	(have) sprung
stand	stood	(have) stood
stave	**stove, staved**	**stove, staved**
steal	stole	(have) stolen
stick	stuck	(have) stuck
sting	stung	(have) stung
stink	stunk	(have) stunk
strew	**strewed**	(have) strewn
stride	strode	(have) stridden
strike	struck	(have) struck (stricken, *adj.*)
string	strung	(have) strung
strive	strove	(have) striven
swear	swore	(have) sworn
sweep	**swept**	**(have) swept**
swell	swelled (*weak*)	(have) swelled, swollen
swim	swam	(have) swum
swing	swung	(have) swung
take	took	(have) taken
teach	**taught**	**(have) taught**
tear	tore	(have) torn
tell	**told**	**(have) told**
think	**thought**	**(have) thought**
thrive	throve, thrived	(have) thriven, thrived
throw	threw	(have) thrown
thrust	**thrust**	**(have) thrust**
tread	trod	(have) trodden
wake	woke, **waked**	(have) woke, **waked**
wear	wore	(have) worn
weave	wove	(have) woven
weep	**wept**	**(have) wept**
wet	**wet**	**(have) wet**
win	won	(have) won
wind	wound	(have) wound
wring	wrung	(have) wrung
write	wrote	(have) written

Made in the USA
Monee, IL
16 June 2022